Praise for *Irregular Army*

"Matt Kennard's careful and judicious investigations reveal an aspect of the modern US military system that should be of deep concern to American citizens—and to everyone, given the unique scope and character of the deployment of US military force worldwide."

Noam Chomsky

"Armies corrupt and disintegrate when they fight colonial wars. Matt Kennard's outstanding, meticulous book exposes the secret recruiting of criminals in an army whose wars are criminal. This is journalism as it should be."

John Pilger

"In his first, gripping book, Matt Kennard delves deeply in the heart of darkness of the US government's so-called War on Terror. *Irregular Army* is required reading for anyone probing the true horror of modern American war. Kennard exposes an organized system of destruction that serves well the generals, the politicians, and above all the profiteering military contractors, but which exploits the poor and vulnerable, and trains and arms the most hateful and vicious in our society, consigning so many millions around the world to displacement, misery and death."

Amy Goodman, host and executive producer, *Democracy Now!*

"A startling and powerful new investigation that reveals the depths of the extremist and criminal elements that have infiltrated the US military over the last two decades. *Irregular Army* exposes both the roots of defective military recruitment and its deadly aftershocks. Kennard's book issues an urgent warning to the American public."

Daryl Johnson, Senior Domestic Terrorism Analyst, Department of Homeland Security, 2004–2010

"Chilling ... Illuminating ... Kennard's nonpartisan portrait of martial waywardness is foreboding."

Publishers Weekly

"Matt Kennard is a fluent, powerful and authoritative writer whose debut book will surely establish him as one of Britain's best-known investigative journalists." David Crouch, *Financial Times*

"Expertly exposes the effect of the American war machine on poor American soldiers as well as the stricken peoples of Iraq and Afghanistan living under them. I hope it is read by many people." Nawal El Saadawi, author of *Woman at Point Zero*

"Matt Kennard is a creative and dogged investigative reporter whose probe of hidden realities inside the US military is a revelation." Esther Kaplan, Editor of the Investigative Fund at the Nation Institute

"An exceptional author, Matt Kennard never tries to paint a pig pretty. Thanks, Matt, for keeping it ugly. In his riveting book *Irregular Army*, Kennard exposes Americans to the real Frankenstein's monsters. Criminal brains in the bodies of some of the finest fighting soldiers in the world. Indispensable." Hunter Glass, former gang investigator, US military

"Provides the first comprehensive account of the lengths the military went to maintain its numbers." *AlterNet*

"An excellent piece of journalism ... It's not only Kennard's long-form, first-person style and sharp, concise writing that keeps you with him to the end, but the fact that solid research is backed up with hundreds of interviews, from neo-Nazis to former generals ... As a result of [Kennard's] research and fresh angle, it stands out amid the vast sea of literature already published on the failings of the War on Terror." *Time Out*

"*Irregular Army* makes a ... strong case that nothing good lies in the future so long as the American government continues to dissolve its standards of human decency to keep the pipeline filled with new soldiers." *Daily Beast*

Matt Kennard is a Fellow at the Centre for Investigative Journalism in London. His second book, *The Racket*, is forthcoming, and he has worked as a staff writer for the *Financial Times* in London, New York and Washington, DC. He graduated from the Columbia Journalism School. He has written for the *New York Times*, the *Chicago Tribune*, and the *Guardian*.

IRREGULAR ARMY

How the US Military Recruited Neo-Nazis, Gang
Members and Criminals to Fight the War on Terror

Matt Kennard

VERSO

London • New York

This paperback edition first published by Verso 2015
First published by Verso 2012
© Matt Kennard 2012, 2015

1 3 5 7 9 10 8 6 4 2

Verso
UK: 6 Meard Street, London W1F 0EG
US: 20 Jay Street, Suite 1010, Brooklyn, NY 11201

www.versobooks.com

Verso is the imprint of New Left Books

ISBN-13: 978-1-78168-563-1 (PB)
eISBN-13: 978-1-84467-905-8 (US)
eISBN-13: 978-1-78168-437-5 (UK)

British Library Cataloguing in Publication Data
A catalogue record for this book is available from the British Library

The Hardback Edition of this Book Is Cataloged with the Library of Congress as Follows:

Kennard, Matt.
Irregular army : how the US military recruited Neo-Nazis, gangs, and criminals to fight
the war on terror / Matt Kennard.
   p. cm.
ISBN 978-1-84467-880-8 (hbk. : alk. paper) — ISBN 978-1-84467-905-8 (ebook)
1. United States—Armed Forces—Enlisting, recruiting, etc.—Standards. 2. United
States—Armed Forces—Enlisting, recruiting, etc.—Corrupt practices. 3. Soldiers—
Health and hygiene—United States—Standards. 4.   Physical fitness—United
States—Standards. 5.   Soldiers—Alcohol use—United States. 6.   Soldiers—Drug
use—United States. 7. Gang members—United States. I. Title.
 UB333K46 2012
 956.7044'34—dc23

                              2012018558

Typeset in Minion by Hewer Text UK, Ltd., Edinburgh
Printed and bound in the US by Maple Press

For all the people whose lives have been ended
or brutalized by these wars

An Army raised without proper regard to the choice of its recruits was never yet made good by length of time; and we are now convinced by fatal experience that this is the source of all our misfortunes.

Flavius Vegetius Renatus, in his military manual
De Re Militari, fifth century, as the decline
of the Roman Empire began in earnest

He served up our great military a huge bowl of chicken feces, and ever since then, our military and our country have been trying to turn this bowl into chicken salad.

Retired General John Batiste, former
commander of the First Infantry division in
Iraq, on Secretary of Defense Donald Rumsfeld, 2006

Contents

Acknowledgments

This is my first book and it spent a long time germinating before it was finally written. Because of that there are lots of people all over the world who helped me make it real as I worked to focus the issues involved. There are two people particularly without whom this book would have been impossible. Jason Yarn helped me put the idea together from its tentative beginnings with great patience and kindness, while Max Ajl gave his time and skills selflessly at the start of the project. Lionel Barber, David Crouch, and Jo Rollo at the *Financial Times* were generous and understanding when I needed time to write.

Most thanks and love to my parents, Judy and Peter, for teaching me always to stand up for what you believe in and in turn believing in both this project and me. In their own different ways, they have dedicated their whole lives to trying to make the world a better place—they are my inspiration. Ana for her love, being the best editor and kindest person too, and more than anyone else making this book what it is. Thanks to my brother Daniel for his unwavering belief that I could do anything I set out to do. My grandma Mary has been steadfast in her support and love all my life—I couldn't have done this without her. Thanks, Nan. Back when this was a seed of an idea Gizem helped me nurture it and was a voice I turned to throughout for sound advice.

Many thanks also to Andrew Hsiao at Verso for his insights into the topic and support throughout the process. Tariq Ali likewise showed faith in the project early on, while Tim Clark improved the final product immeasurably with his stellar editing. The guidance and wisdom of Beech was a constant support the whole way, alongside Rab whose intellectual truculence has taught me a lot over the years. The project started at Columbia University Journalism School where I was taught by Sheila Coronel, who afforded me the financial and intellectual support at the beginning when I was still staring at a blank page. The Nation Institute deserve huge thanks for giving me the financial and moral support needed to continue the initial story—democracy and journalism around the world would be hugely improved if every country could have an institution like the Institute. *Salon* published the first short story which gave birth to this book, so thanks to them and in particular Kevin Berger. There are also those who have kept me sane and laughing while writing, so thanks to: Tom, Nick T., Dave, Jake, Pilar, Steve, Frankie, Patrick, Declan, Billy, Whybrow, Al D., Shane, Ivor, Adam, Lex, Summer, Eugene, Jack, Laurence, Harry, Charlie, Chris, Leah, Ralph, Camilla, Hugh, Lucy, Suey, William, and Shannon.

War is the most traumatic event a human being can experience. That goes for those attacked *and* for those individuals sent to do the attacking. I would like to thank all the veterans who have come home and dedicated their post-combat lives to stopping these wars and fighting for the health and educational benefits that are rightfully theirs. This book is not an indictment of all US service members; it is an indictment of the people who sent them to war on the basis of a lie and knowingly allowed the whole institution to unravel.

It goes without saying none of the people above are responsible for what I have written.

Introduction: Breaking Down

I just can't imagine someone looking at the United States armed forces today and suggesting that they are close to breaking.
                    Secretary of Defense Donald Rumsfeld, 2006[1]

On September 10, 2001, Secretary of Defense Donald Rumsfeld stood in front of the assembled great and good of the Pentagon and delivered an expansive lecture entitled *Bureaucracy to Battlefield*.[2] Its prescriptions were extremely radical—among the most portentous in US military history—but thanks to the terrorist atrocities the following day his words remain buried deep in the memory hole, while their *consequences* are buried under the sands of Iraq and Afghanistan. "The topic today is an adversary that poses a threat, a serious threat, to the security of the United States of America," Rumsfeld began, before revealing the threat to be not Al-Qaeda, but the "Pentagon bureaucracy." "Not the people, but the processes," he added reassuringly. "Not the civilians, but the systems. Not the men and women in uniform, but the uniformity of thought and action that we too often impose on them." In essence, Rumsfeld's speech that day was designed to lay the ground and soften up his workers for a massive privatization of the Department of Defense's services. It was the realization of a long-held dream for Republican politicians and their corporate allies in Washington—who would now be presented with a sweet shop full of lucrative government contracts to chew on. With the tragic events of the next day and the ensuing two-front ground war in the Middle East, Rumsfeld was gifted the perfect opportunity to enact his program with minimal opposition. The results were clear eight years into the War on Terror when the DOD (Department of Defense) had 95,461 private contractors working for them in Iraq compared to 95,900 US military personnel.[3] The use of private contractors was by then so embedded that Barack Obama's initial skepticism about their use displayed while a senator became one more item in a long list of policy climbdowns. But while the privatization of the war effort is a topic that has been explored extensively by a number of journalists, notably Jeremy Scahill,[4] one aspect of the program has received little coverage—namely Rumsfeld's plan for soldiers on the payroll of the DOD. Equally radical, it was a scheme that would prove catastrophic for the troops and the occupied populations living under them. Veiled in the language of business-style efficiency savings, Rumsfeld's plan was intended to eviscerate the US military, which was to become merely an appendage to the massive *private forces* the US would employ in the future.

"In this period of limited funds," he continued, "we need every nickel, every good idea, every innovation, every effort to help modernize and transform the US military."

This could only be done by changing the basics of how the Pentagon worked, in a process that would later be dubbed "Transformation": "Many of the skills we most require are also in high demand in the private sector, as all of you know. To compete, we need to bring the Department of Defense the human resources practices that have already transformed the private sector." Even the DOD itself was to be run like a corporation: "We must employ the tools of modern business. More flexible compensation packages, modern recruiting techniques and better training." What Rumsfeld desired was a scaled-down, streamlined US military—a reversal of what had become known as the Powell Doctrine, named for the Desert Storm general Colin Powell, who believed in high troop numbers, "overwhelming force," and a defined exit strategy. It was a risky approach for Rumsfeld to take. Even before 9/11, Powell, by now Secretary of State, had observed that "our armed forces are stretched rather thin, and there is a limit to how many of these deployments we can sustain."[5] That would prove to be an understatement. But Rumsfeld was backed in his new approach by his boss, President George W. Bush, who much to Powell's consternation shared the same vision. "Building tomorrow's force is not going to be easy. Changing the direction of our military is like changing the course of a mighty ship," Bush said in May 2001.[6]

The oft-repeated cliché is that everything changed on September 11, and indeed it did for millions of Americans. But not for Rumsfeld: his priorities stayed the same while his popularity surged after he was pictured helping victims of the attack at the Pentagon into ambulances. He now had not only the ultimate cover for changing the course of the mighty ship and designing a pared-down business-style war machine, but also the perfect laboratory for his experiments. The war drums began beating in earnest soon after 9/11. The invasion of Afghanistan began with a Rumsfeld-inspired Special Forces mission to bribe local warlords, supported by airstrikes obviating the need for "overwhelming" manpower. But the so-called neoconservatives weren't finished yet: they had their eyes on the ultimate prize of Iraq and, sure enough, eighteen months later and much more controversially, the country with the third-largest reserves of oil in the world was attacked—a move Rumsfeld's deputy Paul Wolfowitz had been advocating (again, with a Rumsfeld-style small force) in the 1990s. Over the next decade, US bombs fell on Syria and Pakistan and Yemen, among others, as the Middle East turned into a conflagration of Dantesque proportions, with civilians, insurgents, and US service members all caught up in the blaze.

Rumsfeld's guinea pigs for his new experiment in "flexible" military planning were the patriotic Americans who believed they were signing up to defend their country—at the height of the War on Terror, 1.6 million of them had served in the Middle East.[7] That number, equivalent to the population of a country like Estonia or a city like Philadelphia, must have come as a surprise to Rumsfeld, who had predicated his whole war plan on a much smaller force and a short war. In fact, soon after 9/11, General Tommy Franks had been asked by Rumsfeld to estimate how many troops an invasion of Iraq would require. The last contingency plan for invading Iraq, dating from 1998, had recommended a force of more than 380,000. But, apparently under pressure from Rumsfeld, General Franks presented his "Generated Start" plan with an initial troop count of just 275,000.[8] Even that was too much for Rumsfeld, who in typical peremptory fashion slapped down the general and pushed for an even smaller force. According to Michael Gordon, military correspondent for the *New York Times*, "They came up with a variant called the running start, where you begin maybe with a division or so, and then the reinforcements would flow behind it. So, you start small but you just keep sending more of what you need."[9] This approach generated what was called a "war within a war," as it pitted Rumsfeld against General Eric Shinseki, the army's popular Chief of Staff, and Secretary of State Powell, both of whom (rightly) believed that large numbers of troops would be needed to ensure security after the initial fighting was over. General Shinseki publicly proposed a force of 200,000, after his frustration with Rumsfeld's intransigence on the issue became insufferable.[10] It didn't matter. Rumsfeld wouldn't listen.

This tactic was so blinded by ideology that it directly contradicted the ostensible goals of the invasion—disarming Saddam Hussein. "The United States did not have nearly enough troops to secure the hundreds of suspected WMD sites that had supposedly been identified in Iraq or to secure the nation's long, porous borders," said Michael Gordon and General Bernard Trainor in their book *Cobra II.* "Had the Iraqis possessed WMD and terrorist groups been prevalent in Iraq as the Bush administration so loudly asserted, [the limited number of] U.S. forces might well have failed to prevent the WMD from being spirited out of the country and falling into the hands of the dark forces the administration had declared war against."[11] But it wasn't just ideology that was to blame for the ensuing damage to the US military and its war aims; there was a sizeable dose of incompetence as well. Declassified war-planning documents from the US Central Command in August 2002 show how ill-prepared the Bush administration was for the occupation which was to follow. The plan they put together assumed that by December 2006 the US military would be almost completely drawn down from Iraq, leaving a residual force of just 5,000 troops.[12] It was madness, but nevertheless music to Rumsfeld's ears.

After much wrangling, Rumsfeld and Franks compromised and the initial force numbered 130,000, much smaller than had been envisioned in the 1990s, but not as slim as Rumsfeld had hoped. It didn't go to plan anyway, and the troop levels were not enough to get a handle on this country of 30 million people. Incrementally more service members were sent out alongside private contractors as the situation descended into chaos after the first viceroy Paul Bremner's decommissioning of the police and military sparked endless violence. By 2005, the US had 150,000 troops deployed in Iraq, and 19,500 in Afghanistan. But the war plan meant the military wasn't prepared in any way for this kind of extended deployment—and it was unraveling. In 2005, just two years into the war in Iraq, people were talking openly about the fact that the US military had reached breaking point. At a Senate hearing in March of that year, General Richard A. Cody expressed these concerns publicly: "What keeps me awake at night is what will this all-volunteer force look like in 2007."[13] But he didn't know the half of it. Worse was to come as in the same year the army missed its recruitment targets by the largest margin since 1979, a time when US society was still afflicted with so-called "Vietnam Syndrome" and the army was much bigger and recruiting twice as many soldiers.

Breaking Point

Around this time a retired army officer named Andrew F. Krepinevich, writing under a Pentagon contract, released a shocking report which was scathing about the US military being able to maintain its troop levels in Iraq without breaking the military or losing the war. His diagnosis was simple: the US armed forces were "confronted with a protracted deployment against irregular forces waging insurgencies," but the ground forces required to provide stability and security in Afghanistan and Iraq "clearly exceed those available for the mission."[14] To compensate, the army was introducing change by the back door at the expense of their troops. Krepinevich pointed to the frequent and untimely redeployment of service members. "Soldiers and brigades are being deployed more frequently, and for longer periods, than what the Army believes is appropriate in order to attract and retain the number of soldiers necessary to maintain the size and quality of the force asking."[15] He offered three solutions for overcoming the desperate shortage of troops: redeploy existing troops more frequently still; redeploy them for even longer; or deploy US Marine ground troops. The first two of these prescriptions had already been undertaken by the army, but it was a dangerous game. "How often can a soldier be put in harm's way and still desire to remain in the Army?" Krepinevich asked. "It is not clear, even to Army leaders, how long this practice can be sustained without inducing recruitment and retention problems."[16] His conclusions were not optimistic: the army, he said, was "in a race against time," in which "its ability to execute long-term initiatives" was compromised by the "risk [of] 'breaking' the force in the form of a catastrophic decline in recruitment and retention."[17] He continued that it would be difficult not to stress the active and reserve components "so severely that recruiting and retention problems become so severe as to threaten the effectiveness of the force."[18] By now, then, everyone—including even Rumsfeld himself—knew the army had to increase in size. "With today's demands placing such a high strain on our service members, it becomes more crucial than ever that we work to alleviate their burden," said Representative Ike Skelton (D-MO), who had a long track record of advocating for a bigger army.[19] But with recruitment down and anger at the war widespread how could this be done?

There was one course of action that would have instantly sewn up the military's unraveling seams, namely: the draft. But it was too controversial. Involuntary conscription had been abolished by Congress in 1973 at the end of the Vietnam War. At the time Krepinevich was writing, it did enter into the national conversation, although the Bush administration remained implacably opposed for reasons of naked self-interest. When Rumsfeld testified at a

Senate Appropriations Defense Subcommittee in April 2005 the issue was raised by Senator Daniel Inouye (D-HI). "For the first time in many years the Army and Marine Corps are not meeting their recruiting targets. There are some who are already discussing the draft," he said with diplomatic tact. An exasperated Rumsfeld shuffled forward in his seat and put his mouth closer to the microphone: "I think the only people who could conceivably be talking about a draft are people who are speaking from pinnacles of near-perfect ignorance," he replied. "The last thing we need is a draft. We just don't."[20]

The Democrats kept pushing until Charles Rangel, a Congressman from New York, reintroduced the Draft Bill in February 2006, which if passed would have reinstated conscription for all those up to forty-two years old. "Every day that the military option is on the table, as declared by the president in his State of the Union address, in Iran, North Korea, and Syria, reinstatement of the military draft is an option that must also be considered, whether we like it or not," said Rangel. "If the military is already having trouble getting the recruits they need, what can we do to fill the ranks if the war spreads from Iraq to other countries? We may have no other choice but a draft."[21] It was rejected by Congress, much to the delight of President Bush. "I applaud the House of Representatives for soundly rejecting the 'Reinstate the Draft' bill," he said in the aftermath. "If this bill were presented to me, I would veto it. America's all-volunteer military is the best in the world, and reinstating the draft would be bad policy. We have increased pay and benefits to ensure that our troops have the resources they need to fight and win the war on terror. I want every American to understand that, as long as I am President, there will be no draft."[22] Reinstating it wouldn't have made the US an anomaly among its allies: many still run compulsory conscription programs, including Israel and (until 2011) Germany. The draft also has deep roots in the US historical narrative: during the Civil War, America's greatest president, Abraham Lincoln, had put forward the Conscription Act which called for the military service of all healthy males between the ages of twenty-five and forty-five for a three-year term. But the opposition from President Bush and his administration should be understood from the perspective of the still-raw memories many Americans have of the last draft. In a war so unpopular and with a president under so much pressure, the administration was aware that conscripting the nation's youth into the military could well be the straw that broke the camel's back. In a 2006 CBS poll, 68 percent of respondents said they opposed reinstating the military draft.[23]

The Vietnam-era draft has also come under concerted attack ever since that war because of its targeted recruitment of certain demographics in the American population. Roughly 80 percent of the soldiers sent to Indochina were from working-class and/or ethnic minority backgrounds.[24] One Vietnam veteran, Mike Clodfelter, who grew up in Plainville, Kansas, wrote in his 1976 memoir: "From my own small home town ... all but two of a dozen high school buddies would eventually serve in Vietnam and all were of working class families, while I knew of not a single middle class son of the town's businessmen, lawyers, doctors, or ranchers from my high school graduating class who experienced the Armageddon of our generation."[25] Even though the draft was never reinstated during the War on Terror, there were symmetries with recruitment trends from the Vietnam era. In the War on Terror, the US military again focused on enlisting society's poorest. Denied the draft, however, it fell back on another method learned from attempts to swell the ranks during Vietnam: changing the regulations on enlistment. In 1965, as the troop buildup in South Vietnam grew, the military started to abandon its standards for recruitment and hundreds of thousands of men who scored among the lowest IQ percentiles were admitted for the first time. "Prior to American escalation in Vietnam such men were routinely rejected, but with a war on these 'new standards' were suddenly declared fit to fight. Rejection rates plummeted," writes one historian.[26] In 1966, Secretary of Defense Robert McNamara instituted a program called "Project 100,000," which aimed to increase the levels of troops by that number within two years by admitting civilians who had previously not met the required standards.[27]

The New Look

Without conscription and with recruitment targets being consistently missed, the Bush administration and the Pentagon devised a similar plan. By subcontracting out myriad operational tasks to private military institutions like Blackwater and DynCorp, who received billions of dollars in government largesse to man the frontlines in the War on Terror, the government had partially dealt with the gap between its demand for cannon fodder and the supply of quality troops. A thin coalition of countries, later including NATO troops in Afghanistan and the UN in Iraq, helped ameliorate the chronic troop deficits. But it wasn't enough. In 2004, Bush took another unusual step to plug the hole: he called up 37,000 members of the National Guard to go to fight in the deserts of Iraq.[28] Not since the Korean War had there been such a mobilization: the National Guard had served in the Gulf War and Kosovo, but in nowhere near such huge numbers. By June 2005, they accounted for 45 percent of the total army in Iraq.[29] Then there were the monetary inducements, which became quite lucrative for service members and crippling for the Pentagon. The Rand Corporation conducted an in-depth study which found that the DOD budget for enlistment and reenlistment bonuses had skyrocketed between 2000 to 2008, more than doubling to $1.4 billion for reenlistment bonuses. The average army enlistment bonus increased from $5,600 to about $18,000 per soldier over the same period.[30] In just three years, from 2006 to 2009, the army dispensed with $1 billion to recruit 64,526 active-duty and reserve soldiers. Army Reserve recruits saw their bonuses more than double over the same period, to $19,500. But the study also found that army recruiters tend to be a more cost-effective way to swell the ranks of the military than enlistment bonuses or pay increases. The Bush administration took that route too. To achieve its 2007 goals, the army increased its 8,000-strong recruiting force with 2,000 new assistants.[31]

At the same time—and perhaps most importantly—those who should have been kicked out were being allowed to stay. In June 2005, the *Wall Street Journal* turned up an internal memo to senior commanders which called the growing dropout rate—called "attrition" in military jargon—"a matter of great concern." "We need your concerted effort to reverse the negative trend," it read. "By reducing attrition 1%, we can save up to 3,000 initial-term soldiers. That's 3,000 more soldiers in our formations." It was an explicit call to drop standards: the message being that soldiers addicted to alcohol and drugs, those who lose their fitness, or their mental poise, shouldn't be discharged. It was batten down the hatches time. The *Wall Street Journal* quoted a battalion commander as saying: "It is the guys on weight control . . . school no-shows, drug users, etc., who eat up my time and cause my hair to grey prematurely . . . Often they have more than one of these issues simultaneously."[32] Such sentiments did not occur in a vacuum. Rumsfeld and the Pentagon were, in fact, allowing the dismantling of the whole regulatory structure for enlistment and retention that the US armed forces had built up in the twenty-five years since Vietnam. The slim military needed fattening up and this was the only way to do it. In the end it constituted a complete re-evaluation of who was qualified to serve in the US armed forces, a full-works facelift of the service unheard of in the annals of modern American history. In the relatively halcyon days of the First Gulf War in 1990, the US military blocked the enlistment of felons. It spurned men and women with low IQs or those without a high school diploma. It would either block the enlistment of or kick out neo-Nazis and gang members. It would treat or discharge alcoholics, drug abusers, and the mentally ill. It would pass up the services of foreign citizens to fight its wars. No more. While the Bush administration adopted conservative policies pretty much universally, it saved its ration of liberalism for the US military, where it scrapped all the previously sacrosanct regulations governing recruitment to the most powerful fighting force in the world. Under the aegis of the War on Terror, the US armed forces became a Mecca for the "different," the weird and wonderful (and dangerous) of America.

Throughout all this, however, the military maintained a rictus, everything-in-order, smile for the public. As late as August 2007, when the crisis befalling the institution had become widely known, Michael Dominguez, Principal Deputy Under Secretary of Defense for Personnel and Readiness, began his testimony to a Congressional hearing with a slap on the back for the US military: "Let me begin by acknowledging an historic achievement that many, including some of our own experts, would have thought impossible a few years ago," he said. "We have taken an all-volunteer military to war. We have done it in a strong economy with 4.5 percent unemployment. We often have asked that force and their families to do more on short notice. And through it all, we have manned this nation's military with people far above average relative to their peers."[33] It was simply untrue. The average member of the US military was no longer far above their average peer. The following chapters will show how the Bush administration, together with a pliant Pentagon (and the succeeding Obama administration), enabled the US military to undergo the biggest and fastest transformation in its history. Each chapter will cover a different group of people who have been enfranchised through the War on Terror as the US military scrambled for troops. The different weightings and amount of reporting on each group reflects the fact that some of these changes in regulation have been explicit (for example, rules on body weight and IQ) while others have been completely denied (from neo-Nazis to gang members). Still others have been hushed up as far as possible—such as the vast numbers of young Americans scarred for life by mental illness, left untreated and forsaken.

It will become clear quite quickly that it is not just American soldiers who have been short-changed by Rumsfeld's vision—the occupied populations have been sacrificed with rivers of their own blood. Many of the wars' worst atrocities are linked directly to the loosening of enlistment regulations on criminals, racist extremists, and gang members, among others. Then there is the domestic US population, which has had to put up with military-trained gang members marauding around their cities; as well as Mexican civilians who have paid with their lives in the drug wars facilitated in part by the US military. The effects of this will be felt for decades to come. Finally, there's the safety of the troops themselves. Loosening standards on intelligence and body weight, for example, compromised the military's operational readiness and undoubtedly endangered the lives of American and allied troops. Hundreds of young Americans may have paid with their lives for this folly.

US society changed profoundly after the September 11 attacks and during the subsequent wars. In many ways, the military is a reflection of the society from which it is drawn, and the changes in the composition of the US military and its regulations over this period reflected a country in political, cultural, and economic reverse gear. As America became increasingly bigoted and inward-looking, so radicalism in the US military increased. As young people became ever fatter, so too did the soldiers. As the criminal justice system locked more and more people up, so the military had to increase the numbers of felons it allowed in. "Today's young men and women are more overweight . . . and are being charged for offenses that in earlier years wouldn't have been considered a serious offense, and might not have resulted in charges in the first place," an army spokesman complained in 2008.[34] At the height of the War on Terror, only one in three men in the general population met the pre-9/11 physical, mental, educational, and other eligibility requirements needed to enlist in the armed forces. "The numbers of people who meet our enlistment standards is astonishingly low," grumbled Under Secretary Dominguez at the end of his testimony lauding the military's success.[35] To enlist the rest, the US military had to change in profound and dangerous ways.

What follows, then, is a soldier's-eye history of the War on Terror, told by the men and women who have often paid the highest price (alongside, of course, the occupied populations). Through it all, the military rationalized its transformation program as an altruistic democratization of the fighting force or denied outright they had loosened regulations. "In the 1990s what you saw was they just kept raising the standards for who they would accept, as a way of weeding out less desirable people, it was a buyer's market," John Pike, a military analyst, told me. "When the war came along they decided that a lot of these standards didn't have anything to do with war fighting."[36] It was a lie, as this book will reveal in its attempt to remedy the relentless propaganda.

CHAPTER ONE

The Other "Don't Ask, Don't Tell"

HITLER IN IRAQ

The military has a "don't ask, don't tell" policy pertaining to extremism. If individuals can perform satisfactorily, without making their extremist opinions overt . . . they are likely to be able to complete their contracts.
US Department of Defense report, 2005[1]

My journey into the dark underworld of the US military begins on a rainy Tuesday morning in March 2008, with a visit to Tampa, Florida, on the south-eastern tip of the country. The mission is simple: to meet Forrest Fogarty, a diehard American patriot who has served the US Army proudly for two years in Iraq, the central focus of America's War on Terror and the country's most controversial foreign adventure since Vietnam. The twist is that Forrest doubles as a white supremacist of the serious Hitler-worshipping type. Over the preceding months, I'd been speaking to him intermittently on his cell phone after his brother had put us in contact. It was a necessarily convoluted route: getting inside the neo-Nazi network in the United States is no cakewalk, requiring endless appeals via phone and email to penetrate the thick walls put up against a hostile mainstream media. I'd been uniquely successful with Fogarty, who is an effortlessly loquacious character with a compelling story, so I take a flight from New York City to meet him.

On arrival, I quickly check into the nearest hotel after the bus drops me off downtown, but it's early afternoon so I walk along the deserted walkway next to the Hillsborough River that runs through the heart of the city, dividing the University of Tampa from the skyscrapers on my side. It is about 5 p.m. before I eventually muster the courage to call Forrest on his cell. He picks up after a few rings. "Oh hey, I didn't think you'd come!" he says in his croaky voice, sounding happy to hear from me. "I usually go get a beer after work, why don't you come?" Sure, I tell him.

A couple of hours later I'm in a cab headed for his favorite hangout, the Winghouse Bar & Grill, which describes itself as "a casual sports-bar with delicious over-sized entrees." I'd assumed the place was downtown, so it's an unpleasant surprise when the taxi speeds along endless miles of pitch-black highway with the full moon barely lighting up the dense forests and thickets whizzing by. The situation is prime for a bit of macabre daydreaming: will I be jumped by a group of his mates, maybe even end up decapitated in the woods? Before too long we pull up at the sparkling Winghouse, located on a plain at the side of the highway, its bright lights a welcome interruption to the surrounding blackness. It's an open-plan restaurant with a bar in the middle and a group of Tampa belles in low-cut tops taking orders. In our brief phone call I'd asked Forrest how I would recognize him. "Just look for the skinhead with the tattoos," he said, laughing. And sure enough, sitting straight to my right as I walk in is a youngish looking man, plastered in tattoos, with tightly cropped hair, wife-beater vest, and bulging biceps—a poster-boy skinhead, the archetypal American Nazi. "Good to meet you," I say, not bothering to get confirmation. "Hey Matt," he replies. "Sit down." He is bright and alert, his keen eyes darting around as he speaks. We order some chicken wings with buffalo sauce, and a pitcher of beer. "You're British, right," he says. "I remember seeing black guys with British accents in Iraq, shit was so crazy."

Forrest is obviously in his element in the Winghouse as he slouches in his chair, beer in one hand, chicken wing in the other. He doesn't take long to start in with his life story, which, for shock value, is admittedly hard to beat. He tells me he grew up in Los Angeles and moved to Tampa at fifteen with some serious psychological baggage. In high school in LA he was bullied by Mexican and African American children and was just fourteen when he decided he wanted to be a Nazi. By the time his family moved and he switched to Leto High in Tampa, he had found his identity: "I eventually got kicked out of Leto High, for being a racialist," he says, his voice quivering with anger still. "I was getting in a few fights. What they do in desegregation is bus blacks into the neighborhood. On the first day, a bunch of niggers, they said 'Are you in the KKK?' to me, and I said, 'Yeah,' and it was on. After this, I kept getting in fights, eventually they expelled me."

It's nerve-wracking sitting in a bar with Forrest as he vents openly against black people and Jews. He has no qualms about flaunting his Nazism and I look like his friend. "I get into fights myself twice a month because I'm a Nazi," he assures me, pouring a pint of beer and smiling. "I'm completely open about it." When black people come into the bar he emits a hiss of disapproval. "I just don't want to be around them," he tells me. "I don't want to look at them, I don't want them near me, I don't want to smell them. And people say, 'Oh people who are racialist you've never hung around black people' . . . bullshit, I've showered with them, I've lived with them, I don't like them . . . they're fucking savages, they're tribal motherfuckers, they are different to us, how they think, how they conduct themselves." Although he has two kids to look after, aged nine and thirteen, he has the mannerisms of an adolescent. He speaks a lot about "chasing pussy" and getting into fights, and bloviates about Jews and Arabs in between. I nod my head insincerely.

But there's more to Forrest than just bravado. As he downs our pitcher of Bud he becomes freer and talks about his other great passion in life: music. As a young man he was obsessed with Ian Stuart Donaldson, the legendary singer in the British band Skrewdriver, who is hero-worshipped in the neo-Nazi music scene with a fervor akin to a thirteen-year-old Goth's veneration of Marilyn Manson. This adulation was so strong that at sixteen Forrest had an image from one of Skrewdriver's album covers—a Viking carrying an axe, an icon among white nationalists—tattooed on his left forearm. Soon after he had a Celtic cross, an Irish symbol appropriated by neo-Nazis, emblazoned on his stomach. A few years later he started his own band, Attack, now one of the biggest Nazi bands in the US, playing all over the country to crowds of white power fans. But it was never his day job. "I was a landscaper when I left school," he says, leaning back in his chair. "I kind of fell into it, I was a kid back then. I didn't give a shit what I was doing, I was just drinking and fighting."

For the next eight years he drifted through jobs in construction and landscaping and began hanging out with the National Alliance, at the time one of the biggest neo-Nazi organizations in the US. He soon became a member. The group's founder was the late William Pierce, author of *The Turner Diaries*, a novel describing the violent overthrow of the American government, and which is believed to have inspired Timothy McVeigh to carry out the 1995 terrorist attack in Oklahoma.[2] The Alliance is one of the few durable fixtures in the American extremist firmament, where groups often start up and die within a hummingbird's lifetime. At the time of Forrest's involvement with them, they were arguably the most powerful far-right force in the US. It has called for "a long-term eugenics program involving at least the entire populations of Europe and America."

With his music and friends in place, Forrest turned his attention to his lackluster work. Construction was never what he had wanted to do. He had always seen himself as a fighter and warrior. So he resolved to do what two generations of Fogartys had done before him: join the military. "I wanted to serve my country," he says as he chews on the last remnants of chicken. "Every male part of my family has served in combat; my father was in Vietnam for two tours as part of the Marine Corps, and my grandfather was in World War Two, Korea and Vietnam."

Forrest would not be the first extremist to enter the armed forces. The neo-Nazi movement has had a long and tense relationship with the US military, documented for decades. Since its inception, the leaders of the white supremacist movement—which is as old as the country—have encouraged their members to enlist. They see it as a way for their followers to receive combat and weapons training, courtesy of the US government, and to bring what they learn home to then undertake a domestic race war. The concept of a racial "holy war," often called "Rahowa," is adhered to by a host of extremist groups—from the Nation of Islam to neo-Nazis—and advocates an apocalyptic eruption of all-against-all racial violence that pitches races against each other and into open conflict with the government. Not all far-right groups subscribe to this vision—some, like the Ku Klux Klan, claim to prefer a democratic approach. But a large portion see themselves as insurrectionary forces challenging the moral bankruptcy of a government that is unreformable. To that end, professional training in warfare is a must. The US military has long been aware of these groups' attempts at infiltration. Even so, the first military directive pertaining to "extremism" didn't appear until the Vietnam War and the target of the new guidelines wasn't racist extremists, but rather anti-war elements. The Department of Defense Directive *Guidelines for Handling Dissent and Protest Activities Among Members of the Armed Forces* was aimed at curbing the influence of dissidents within the military by prohibiting the publishing of "underground" newspapers, the formation of military unions, and other actions that could be used by anti-war protestors to further their agenda.[3]

The presence of white supremacists in the military first triggered concern in 1976. At Camp Pendleton in California, a group of black marines attacked white marines they mistakenly believed to be in the KKK. The resulting investigation uncovered a KKK chapter at the base and led to the jailing or transfer of sixteen Klansmen. But the Vietnam-era legislation was the extent of provisions until 1986, when reports again surfaced of army and Marine Corps members participating in Ku Klux Klan activities. This forced President Reagan's Secretary of Defense at the time, Caspar Weinberger, to issue a directive stipulating that "military personnel must reject participation in white supremacy, neo-Nazi, and other such groups which espouse or attempt to create overt discrimination."[4] The 1986 policy change was modified further in 1996 when language was added to the DOD Directive that specifically banned white supremacist and neo-Nazi groups. It explicitly "prohibited activities" by these groups in the military. This change came after the murder in 1995 of two African Americans by a neo-Nazi paratrooper

stationed at Fort Bragg, North Carolina. The killings led to an investigation that ultimately revealed twenty-two soldiers at Fort Bragg
with known extremist tendencies. Fogarty was recruited the year after.

As we finish up our drinks at the Winghouse, I ask if I can meet
Forrest again while I'm in the city, which is for just another three
days. "I'm working tomorrow, and with the kids on Saturday," he
says. Thinking quickly, I suggest taking them all to the local zoo, the
first attraction I can remember from my hotel tourist pack. "Yeah,
why not," he says, and we set a date for Saturday afternoon.

A Narrative of Mistakes

Driving out from downtown Tampa, it takes twenty minutes to
arrive at the fifty-six-acre Lowry Park Zoo, tucked away behind the
tree-lined highway. The place is overrun with kids and their parents
even as the inclement weather beats down rain and hail. Forrest
turns up a bit late with his two kids and we set off around the enclosures. Before the rain gets too much we take in the seals, the tigers,
and the camels. "Goddamn camels," says Forrest, looking peaked, "I
hate them things." We talk candidly about his racism and violence in
front of his kids, who are a smart pair, not yet set on the same political trajectory as their dad. "There's nothing they don't know. I just
tell them it's OK to be white," says Forrest. "In school they teach
about slavery and the Holocaust, they teach them about indiscriminately murdering Jews. I say there's two sides to every story, you're
hearing from the people who won the war. I don't care if they have
non-white friends, but they will become gang-bangers and not like
you when they are older." The younger kid is "hardcore" according
to Forrest, but his ex-wife doesn't want him joining the military. The
older one is obviously very intelligent, outlining the evolutionary
reasons for various animal quirks to me effortlessly.

After a good period, the rain sends us all to seek refuge under an
umbrella-covered table by a restaurant. While Forrest's sons play by
themselves, he delves deeper into how he joined the military in the
first place, with his five-star neo-Nazi credentials. He knew back then
that the tattoo he had riding up his forearm could be a problem

when it came to enlistment. In a neo-Nazi underworld obsessed with secrecy, racist tattoos remain one of the biggest indicators of extremism for a recruiter, and in an effort to police the matter the US military requires recruits to explain any tattoos. An army manual published in 2000 notes, that "Extremist groups frequently use tattoos to show group association" and offers recruiters a list of specific images to look out for, among them "lightning bolts, skulls, Nazi swastikas, eagles, and Nordic warriors."[5] It instructs recruiters that any would-be soldier who refuses to remove an offending tattoo should not be allowed to enlist. Fogarty's are quite clearly the kind written about in the manual—a Nordic warrior and a Celtic cross. This didn't hinder his application. "They just told me to write an explanation of each tattoo and I made up some stuff and that was that," he says, chuckling. Maybe it's not so surprising. According to the military itself, the education of recruiters about how to identify extremists fell by the wayside during the War on Terror. A 2005 report by the Defense Personnel Security Research Center (DPSRC), which is a DOD entity, concluded that recruiting personnel "were not aware of having received training on recognizing and responding to possible terrorists"—a designation that includes white supremacists— "who try to enlist." It found, on the question of extremist tattoos, that recruiters lacked "completeness, accuracy, timeliness, and accessibility of intelligence for screening tattoos."[6]

After hanging out with Forrest, I decided to test it out. I contacted a random pool of recruitment centers and found that the level of awareness was low to minimal. I spoke to five different stations around the country pretending to be a prospective soldier, with the caveat that I had a pair of "SS lightning bolts" tattooed on my arm. Despite being outlined in army regulations as a tattoo to look out for, none of the recruiters reacted negatively and, when pressed directly about the tattoo, not one of them said it would be an outright problem. The conversations began in the usual fashion: I told them I wanted to join the military, and covered up for my British accent by saying I was just married to an American. The recruiter at Houston station hadn't heard of SS bolts. "I don't know what they are; you'll have to come in. They might be OK, might not be OK," she said. At the Houston Willowbrook office I was told, "I don't know, will have to crack the regulation open." At Waldo in Kansas City the recruiter's response was again ambiguous. "I'm not saying it means you can't get in," he said.[7] No wonder Forrest found it so easy. Not long after, my suspicions were given further validation when I was flicking through a long 2009 *Newsweek* profile of army specialist Terry Holdbrooks, who converted to Islam after being positioned at Guantanamo Bay. Deep into the article, with breathless ambivalence, the journalist recalls being at Holdbrooks's Phoenix apartment when "he rolls up both sleeves to reveal wrist-to-shoulder tattoos." Holdbrooks goes on to describe the "ink work as a narrative of his mistakes and addictions." These "mistakes" include "religious symbols and Nazi SS bolts, track marks and, in large letters, the words BY DEMONS BE DRIVEN."[8] The journalist fails to raise the obvious question: How did someone with a tattoo of Nazi SS bolts get into the US military in the first place?

But even if the tattoos are missed for whatever reason, it's not the last chance the military has to rid itself of a neo-Nazi soldier. An Army Command Policy manual devotes more than one hundred pages to rooting them out. But no officer appeared to be reading it. It states the policy generally: "Participation in extremist organizations and activities by Army personnel is inconsistent with the responsibilities of military service."[9] Specifically, soldiers are prohibited from participating in such organizations through public demonstrations or rallies, attending meetings or activities, fundraising, recruitment or training, taking a visible leadership role or distributing literature. The options available to a commander should these rules be transgressed are involuntary separation, reclassification action or bar to reenlistment actions, or other action "deemed appropriate." None of that appeared to be of interest as the War on Terror raged.

Medals and Everything

Soon after Fogarty was approved, he was stationed in the Third Infantry Division based at Fort Stewart, Georgia, the largest army installation east of the Mississippi River. Once at the base, the army got a helping hand from an unlikely source who alerted them to the extremist in their midst. As we stroll on again around the zoo, Forrest recounts the story of how his ex-girlfriend and mother of his eldest child was livid when he joined the military and tried to scupper his plans when he was positioned in Georgia, away from the family. "She hated that I was in the military," he says as he looks at his kids. Her anger became so acute that, according to Fogarty, she sent a dossier of pictures to his military command that showed him at white suprema-cist and neo-Nazi rallies, as well as performing his racist rock with Attack. "They hauled me before some sort of committee, and showed me the pictures and asked me what they were. I just denied it and said my girlfriend was a spiteful bitch, which is true." Although he talks a lot about chasing all sorts of women, Forrest claims he doesn't go for women who are like him, which might explain her exaspera-tion. He is currently single but says, "I try to keep some chicks, but I don't like skinhead girls, I don't like girls with tattoos."

The committee, he says, "knew what I was about, but they let it go because I'm a great soldier, and they knew that." The investigation, Fogarty tells me, was headed by Command Sergeant Major Tommy Dunne, now retired. When I contact Dunne by phone, he initially denies knowing Fogarty, but when I try again some months later he acknowledges that he remembers the soldier. I ask if he recalls seeing Fogarty's prominent racist tattoos. "I didn't see any tattoos like that," he says. At one point in our conversations, Fogarty claimed that Dunn had told him "The only reason I like you is you're racist!" I ask Dunn about this. "I don't remember saying anything like that," he says. "He was just an average soldier." "It's funny," says Fogarty when I tell him. "He gave me medals and everything." Even Colonel Todd Wood, the highest authority at the military installation, doted on him, according to Fogarty. I ask him whether that was because of his fighting prowess. "Yes, exactly," he says, "They didn't want me to get out, they were taking me to dinner, taking me and my wife out." A roadside bomb in Iraq killed Colonel Wood in October 2005.[10]

The brave efforts of Fogarty's girlfriend having gone unheeded, Fogarty remained in the reserves, until finally, in 2004, he was sent where he had always wanted to go: Iraq. "I'm a fighter, I love combat,

I wanted to be in the action," he says. At the time, the Tampa local newspaper, the *St. Petersburg Times*, interviewed him at Fort Stewart. There was no mention of his Nazism. "We didn't come over here to hang out at Fort Stewart," Forrest told them.[11] Before he left for the Middle East, Forrest joined the Hammerskin Nation—described by the Anti-Defamation League as the "the most violent and best-organized neo-Nazi skinhead group in the United States."[12] He was a probate for the Hammerskin Nation while in Iraq, a process that guards against infiltration, and on his return to the United States became a full-fledged member.

The degree of impunity encountered by Forrest and countless other extremists caused tensions within the military. The blind eye turned by the recruiters angered many investigators whose integrity was being compromised. Hunter Glass was a paratrooper in the 1980s and became a gang cop in 1999 in Fairville, North Carolina, next to Fort Bragg. "In the 1990s the military was hard on them, they could pick and choose," he recalls, "that was after the Burmeister trial, so they were looking for anybody, they were looking for swastikas, they were looking for anything." (James Burmeister was the army paratrooper convicted of murdering two African Americans in a 1995 racist gun attack in Fayetteville, while he was stationed at Fort Bragg.) But the regulations on racist extremists and fear of other Burmeisters did not continue with the inception of the War on Terror. "The key rule nowadays is ignore it until it becomes a problem," Glass tells me. "We need manpower, so as long as the man isn't acting out, let's blow it off." He recounts one episode in early 2005 when he was requested by the military police investigators at Fort Bragg to interview a soldier with blatant skinhead insignia—SS lightning bolts and hammers. "He was already in with this tattoo!" Glass exclaims. "I asked him about it, and he said he had dreamed it up. I asked, 'Where are you from?' He said Birmingham, Alabama." But Glass knew what it really was. "He had a hammer above it; he was a Hammerskin." Even so, the soldier claimed "it was because he was in an engineer unit." Glass worked with the base's military police investigators, who filed a report. "They recommended that he be kicked out," he recalls, "but the commanding officers didn't do anything." He says there was an open culture of impunity. "We're seeing guys with tattoos all the time . . . As far as hunting them down, I don't see it. I'm seeing the opposite, where if a white supremacist has committed a crime, the military stance will be, 'He didn't commit a race-related crime.'" Former Department of Defense investigator Scott Barfield had a similar experience: "Recruiters are knowingly allowing neo-Nazis and white supremacists to join the armed forces, and commanders don't remove them from the military even after we positively identify them as extremists or gang members." Speaking in 2006, he added, "Last year, for the first time, they didn't make their recruiting goals. They don't want to start making a big deal about neo-Nazis in the military, because then parents who are already worried about their kids signing up and dying in Iraq are going to be even more reluctant about their kids enlisting if they feel they'll be exposed to gangs and white supremacists."[13]

The War on Terror produced no official acknowledgment from Pentagon brass that regulations have been loosened on neo-Nazis. Individually, however, officials seem to accept that it has happened by stealth. One is Douglas Smith, the public affairs officer at the Recruitment Command who spoke openly to me about the policy on extremists: "We don't exclude people from the army based on their thoughts," he explained. "We exclude based on behavior. But a tattoo of an offensive nature, racial, sexual, or extremist, might be a reason for them not to be in the military . . . The tattoo is a relatively subjective decision . . . We try to educate recruiters about extremist tattoos, but it's going to depend on their general knowledge of tattoos." He says that a racist tattoo shouldn't automatically bar enlistment: "A tattoo in and of itself is not a bar to enlistment. It is behavior that would prohibit someone serving or enlisting. There are First Amendment rights . . . The concept seems to be if the tattoo is so patently offensive that it would cause disruption, it could require action." Even a swastika might get through, he continues. "A swastika would trigger questions, but again if the gentleman said, 'I like the way the swastika looked,' and had a clean criminal record, it's possible we would allow that person in."

It's in the interest of recruiters to interpret recruiting standards loosely, as failure to meet their targets means they have to attend a punitive counseling session, and persistent failure hurts their chances for promotion. When, in 2006, the army relaxed the regulations on non-extremist tattoos, such as body art covering the hands, neck, and face, this cut recruiters even more slack.[14]

Letting Everybody In

Leaders in the neo-Nazi movement agree that Forrest's journey has become even more common as the military needs more fighters. One of those leaders is Tom Metzger, the seventy-year-old godfather of contemporary national socialism in the United States. "Ah, Metzger!" says Forrest, when I mention him at the zoo. "I know him pretty well, hung out a couple of times." On the phone Metzger is quick to crack a joke, talk about his idiosyncratic political philosophy, and work out how he can help me with anything I want to know. Metzger's journey around the white supremacist movements started in the 1970s with the Ku Klux Klan, for whom he served as Grand Dragon in California. He twice ran for the Senate as a Democrat, against the party's wishes, and, when that failed, set up his own organization: White Aryan Resistance, or WAR. He has been in prison, declared bankrupt, and the subject of a BBC documentary. "Now they are letting everybody in," he says of the US military. "All the gang-bangers, all the blacks, Mexicans, and white supremacists. I would say that 10 percent of the army and Marines—they are not in the navy and air force so much—are racist extremists of some variety."

Metzger's organization is not your typical white power outfit. "I run an association of independent people who work in cells to the best of their talents," he says. "I would encourage them to join the military, if they have a scratch they can't seem to itch. Then go in to bring some training back to the US to make the federal government aware of our existence." Metzger's philosophy is a strange mishmash of the far left, far right, and, in fact, everything in between. When he starts dilating it sends the unsuspecting listener into an ideological daze. One minute he's praising left-wing intellectual Noam Chomsky—"we disagree radically on race but his opinions on transnational corporations and how we are destroying the environment are spot on"—while the next he's on to Adolf Hitler. "I used to call it White Aryan Resistance. Now I call it The Insurgents," he says. "We are now a non-violent insurgency, but we are prepared to turn violent if the need be. It's up to the government. There are moves to suppress free speech and it won't be too long before they get their hands slapped . . . I'm no military general, I meet military people; there are no plans, just an insurgency that could become hot I would say by any means. Like any unconventional warfare it would involve whatever we would be capable of using. The white working class don't have jet planes and atomic bombs, we would work along other lines."

One veteran neo-Nazi who agrees is Billy Roper, who left the National Alliance after a power struggle in 2002 to start his own outfit, White Revolution. While in Tampa meeting Forrest I decide to call Roper. "We have some members in the military," he tells me. "There are a few in the 101st Airborne, some at Fort Campbell, and some Marines in Iraq . . . There's about twelve in there, some of them have tattoos, because anyone can walk in and get in the military now." Roper tells me he knew two members who had swastikas and were barred but had them re-tattooed into sun wheels and the military allowed them back in. One group who don't shy away from swastikas is the NSM, or National Socialist Movement. It claims to be the biggest Nazi organization in the US but activists like Forrest and Roper call them "clowns" because of their propensity to dress up in World War Two fatigues. Someone calling himself Willem Herring, their spokesman, says he doesn't believe swastikas are a problem at all. "I do believe you can join the service with tattoos," he says. "I'm sure you can join with a swastika. There's a big gang problem in the armed forces right now: if you went to a recruitment station with a swastika I don't think they would stop you; it would be noted in your record."

The NSM is undoubtedly the most media-savvy group, in terms of their showiness and their accessibility. Through their media spokesman I am put in contact with Mark Connelly, the head of the SS division in New York, who I'm told is a college student and a "genius." I'm not given a number but rather told I will be called. "You limey bastard" is the first I hear from Mark. He suspects me of being part of the Jewish Defense Force, a radical Jewish organization. I call up the spokesman who pledges to sort it out for me. A few weeks after I get another call from Mark and this time he is less truculent. "Sorry about that," he says. "We just had a problem with the JDF; they were trying to mess us up." I assure Mark that I just want to find out what's going on with the NSM, and he seems to have the arrogance of youth, so I play to that. "I do the job pro bono," he says of his role. "It's something that you have to have a love for, it's hard, it takes character for people who want to learn about history. This is about the reality of World War Two and the demonized German society, and being in support of National Socialism." What brought him in? "I got into the movement when in high school, when I was learning things about certain events. They only tell you the victors' side of the war; I found many discrepancies. I used to be Republican, but it comes to the point where you can't trust the system."

Connelly won't give his age but by the sound of his voice he's young. He lives in upstate New York, near the capital, Albany. "I've been disowned by my mother," he says. The NSM are the most explicit Nazis in the US. They unashamedly worship Hitler, and dress up in 1940s Nazi regalia at their events. I attended their "historic" march on Congress in April 2008, billed as the biggest in decades. As the hundreds of cops and large numbers of anti-fascist protesters lined the streets before the march there was a feeling of great foreboding—until the NSM contingent arrived in a beat-up old van, containing perhaps thirty people, all waving swastikas, and dressed in jackboots. Scary it wasn't. Metzger calls them, without irony, "right-wing reactionaries": "They try to get in to the military covered in tattoos; my kind of people are taught to keep their mouth shut, to pretend they are race-mixing liberals; they don't join any racial organization," he says. "They are all nerds to me," adds Forrest. "I fit in more with the Hammerskin agenda: they are more political, we are more for street activism. We're skinheads, we're not politicians, we're street soldiers."

Away from the NSM's ostentatious pageants are the genuinely dangerous underground operators. One such is Dennis Mahon, who has been on the extremist scene for decades and had links with the Oklahoma bomber, Timothy McVeigh, although he remains coy with me as to what they were. "It drives you crazy," he once said. "Thousands think I was involved. I've started to believe it myself. Maybe I was there. Maybe they brainwashed me and I forgot about it. Maybe I can get hypnotized and remember it. Everybody said I was there. Everybody said I drove the truck. They saw me."[15] Tom Metzger, an old friend of Mahon's, puts me in contact with him, and when I get hold of him he picks up the phone panting like someone who has been doing strenuous exercise. He's at home and it's 2 p.m. "Now's not a good time," he says. "What are you doing?" I ask. "Oh, I really can't say," he replies. When I finally get him for the interview he talks about how he started out in the White Knights of the Ku Klux Klan before joining the National Alliance in 1980. "I thought they were too conservative," he says initially. "I read a lot of books, like the Turner diaries, but then I was in Miami when we had the Haitian invasion." Mahon is alluding to the "Mariel boatlift," which saw an influx of asylum seekers during a seven-month period in 1980 when approximately 125,000 Cubans and 25,000 Haitians arrived by boat to South Florida. At the time Mahon was in the National Guard and was drafted in to help out. "I had to take them from federal prison; they were defecating and urinating in the back of the bus." His ideas started to change. "I thought the National Alliance wasn't radical enough, I went back to join the KKK in Columbia, Alabama." Now, Mahon acts as a "lone warrior," much like Metzger, not bogged down by the politics of petty rivalries which distract from his central mission: causing carnage in his race war against the government. "I guarantee something will happen—we've all got our targets. The Weathermen is a book about how to destroy America. The Achilles' heel is the grid system: when energy is needed the most you blast the stations, and once the power goes out the cities go out. I know of a lot of vulnerable areas. I'm not going to say

I'm going to do this, but there are some lone wolves. Chicago will be out for a week."

Mahon received basic training while in the National Guard and, he says, put it to good use at the time. "I was in National Guard and I was doing some real serious shit," he continues. "No one was ever the wiser—shootings and bombings." He pauses. "No I can't say, they can get you on civil rights violations, believe you me; the Klan can see what the results are, but you don't see them." He talks about a legendary "lone wolf" in Arizona, who goes by the code name Tom E. Gunn, a former Marine. "He does a lot of damage to people's business and harasses people; he's kind of nuts, I hear he's a master of unconventional warfare, he does some damage to people and he was in the Marines. I've tried to talk to him," he continues, "I talked to him one time, he is above ground; the underground guys, they are not supposed to contact me, but they send me newspaper clippings, there's so many organizations getting busted." Tom E. Gunn can be found attacking Tom Metzger— "Metzger, you are an old nobody, a has-been, and a never-was. Go away and nobody gets hurt. Show up with ANY of your kind and it will be your LAST mistake"—in a *Phoenix New Times* article about an Arizonian neo-Nazi icon named Elton Hall being hit by a vehicle while taking part in a protest,[16] but that's about the extent of the evidence of his existence. Because he goes by an alias, tracking him down is near impossible.

Although joining the armed forces has been a frequently successful mission in the past, Mahon says now it's even easier. "I know two people in the military—one in Marines and one in the army. One has done two tours of Iraq," he says. "They are so desperate at the moment; they are going to let you in with a small swastika. If you are an obvious racist and shoot niggers and queers you might find it difficult, but generally you are fine. I've got reports from some of my sources in the military," he continues. "They say they are getting a lot more skinhead types, quasi-racists, more tattoos; essentially they want guys that want to kill. In Iraq you don't know who your enemies are, there's no frontline." But, he believes, this new liberalism will come back to haunt the authorities. "They are hard to stop," he says. "The soldiers learn from unconventional warfare in Iraq and they realize that they can use that type of warfare in America, and it's impossible to stop. I tell people to learn as much as you can to improve munitions capabilities, patrolling; I want them to learn sniping and explosives, the Green Berets. Once they go in they are not supposed to tell anyone who they are."

By the time this book hit the press, Mahon had been sentenced to forty years for a bomb attack that injured a black city official in Phoenix.

It's Kill or Be Killed

Back in the zoo, Forrest plays around with his boys, throwing them about as the rain subsides and we once again start off around the enclosures. The zoo is divided into different themes: we hang out with the cats for a while, then we head over to the elephants under duress from the youngest. According to Mahon's rhetoric the US will erupt in flames when soldiers like Forrest return from Iraq, but looking at him languidly walking around with his kids, talking about his girl troubles and boredom at work, I find it hard to imagine. He laughs a lot when I mention the grandstanding rhetoric of his fellow-thinkers. "Talking about race war right now, we'd be wiped off the planet!" he cries. Despite this, Forrest says a lot of his friends in the Hammerskins are under constant surveillance by the authorities. "All my friends have been to prison. The FBI paid $30,000 to infiltrate the 'skins . . . They learn that, guess what, we drink a lot of beer and chase pussy!" He continues, "I know my name has been brought up a lot of times by the FBI, they are out for my mates Cobi and Richie, they are trying to put something together, it's totally crazy. They are on the Terrorist Watch List. The FBI contacted them, came to their house, the cops came to my house when I busted up the anti-war protest."

As the afternoon wears on the animals start to blend into each other and the only thing that keeps sparking Forrest up is his time in Iraq. He returns again and again to the period he spent there from 2004 to 2005—it seems his most cherished life experience. For two years he served in the military police, escorting officers, including generals, around the hostile country. He says he was granted top-secret clearance and access to battle plans. "I was always on the move . . . Some of my actions led to the deaths of Arabs." He shot at people but he can't know how many he killed because he was always on the move: "If you stopped you'd get hit back. It's a big rush," he tells me. "It changes a human being. I never had any kill counts; some soldiers do." But there's no love lost for the local population. "To tell you the truth I hate Arabs more than anybody," he continues. "For the simple fact I've served over there and seen how they live. They're just a backward people . . . them and the Jews are just disgusting people as far as I'm concerned, their customs, everything to do with the Middle East is just repugnant to me." He wasn't happy with how the war was being fought either. "You have to break these people's will to fight; the only reason they are fighting is that there is some sort of profit to it, or it's not that bad, that the Americans are not going to do what they did in World War Two and kill everybody." Would he nuke Baghdad? "Fuck yeah! If we had an occupying force cracking down on spitting on sidewalks would you spit on the sidewalk if they shot you in the head for it? Go in with an ironfist: this is how you will live, if you don't we'll kill you. Quit pussy-footing around, listen to us or die."

Forrest maintains that a good portion of those around him were aware of his neo-Nazism. "They all knew in my unit," he says. "They would always kid around and say, 'Hey, you're that skinhead!'" Did anyone rat on him? "No, I was hardcore, I would volunteer for all the hardest missions, and they were like, 'Let Fogarty go,' you know what I mean, they didn't want to get rid of me." He was confident enough of his carte blanche from the military that during his break from service in 2004 he flew not to see his family in the US but to Dresden, Germany, to give a concert to 2,500 skinheads, on the army's budget. "What happens is you get to choose whether you want to go to Europe or America, and I put down Germany. The military didn't care. My friends picked me up from Frankfurt airport and I played two shows." What about getting caught? "Ah, fuck it," he sighs. When he was at Camp Victory in Baghdad, Forrest even says a sergeant came up to him and said plainly, "You're one of those racist motherfuckers, aren't you!" Fogarty's driver in Iraq was black and he rebutted, "Only I can call him racist!" I ask him how the sergeant knew about his racism. "The tattoo, I suppose. I can't hide every-thing—people knew—even the chain of command."

He starts getting really misty-eyed recollecting some of his close shaves in the warzone. "One time, I was pulling out of Camp Anaconda, which is about fifteen miles west of Baghdad. Some convoy had blocked lanes of traffic, so we had come out with a Humvee at 5 a.m. We were chilling, but there was this truck hauling at us and not stopping. I'm looking at my driver, he can't see, but my gunner is up there; he said, 'This guy's not stopping,' and I said, 'You know what to do,' and right when I said that, he was just hitting him up with a 50 cal, cha cha cha! Just shooting him up and it was coming towards at us and it was getting all blown to pieces, dude, and as we're pulling out it missed us by like two foot and just fell into the ditch . . . My gunner let him have it with a 50 cal; the gunner was a cool guy. Once you papped him up, I didn't get out the vehicle but I looked in, and there was nobody living."

Another time he was at Camp Victory North at Baghdad airport. "I was in the chow hall, a mortar round came in and blew up a bunch of guys, cut some chicks' legs off. Me and my gunner, I was drinking non-alcoholic beer for the 4th of July, we were like 'Welcome to Baghdad!'" On another occasion he came across the soldiers who had leaked the pictures of torture at Abu Ghraib. "Abu Ghraib was a torture center before the Americans, Saddam will cut your tongue out. Those guys' lives are ruined for harassing a bunch of dirty scum-bags, I guarantee when an Iraqi captures us it's ten times worse," he says. "I met them in Camp Arifjan in Kuwait. We were in the chow hall, we were talking, I forget how it came up, one guy was like, 'I was pulled out of mission because I told someone about the pictures.' I said, 'You punk motherfucker' . . . pussy faggots, I cussed them out."

Although Fogarty gets excited talking about various operations in Iraq, he says he would never say anything "that would put the mili-tary in a bad light." In fact, he has so much antipathy for people who denigrate the military he was arrested by police for breaking up an anti-war protest in 2006. "They threw shit at my dad when he came back from Vietnam, I mean who are these left-wing scumbags?" he asks. "They tried to say I had PTSD [Post-Traumatic Stress Disorder] whenever I got arrested. The VA [Department of Veterans Affairs] said I had PTSD, but because I bust up the anti-war thing doesn't mean I'm suffering from PTSD." Despite all his pro-military rhetoric, Forrest is characteristically contradictory when he waxes lyrical about the hell of war. "You are trained to accept you are going to see dead people," he says. "War is not pretty, there's nothing good about war." He concedes, "The niggarabs are human beings."

After three hours trucking around we all resolve to head out of the zoo. We walk to the gate and I say goodbye. "I've got to get you the CD!" Forrest remembers. And before long he has run to his car and come back with his latest album, *Survival*. The jacket has a picture of him in military fatigues in Iraq. Back at the hotel I cast an eye over the lyrics, which are written in Gothic type on the inside sleeve. "Eye For An Eye" opens with the lines: *A slow painful death I strive / Why are you still alive?* The chorus goes: *It's our turn to watch you bleed / It's our turn to tear you limb from limb . . . We will leave no survivors of this bloody war.* Another one, "In Battle": *In battle there are no laws . . . It's kill or be killed, die with the rest . . . Relief came when I pulled the trigger and watched you die / I can't stop laughing everytime I remember you start to cry / Watch you cry!*

Kill a Couple of Towel Heads for Me OK!

Perhaps ironically considering their general warmongering, the American neo-Nazi movement was for the most part virulently against the war in Iraq. Most of the groups hold to an updated conspiracy theory about Jewish power, which they call ZOG, or Zionist Occupation Government. It is premised on Western governments' supposed submission to Jewish and Israeli power. On their internet forums, US soldiers are often greeted with incendiary comments about being "Jewish warriors" and "Zionist crusaders" for fighting in the War on Terror. This should not be surprising. The white supremacist movement across America has ebbed and flowed since the heyday of the Ku Klux Klan in the 1950s South. It is plagued by fissures and rivalries and ideological nitpicking that have always damaged its ability to form a large-scale and coherent movement. In

2008, there were over 150 different far-right groups—ranging from the Hitler worshippers to Christian nationalists—nestled all over the country. But as the War on Terror raged, extremism was increasing around America generally, according the Southern Poverty Law Center (SPLC), a group that investigates hate and racist groups. In its report *Rage on the Right* it said that in 2008 extremist groups had come "roaring back to life," increasing by nearly 250 percent as well as building links to the mainstream right-wing.[17] It was a grave concern given their willingness to kill innocent Americans (as Timothy McVeigh had demonstrated), even more so now that they had military training.

Charles Wilson, spokesman for the National Socialist Movement, tells me the group is "150 percent against the war in Iraq. It was a total mistake to invade Iraq; we can't even secure our own borders. By 2015 white people will be a minority in America." The IKA, or Imperial Klans of America, is based on the original KKK. "I am, as many of us are, a vet," Truitt Lilly, the spokesman, writes in an email because he wants to remain faceless (and voiceless). "I do not encourage anyone to join any part of Z.O.G. However, military training is good training for anyone: tactics and physical and self defense and discipline are key to any Christian's way of life and should be taken into one's consideration." The original KKK is against it too. "We have opposed the war in Iraq since day one," national director Pastor Thomas Robb tells me. "If we are going to have a war then it needs to be done constitutionally."

But none of this anti-war sentiment has stopped them taking advantage of the opportunities for training. "We do encourage them to sign up for the military. We can use the training to secure the resistance to our government," says Wilson. "Every one of them takes a pact of secrecy . . . Our military doesn't agree with our political beliefs, they are not supposed to be in the military, but they're there, in ever greater numbers." He claims to have 190 members serving. Billy Roper, founder of White Revolution, is another advocate. "A number of skinheads have gone into armed forces for education, college, tuition, and the military training provided," he says. "They are using it to secure the future for white children. Anyone in the movement overseas knows they are getting training and financial help. America began in bloody revolution and it might end that way." Even Forrest, who talks with a glint in his eye about his time in Iraq, is actually against the war in essence. "I don't believe in the War on Terror," he says. "It's a war to protect Israel; I don't think we need to be over there, I just went. I get in this conversation a lot, but I don't like it when people call me a warrior for Israel."

Tom Leyden was in the movement for fifteen years before he managed to extricate himself in 1996. "I had to get out mostly because of my kids," he says on the phone. "I realized that the movement wasn't after me but my children. I was an organizer and recruiter, and I realized it wasn't me they wanted but my children, my boys would be the next generation and militants are much more hardcore than their predecessors." Forrest knows about Leyden and isn't impressed. "That guy is a punk—I'll eat him for lunch," he says. "He's milking the Jews—he had a couple of tattoos, said he was leader of the Hammerskins, there's no rank structure in the 'skins like he says. He has everything to gain by doing this—he has to stay employed, so he says, 'Skinheads are back!'" Leyden provides me with photographs of current servicemen with racist tattoos riding up their arms. "The military says maybe 1 percent is gang members," he says, "well, that's 14,000 people: they don't do training exercises that big! 90 percent of the gangs in the US are street gangs but 9 percent are white supremacists. That's 1,400 people are being trained by the armed forces who are extremist racists."

I stalk neo-Nazi forums for a period and they are still replete with bravado and machismo from people who claim to be soldiers serving in Iraq and Afghanistan who are shooting the locals not to further the military's strategic goals but because killing "hajjis" is their duty as white militants. The website New Saxon is a social networking website for "people of European descent."[18] One of the possible professions when making a profile is the military. There are currently forty-six members who claim to be serving. There is even a group—populated by six professed soldiers called "White Military Men"—started by a young man whose page is headlined with the phrase "FightingforWhites." "All men with military experience, retired or active/reserve should join this group to see how many men have experience to build an army. We want to win a war, we need soldiers," his profile reads. "FightingforWhites" is actually Lance Corporal Burton of the Second Battalion Fox Company Pit 2097, from Florida. In his About Me section, he writes: "Love to shoot my M16A2 service rifle effectively at the Hachies (Iraqis)," and among his passions is: "Love to watch things blow up (Hachies House)." His turn-offs include: "Overweight, lazy, illegals, *WIGGERS*, rape crimes, soldiers that died in Iraq, the Air Force (I called in an airstrike and they apparently had 'tea time' when it was called in)." On his wall his friend writes: "THANKS BROTHER!!!! kill a couple towel heads for me ok!"

There are other examples of the same ostentatious advertising of military credentials on neo-Nazi websites. On the forum of the website Blood and Honour, neo-Nazis encourage their serving comrades to commit indiscriminate murder, and allude to the training they are getting. "I am in the ARMY right now," writes 88Soldier88. "You have no idea how 'nice' we have to treat these fucking people. I work in the Detainee Holding Area so I see these fuckers every day (Terrorists) and we have to treat them better than our own troops. Its sick. I am in this until 2013. I am in the Infantry but want to go SF [Special Forces]. Hopefully the training will prepare me for what I hope is to come."[19] "I get out in 2009. I have the training I need and will pass it on to others when I get out," writes AMERICANARYAN. 88Soldier88 says he is leaving for Iraq in three days. "Aye bro stay safe!!" says AngryAryanHitman, "try get a few notches on ya rifflebutt from the filthy sand nigger cunts." "Good Luck Mate, Stay safe, Get a few Kills, and come Home," says "Paul." "Good luck and i hope everything goes well stay safe keep your head down and try to bag a few sand niggers," says 14 callum 88.

Via the website I wrote to a soldier, Jacob Berg, who claimed to be serving in Iraq. "There are actually alot more 'skinheads' 'nazis' White supremacists now then there has been in a very long time," he wrote back. "Us racists are actually getting into the millatary alot now because If we dont every one who already is will take pitty on killing sand niggers. yes I have killed women, yes I have killed children, and yes I have killed Older people. But the biggest reson Im so proud of my kills Is because by killing a brown many white people will live to see a new dawn."

In 2009, the whistle-blowing website Wikileaks released the internal emails of the NSM, including mine, and uncovered a number of military members conversing with the leadership back in the US. As the SPLC documents:

Among those who contacted NSM was an infantryman who identified himself as Kyle R. Wrobel. Writing from a hotmail contact, Wrobel told NSM that he was from Cleveland, Ohio. "i am a sergeant in the US Army infantry, currently serving my second combat tour to iraq," he wrote on Jan. 17, 2008. "i vehemently support your cause, and want to become heavily involved. my wife and i both advocate and support the cause. i want a lifetime membership and want to become involved and do whatever i can as soon as possible."

Wrobel served for four years in the Army and was discharged in November 2008 as a specialist, according to an Army spokesman. The type of discharge is not public information, the spokesman said, though an acquaintance of Wrobel said it was honorable. (It's unclear why Wrobel stated in his E-mail to the NSM that he was a sergeant, which is higher ranking than a specialist.) Wrobel received seven awards for his service, including the Combat Action Badge and the Iraq Campaign Medal for two year-long tours in Iraq, as well as the Army Good Conduct Medal.[20]

I had tried to get an interview with a NSM soldier (which was never forthcoming), but the Wikileaks release revealed the private correspondence between the group's members about my request which gives a shocking insight into how prevalent their members were in the military: "I did my part and forwarded his inquiry to NSM Colorado who is lead by Davi the guy who got the purple heart in Afghanistan," said Commander Jeff Schoep, the head of the organization and arguably the most powerful Nazi in America. "He . . . did not respond back. I know the Colorado guys are active and recruiting, just processed 2 or 3 new members from there. I cannot force them to talk to student reporters. Apparently they just don't want to do it. I agree with you, its an opportunity to reach people, but it seems most of our members will not talk with any Press. 88."[21] (In Nazi code, 88 symbolizes Heil Hitler, H being the eighth letter in alphabet.)

The more public internet bravado is hard to vet for truth, but there has been a real-life high-profile case of murder involving a soldier in Iraq who had SS bolts tattooed on his arm. The victim, Kevin Shields, was murdered on December 1, 2007, in Colorado Springs by three of his fellow soldiers, Louis Bressler, Kenneth Eastridge, and Bruce Bastien, Jr., who all served in Iraq as part of the Second Brigade Combat Team, Second Infantry Division in their early twenties. Bressler and Bastien were each put away for sixty years for their part in the murder alongside a litany of other crimes in Colorado Springs, while Eastridge is now serving a ten-year prison sentence for his part. But in the aftermath of the arrests, National Public Radio publicized the MySpace page of Eastridge.[22] It showed him proudly displaying his SS bolts tattoo. It also had a picture of him holding a cat in Iraq with the caption, "Killed another Iraqi pussy." There is a picture of a gun and a cache of ammo. "Ready for Whatever!!!!" says the caption. He has another tattoo that reads: "Killing is what I do." After his arrest, Bastien told investigators that he and Eastridge had randomly fired at civilians in Iraq during patrols through the streets of Baghdad. In broad daylight, Bastien alleged, Eastridge would use a stolen AK-47 to fire indiscriminately at Iraqi civilians. At least one was hit, he said.[23] "We were trigger happy. We'd open up on anything. They even didn't have to be armed. We were keeping scores," said another member of the platoon, José Barco, who is serving fifty-two years in jail for shooting and injuring a pregnant woman in Colorado Springs.[24] So far, no one has been charged with shooting civilians in Iraq.

The military not only ignored Eastridge's extremism, but on his return from combat awarded him a Purple Heart and Army Achievement medals. Eastridge's lawyer, Sheilagh McAteer, becomes palpably angry when I talk to her on the phone. She claimed that the military were now knowingly sending mentally unstable young men to Afghanistan and Iraq. "The military is to some extent desperate to get people to go to fight, soldiers who are not fit, mentally and physically sick, but they continue to send them," she told me. "Having a tattoo was the least of his concerns." Another white supremacist soldier, James Douglas Ross, a military intelligence officer stationed at Fort Bragg, was given a bad conduct discharge from the army when he was caught trying to mail a submachine gun from Iraq to his father's home in Spokane, Washington. Military police found a cache of white supremacist paraphernalia and several weapons hidden behind ceiling tiles in Ross's military quarters. After his discharge, a Spokane County deputy sheriff saw Ross passing out fliers for the neo-Nazi National Alliance.[25] On top of this, in early 2012, a photo emerged of a ten-strong US Marine Scout sniper unit posing for a photo with a Nazi SS bolts flag in Sangin, Afghanistan. According to the military, the symbolism was unknown to the soldiers. "Certainly, the use of the 'SS runes' is not acceptable and Scout Snipers have been addressed concerning this issue," Marine Corps spokesman Captain Gregory Wolf said.[26] But nothing about the SS bolts was unacceptable, and the claim that it could result in punishment was laughable. There were countless similar examples throughout the War on Terror that the military had known about—and brushed under the carpet.

Emerging Terrorists

The magnitude of the problem within the army and other branches of the military is, however, hard to quantify. The military does not track extremists as a discrete category, coupling them with gang members. People in the neo-Nazi movement claim different numbers. The National Socialist Movement claimed 190 of its members are inside. White Revolution claimed twelve. Tom Metzger claimed that 10 percent of those serving in the army and Marines are extremists of some sort. But the problem was conceded by the Department of Homeland Security in a 2009 report, *Rightwing*

Extremism: Current Economic and Political Climate Fueling Resurgence in Radicalization and Recruitment, which noted that "the willingness of a small percentage of military personnel to join extremist groups during the 1990s because they were disgruntled, disillusioned, or suffering from the psychological effects of war is being replicated today."[27] On the back of the publication, DHS Secretary Janet Napolitano had to apologize to veterans' groups about her department's findings that "the return of military veterans facing significant challenges reintegrating into their communities could lead to the potential emergence of terrorist groups or lone wolf extremists capable of carrying out violent attacks." But the report was right. Following an investigation of white supremacist groups, a 2008 FBI report declared: "Military experience—ranging from failure at basic training to success in special operations forces—is found throughout the white supremacist extremist movement."[28] In white supremacist incidents from 2001 to 2008, the FBI identified 203 veterans. Most of them were associated with the National Alliance and the National Socialist Movement, which promote anti-Semitism and the overthrow of the US government, and assorted skinhead groups.

Because the FBI focused only on reported cases, its numbers don't include the many extremist soldiers who have managed to stay off the radar. But its report does pinpoint why the white supremacist movements seek to recruit veterans—they "may exploit their accesses to restricted areas and intelligence or apply specialized training in weapons, tactics, and organizational skills to benefit the extremist movement." In reality, white supremacists were using their military status to build the white right. The report found, for example, that two army privates in the Eighty-Second Airborne Division at Fort Bragg had attempted in 2007 to sell stolen property from the military—including ballistic vests, a combat helmet, and pain medications such as morphine—to an undercover FBI agent they believed was involved with the white supremacist movement (they were convicted and sentenced to six years in prison). It also found multiple examples of white supremacist recruitment among active military including a period in 2003 when six active-duty soldiers at Fort Riley were found to be members of the neo-Nazi group Aryan Nations, working to recruit their army colleagues and even serving as the Aryan Nations' point of contact for the State of Kansas.

It seemed everyone knew what was happening. A 2006 report by the National Gang Intelligence Center noted that "various white supremacist groups have been documented on military installations both domestically and internationally."[29] Neo-Nazis "stretch across all branches of service, they are linking up across the branches once they're inside, and they are hard-core," Department of Defense gang detective Scott Barfield told the SPLC. "We've got Aryan Nations graffiti in Baghdad," he added. "That's a problem."[30] Harold Cloverdell served in the army in Afghanistan for a year and in Iraq for two years. "You can go in any restaurant you can find graffiti, maybe a swastika," he says. "Or 'I hate hajjis'—what they call someone with Middle Eastern heritage . . . It pisses you off that you see it," he continues, "as it effects someone's performance, most guys are white in the infantry, a lot of them tend to be of European descent, it may have made someone else uncomfortable." Aaron Lukefahr is now a member of the Aryan Nations, but served two years as part of the Marine Corps in Okinawa in Japan. "I know of at least one other racialist," he tells me. "Once I saw some swastikas in our barracks, stationed in Japan, I don't know who that was, they never found out who it was, but there wasn't much investigation into it as an extremist act rather than an act of vandalism."

Despite the mounting evidence, the government itself did nothing, apart from to issue denials. The US Senate Committee on the Armed Forces has long been considered one of Congress's most powerful groups. It governs legislation affecting the Pentagon, defense budget, military strategies and operations. When I contacted the committee, it was led by the influential senators Carl Levin and John McCain. An investigation by the committee into how white supremacists permeate the military in plain violation of US law could result in substantive changes. Staffers on the committee would not agree to be interviewed. Instead, a spokesperson responded that white supremacy in the military has never arisen as a concern. In an email, the spokesperson said, "The Committee doesn't have any information that would indicate this is a particular problem." But in June 2011, the SPLC reported that the Department of Homeland Security (DHS) had "virtually dismantled its unit responsible for investigating homegrown extremists." Daryl Johnson, an analyst who authored a 2009 DHS report warning of a "growing threat" from far-right radicals, told the group: "My greatest fear is that domestic extremists . . . will [carry] out a mass-casualty attack. That is what keeps me up at night."[31] Johnson's fears came closer to being realized in April 2012, when neo-Nazis started "heavily-armed" patrols around the area of Sanford, Florida—it was the natural conclusion of a decade of hard training by the US military, and a complement to similar work on the US–Mexico border. This new paramilitary garrison in Florida was organized by the National Socialist Movement—who, as we have seen, included a large number of veterans—in the aftermath of the shooting of black teenager Trayvon Martin. The *Miami New Times* reported that the group and their shock troops were "prepared" for race riots, and they would "defend" the white population. "Further racial violence . . . is brimming over like a powder keg ready to explode into the streets," said Jeff Schoep, the NSM Commander. "In Arizona the guys [in NSM] can walk around with assault weapons and that's totally legal," he added.[32] Schoep, however, refused to divulge what kind of "firepower" they had with them on the patrols of between ten and twenty American-style Waffen-SS. But with the military experience running through the movement, along with years of access to the highest-grade weaponry in the world, it can safely be assumed that it wasn't just 9mm handguns.

Begging

During the whole time I spend with him, the only time I see Forrest angry, aside from when his kids are messing around, is when he talks about he was treated after his tour of Iraq. He left in June 2006 and was later honorably discharged from the army before being asked to reenlist. "They were begging me to reenlist, they didn't want me to get out, my whole military career they didn't want me to get out," he says. He wanted to join Blackwater, become a private contractor and go back to Iraq. "You make a lot of money at Blackwater, $100,000 a year, I was getting $30,000 when I was in the army," he says. "They are hardcore, they're doing cool stuff, the army is fighting with boxing gloves on, Blackwater is gloves off." Unfortunately for Forrest the SPLC would intervene to stop his dream of going back to Iraq with immunity. In between honorable discharge from the civilian army and application for Blackwater, the SPLC had publicized his neo-Nazi connections.[33] After putting his application in to Blackwater, he was told that they "couldn't touch" him because he had been put on the Terrorist Watch List, kept by the FBI's Terrorist Screening Center in a bid to identify all potential terrorist threats to the US. "They defamed me," says Fogarty with real emotion. "It was slander-ous, they painted me as a dumbass . . . I would have been able to stay in without the SPLC," adds Fogarty. "They [the army] wouldn't care unless I made an incident at work, but now the SPLC comes out it looks bad." Fogarty is right that he was unlucky. Despite his girl-friend's dossier, his tattoos, and his impromptu trip to Germany, he had been allowed to stay in, and would seemingly have been fine reenlisting had the SPLC not intervened. Following their report, the President of the SPLC, J. Richard Cohen, wrote a letter to the Under Secretary of Defense, David S. C. Chu, stating that "a combination of manpower shortages and poorly written inconsistently enforced regulations has resulted in the recent reappearance of significant numbers of extremists in the armed forces."[34]

John Fain is another. A soft-spoken and more thoughtful charac-ter, he spent two years fighting in the War on Terror, but has none of the bravado of other military extremists. He tells me he joined up "Not to learn combat, but to make myself a better person. I wanted a better work ethic, not just the training to be a soldier. It wasn't so much for a political thing when I joined the military . . . I'm concerned with the welfare and wellbeing of white Americans," he continues, "but the main thing with me is not so much how people look, but there's a particular interest that there is in the media, most of the people are Jewish, they'll admit it. It's not good when you have a population of three percent brainwashing the rest of the populace. People should be made free to have information, because the masses are stupid." His neo-Nazi affiliations did nothing to stop the military trying to reenlist him. Fain claims he has never been a member of the National Alliance, but considers himself a "patriot, which liberals in the military deem as extremist," and admits that he "support[s] the National Alliance" and "agrees with most of what they say." Erich Gliebe, the leader of the Alliance, seems surprised when I tell him Fain wasn't a member. "He isn't?" he asks. "I'm a separatist," says Fain. "I'd be willing to state it out in the street. I've worked with a black guy who had been member of the Black Panthers; he said, 'I don't have problem with white people but I don't want my daughter bringing home white men.' I feel the same, we're both racists. We had an understanding."

Fain joined the military in 1999 when he was eighteen years old, and since he had no tattoos or criminal convictions, he passed through recruitment easily. "I was kind of at a crossroads in my life, doing a dead end job," he says, in a familiar story. "I wanted to try to better myself, and I thought about joining the military. I was going to join the Navy but when I was there the army recruiter said, 'Can I talk to you in a sec?'" Within a week Fain had signed up. Between 2003 and 2004 Fain served two tours in Iraq, going all over the country, from Baghdad to Basra. "Most people keep their opinions to themselves," he says of fellow extremists. "But I've met quite a few of them actually. Last year I ran across a lot of people. I was sitting in the barracks in the US," he says. "There were some guys I overheard on their laptop and they were playing music from Resistance Records [a neo-Nazi music label]. I never noticed people causing a ruckus; the unit I was with was what would be considered good ol' boys from the country." Fain is actually relatively pro-Arab, for good racist reasons. "It's more what's in someone's head than color of their skin. Arabs aren't European, but they are governing themselves. They are not coming over to mingle with us. And they are against Zionist control of governments; they just want to have their own country and own lands."

When Fain returned from Iraq in 2004 he started to work for Vanguard Books, the literary arm of the National Alliance. It sells US army books: $9.95 will get you a tome on *Explosives and Demolitions*. And when Fain left the army, this spell working for the National

Alliance came back to haunt him. The army refused him security clearance, which is a privilege conferred on soldiers and other civil servants after service that gives them access to classified information of a certain sensitivity. "They had found out information about me," says Fain. "I had worked for National Vanguard books, and they were like, 'Who owns it?' and I said, 'It's owned by a corporation.' So they said, 'Isn't it owned by the National Alliance?' I said, 'I don't know,' 'Are you member?' 'No, I don't hold membership but I work for them.'" The army had procured information on his employment through tax returns, and pursued their investigations of Vanguard Books. Despite this, Fain claims he was asked to reenlist. "I'm not going to do it, I've had enough now," he says. Does he think they relaxed standards? I ask him. "It's quite possible. I can't say that it is, I don't know what the government has issued, but I would say it's quite possible. Before they could be picky, now that they need to keep troop numbers high they are accepting no high school diploma, which is more detrimental. I'd rather see swastika than an idiot with no tattoos." Elsewhere the SPLC quotes Fain as saying, "Join only for the training, and to better defend yourself, our people, and our culture. We must have people to open doors from the inside when the time comes."[35]

The discharge figures confirm the experiences of Fogarty and Fain. They show that the avenues the army guidelines stipulate for dealing with extremists already serving in the military have been drastically reduced since 1998, and increasingly so since the War on Terror was initially announced. One such avenue is the denial of reenlistment, which fell from a high of 4,000 soldiers rejected in 1994 to a low of 81 in 2006. Another is a soldier receiving misconduct charges resulting in discharge from the army. In the five-year period from 1998 to 2003 the number of discharges for misconduct teetered from a high of 2,560 to a low of 2,307. But by 2006 this number had fallen off to 1,435.[36] Again, misconduct is a broad category but the decline shows clearly that standards dropped.

The US Army Criminal Investigation Command (CID) is set up to investigate criminal behavior by army personnel and their reports have often touched on the problem of extremist soldiers. A number of internal investigations into extremist soldiers I obtained through the Freedom of Information Act show that CID consistently ignored evidence of violent neo-Nazis and white supremacists. One case at Fort Hood included evidence that a soldier was making internet postings on the white supremacist site Stormfront.org. But the investigator seems to have been unable even to locate the soldier in question. Due to "poor documentation," he writes, "attempts to locate with minimal information met with negative results . . . I'm not doing my job here," he notes. "Needs to get fixed."[37] Another investigation into another soldier at Fort Hood is even more distressing. The investigators found that he belonged to the neo-Nazi Hammerskins and was "closely associated with" the Celtic Knights of Austin, Texas, another extremist organization, a situation bad enough to merit a joint investigation by the FBI and CID. The army summary states that there was "probable cause" to believe that the soldier had participated in at least one white extremist meeting and that he had "provided a military technical manual [Improvised Munitions Handbook] to the leader of a white extremist group in order to assist in the planning and execution of future attacks on various targets." Of four preliminary probes into white supremacists I obtained, CID carried through on only this one. On March 22, 2006, the suspect provided the Improvised Munitions Handbook to the leader of the Celtic Knights, it notes, "to assist in the planning and execution of attacks on five methamphetamine laboratories in the Austin, TX area." It adds, "these attacks were not carried out and the [Joint Terrorism Taskforce] indicated a larger single attack was planned for the San Antonio, Texas after a considerable amount of media attention was given to illegal immigrants. The attack was not completed due to the inability of the organization to obtain explosives." The document notes that despite these grave threats the subject was only interviewed once, in 2006, and the investigation was terminated the following year because the action commander or prosecutor indicated intent to do nothing or at least only "action amounting to less than a court proceeding." The report added, "no further investigative assistance of CID is required."

Another internal report documented the case of an Army National Guard member who investigators believed was "the leader and recruiter" for the Alaska Front, yet another white supremacist organization. The summary describes the soldier as "a person of interest to the FBI due to statements made by the Soldier relating to the robbery of armored cars." The soldier and another member of the Alaska Front were, the report notes, employed by the security company in Anchorage responsible for transporting money using armored cars. Once again, after noting clear affiliations and concrete threats of criminal activity, the narrative indicates that the investigation was closed. "The Soldier's Commander was briefed," it reads. "No further investigation has occurred by the FBI since the Soldier has been mobilized to Camp Shelby, MS in preparation for deployment to Iraq."[38]

The 2005 DPSRC report found that because recruiters and basic training officers lack clear instructions on how to handle evidence of extremist affiliations and also fail to share information, "military personnel cannot evaluate the full extent to which problematic persons associated with particular groups are trying to enlist in the military and their apparent strategies for doing so." It concludes, "Personnel are unlikely to be able to detect anything beyond what would appear to be isolated incidents." Finding evidence of participation on white supremacist websites would be another easy way to screen out extremist recruits, but the same report found that the DOD had not adequately clarified which web forums were gathering places for extremists. In fact, even in cases where active-duty soldiers have been caught posting to such sites, the investigations have been terminated. It appears to some insiders that this incoherence and confusion is consciously fostered to allow the recruitment of extremist soldiers to continue, and to avoid their discharge. "Effectively," the report concludes, "the military has a 'don't ask, don't tell' policy pertaining to extremism. If individuals can perform satisfactorily, without making their extremist opinions overt . . . they are likely to be able to complete their contracts."[39] This went for Islamic fundamentalists, too. When Nidal Malik Hasan allegedly murdered thirteen of his fellow soldiers at Fort Hood in Texas, it was revealed afterwards that the military had been aware of his Islamic extremist ideology but had done nothing to stop it. Hasan had been in contact with his ideological hero Anwar al-Awlaki—the extremist cleric exiled in Yemen who was assassinated by the Obama administration in 2011—and the military had either not trained its personnel well enough or had told them to turn a blind eye to extremism.

Carter F. Smith, another former military gang investigator, defends CID, who he worked with in 2004–6, telling me, "They don't bend to the whims of the commander as much as people on the outside say. They piss a lot of people off. If they wanted to push something they could, but it takes a lot of emphasis on what's right." But he is not surprised by the lax 2006 CID "investigations." "When you need more soldiers you lower the standards whether you say so or not," says Smith, who served as military investigator from 1982, and from 1998 to 1999 was the chief of the gang-hate group investigations team. "The increase with gangs and extremists is an indicator of this." He says the pressure to maintain numbers might make an investigator "ignore stuff . . . Say an investigator sees a soldier with a tattoo that reads '88,'" he says, "if you know 88 is Heil Hitler, but the soldier gives you a plausible reason and you don't look for any memorabilia, you can let him go . . . It's not that they aren't concerned about white supremacists," he adds, "but they have a war to fight and they don't have any incentive to slow down."

Iraq as Race War

For neo-Nazis to prosper in the US military, a general culture of racism is undoubtedly a prerequisite. Forrest stood out because of his skin-head appearance and tattoos, but his casual use of the derogatory term "hajjis" and perception of Arabs as "backward" became endemic throughout the military during the War on Terror. "Racism was rampant," recalls veteran Michael Prysner, who served in Iraq in 2003 and 2004 as part of the 173rd Airborne Brigade. "All of command, everywhere, it was completely ingrained in the consciousness of every soldier. I've heard top generals refer to the Iraqi people as 'hajjis.' And it wasn't auto-ingrained in the soldiers, the anti-Arab racism came from the brass, it came from the top and was pushed into the mind of subordinate soldiers." Prysner believes this kind of racist attitude is consciously fostered to make the military operations easier to carry out. "Even before the invasion racist language was always used against the Iraqi people," he said. "Attributing their condition to cultural backwardness, painting a picture of backward people helped this idea that they needed the US to go in. When you are carrying out missions this is what was on the mind of the soldiers, so the soldiers conduct themselves terribly; we weren't acting with human beings to protect them, we were there to control every Iraqi who was subordinate to us, and everything was justified because they weren't considered people."

Another vet, Michael Totten, who served in Iraq with the 101st Airborne from 2003 to 2004, agrees: "I think at a fundamental level there's a type of superiority complex, a heightened sense of importance; the military carries this attitude, in my experience, towards the people of Iraq. The Iraqis were seen as substandard, second class, a lot of times they weren't seen as human, they were seen as an obstacle, more of a burden, I didn't feel that we were going in as liberators, I felt I was there for the sake of being there." On neo-Nazis like Fogarty, he doesn't think they would stand out at all. "It wouldn't stand out if you said 'sand-niggers,' even if you aren't a neo-Nazi. At the time, I used the words 'sand-nigger,' I didn't consider 'hajji' to be derogatory. I have changed since I came back, obviously." Even racism between soldiers was rife. In late 2011, eight soldiers were charged after the suicide of Chinese-American Private Danny Chen, a nineteen-year-old infantryman from New York, who shot himself in Kandahar, Afghanistan. The charges were brought against the soldiers for an alleged long history of assaults and racist taunts which led to him taking his life. Geoffrey Millard served in Iraq for thirteen months, beginning in 2004, as part of the Forty-Second Infantry Division. He recalls General George Casey, who served as the commander in Iraq from 2004 to 2007, addressing a briefing he attended in the summer of 2005 at Forward Operating Base, outside Tikrit. "As he walked past, he was talking about some incident that had just happened, and he was talking about how 'these stupid fucking hajjis couldn't figure shit out.' And I'm just like, Are you kidding me? This is General Casey, the highest-ranking guy in Iraq, referring to the Iraqi people as 'fucking hajjis.'" (A spokesperson for Casey, who later served as the Army Chief of Staff, said the general "did not make this statement.") "We had a frago [fragmentary order] come out one day that actually talked about how the DOD wanted us to stop using the word 'hajji' because it was seen as a racist slur, but I still heard [another general] use the word hajji. He'd have to correct himself, but it didn't change his thought pattern." Millard was later an organizer for Iraq Veterans Against the War and says he has seen white nationalist tattoos during outreach operations. "Since we've been doing outreach to bases there's this [White Power] tattoo that I've seen a couple of times, and a couple of other different racial symbols. They've got rid of the regulations on a lot of things, including white supremacists . . . The military is attractive to white supremacists," he adds, "because the war itself is racist."

Forrest never saw what the beef was—much like the military itself. "As long as you don't bring personal beliefs to the military it's not a problem," he tells me. "If I was goose-stepping maybe, but I served my country honorably. I'm a soldier who is trying to come home, I have got two children, I'm not gonna be preaching politics while my driver's a nigger." He pauses. "What about the Bloods and Crips?" he asks, exasperated, before we go our separate ways. What about them? I ask. "I seen a million Bloods and Crips," he says nonchalantly. The Bloods. The Crips. Two of the biggest and most dangerous gangs in the US or any other country on the planet. "I seen a million."

STRAIGHT OUTTA BAGHDAD

When these cats, these gang members, come back, we're going to have some hell on these streets.
Miguel Robinson, Airman First Class and Los Angeles Crip, 2007[40]

On the eve of America's most patriotic day in 2005 a group of US soldiers from the army base in Kaiserslautern, southwest Germany, took a drive down to the park pavilion in a nearby forest. The twelve soldiers in the group were in high spirits: aside from the

July Fourth festivities coming the next day, some of them were due to finish their first eighteen-month tour of duty, including a spell in Iraq, within a matter of weeks and would be returning home to their long-suffering families. Among them was twenty-five-year-old Sergeant. Juwan Johnson, or J. Rock to his friends, a member of the Sixty-Sixth Transportation Company who was looking forward to returning home to his pregnant wife within the fortnight. It was to be a welcome relief; the past year had been a difficult one. During his tour of Iraq, he had seen the sharp end of the conflict, reportedly surviving an IED (improvised explosive device) attack which blew up his vehicle, and finding the toil of war difficult to cope with. But nothing would prepare him for the treatment he was about to receive from his comrades shortly after 9 p.m. that night. In the park pavilion, J. Rock was set to become a full-fledged member of the Chicago-based gang the Gangster Disciples, listed by the FBI as one of the fifteen biggest gangs in the US. The purpose of the trip that night was to conduct his initiation ceremony, a rite of passage he had to endure to realize his dream of becoming part of one of America's fiercest street gangs. In gang lingo the ceremony is called "jumping in," also known as a timed beating. Soon after they arrived, the pack of men Johnson had gone down with began to circle their new recruit. The leader of the gang at the base, Rico Williams, a former airman, struck the first blow, lamping Johnson straight across the face—a blow that knocked him unconscious. The ferocious beating that ensued soon "escalated from reckless to a free-for-all."[41] Johnson's lifeless body was treated to a six-minute orgy of violence in which he received 200 blows all over his body and head from the fists and feet of his fellow soldiers.

Still in an unconscious state, Johnson was placed back in his bed by his attackers. He would never wake up. The next morning one of Johnson's roommates found him in his barracks room but could not rouse him. After trying desperately to resuscitate him, a German physician was called who pronounced him dead on arrival. The resulting autopsy report, signed by an Army Forces regional medical examiner, concluded: "The cause of death of this twenty-five-year-old male is multiple blunt force injuries reportedly sustained in a physical assault resulting in fatal injury to the heart and brain." It added, "The manner of death, in my opinion, is homicide."[42] Despite the unambiguous verdict, more than three years later only three of the eleven suspects had been convicted and given confinement terms.[43] One reason for this abysmal bit of police work may have been the intense fear running through the veins of the suspects which had stopped them speaking out. At a Gangster Disciples barbeque in the aftermath of the murder, the gang's ringleader Williams had warned the rest of them that he would kill anyone who snitched to the authorities, along with their families. The more likely reason for the failure to bring Johnson's killers to justice, however, was reluctance on the part of the military to prosecute the case as it tried to keep a lid on public recognition of the developing crisis arising from the gangs' infiltration of the military.

In the end, it took until February 2009 for the police to arrest the main suspect Williams in his hometown of Chesapeake, Virginia, and charge him with second-degree murder as well as three counts of tampering with a witness, including intimidation and threats.[44] The military decided to try him through a court-martial—a legal process much more secretive and less independent than civilian trials. He was found guilty of second-degree murder in November 2010, nearly six years after Johnson was slain, and was acquitted of tampering with a witness.[45] If the military's goal was to keep the embarrassing press to a minimum, it was a success. In another trial by court-martial, suspect Private Bobby Morrissette was acquitted in Germany on charges of voluntary manslaughter and conspiracy to commit aggravated assault, which carried a possible fifty-five years confinement.[46] It was a stunning verdict—Morrissette had been found to have taken part in the "jumping in" that had led to Johnson's death. He was instead found guilty of impeding the investigation and the trial, and willfully disobeying a superior commissioned officer. In a separate incident, giving a further indication of his questionable moral fiber, he was convicted of committing an indecent act on a female in the presence of another person and wrongful use of a controlled substance. In the end, he got away with forty-two months confinement and a bad misconduct charge.

Understandably the acquittal and weak sentencing angered Johnson's grieving mother, Stephanie D. Cockrell. "I'm angry, and

I'm outraged that we have gangs in the military," she said. "The court system is sending a message that it's OK."[47] Her complaint would be vindicated not long after when another soldier involved in the beating, senior airman Jerome A. Jones, was also acquitted of involuntary manslaughter in another court-martial, despite being present at the beating. After denying all charges, Jones was given the lesser conviction of aggravated assault, as well as being found guilty of marijuana use and assisting in hiding gang members and conspiracy to cover up the murder—including tampering with their gang tattoos.[48] He was given a dishonorable discharge and sentenced to two years in prison by the five-member panel which comprised two air force officers and three air force non-commissioned officers from the Little Rock base—where Jones was stationed. In the subsequent months, the military cover-up became even more scandalous as it emerged that the authorities had actively suppressed intelligence from a whistle-blower on the growing threat of gangs in the Sixty-Sixth Transportation company. In the period before the murder, another soldier in the company, Private Nick Pasquale, had taken copious pictures of gang graffiti in Iraq and on the base and handed them to his superiors in an attempt to press them into action. It had resulted in an investigation into the unit over the course of its thirteen-month deployment to Iraq, which turned up ironclad evidence of gang activity. According to the military newspaper *Stars and Stripes*, "the probe involved soldiers believed to be members of the Chicago-based Gangster Disciples. Numerous photos of Disciples had been found, along with graffiti and a list of potential gang members, in the soldiers' living quarters."[49] But the investigation reported to have found no evidence "validating or disproving" the rampant gang activity in the unit.

Just two months later Johnson was dead. "The only thing that came from the investigation downrange was that I was a disgruntled soldier, causing problems," Pasquale said. He had even written down the names of those he suspected of gang activity and given them to his superiors, who refused to take action. "Then we come back from Iraq and wham, bam a soldier's dead. I want [Johnson's] family to know that your son, your husband, the father of your child did not have to die. I want his family to know that he didn't have to die if someone had done their job and not swept this under the rug," said Pasquale. In the aftermath of his testimony, Pasquale was the target of relentless abuse and intimidation, including threats to his life and gang graffiti daubed on his barracks. He even had alarms fitted and slept with knives. "If I do get killed, I don't want to be another Sgt. Johnson with people wondering, 'What happened to him? Why?'" he said. "I don't want my mother going through what Sgt. Johnson's mother's going through, trying to get answers from the army."

Getting Answers

That Pasquale didn't want his mother asking the military for answers is understandable. Throughout the War on Terror, getting genuine answers from the army or any other branch of the military about gang infiltration was impossible. The reaction from the military brass when presented with evidence of the vast numbers of gang members in their midst—even from federal investigators or their own troops—oscillated from outright denial to ad hominem attacks on those making the charges. The threat to the wellbeing of troops, the occupied populations and those back home in American cities didn't seem to trouble them. The most serious and important work undertaken to collect information had, therefore, to be undertaken outside of the military establishment—primarily, by the FBI and civilian police. An extensive report on the problem was published by the FBI in 2007, but at the time it barely registered on the radar of the mainstream media and became another important military-related document read only by the initiated.[50] This time around, however, it was more surprising than usual as the findings were particularly worrying for the *domestic* population of the US. Gang-bangers know a lot about fighting and violence—it's their *raison d'être*. But until the War on Terror that "expertise" had never been shifted wholesale from the inner city to the US military, from South Central to Baghdad and back again. "Gang-related activity in the US military is increasing and poses a threat to law enforcement officials and national security," the investigators concluded. "Members of nearly every major street gang have been identified on both domestic and international military installations." The FBI did not mince words when outlining the problems this could cause for the military. Gang membership in the ranks will "result in disruption of command, low morale, disciplinary problems, and a broad range of criminal activity," as well as the "risk of transferring their weapons and combat training back to the community to employ against rival gangs and law enforcement officers."

Despite this prognosis, in its long history the US military had never instituted regulation prohibiting gang members from joining its ranks. It is true that gang members tend to have criminal records, which can bar an individual from enlistment, but if they are clean, there is sufficient ambiguity in regulations to allow them through. And even criminal records aren't always a bar. Another strange feature of the military's enlistment process is that it relies on recruits to voluntarily reveal their past records, rather than actively investigating them. If the recruit is upfront enough they will go through a "suitability review" which includes a police record check. If that record contains frequent offenses for a number of misdemeanors, the recruit will require a "moral waiver" in order to serve.[51] The FBI fingered this as a serious problem which had allowed gang members to fly through recruitment. "Gang members have been known to enlist in the military by failing to report past criminal convictions or by using fraudulent documents," said the report.[52] And once they are in, a whole new complex of problems appears. The FBI lamented the impossibility of gauging the extent of the gang members in service because "military authorities may not recognize gang affiliation or *may be inclined not to report such incidences*" (my emphasis). It's an incredible suggestion: the federal government's investigative branch cannot gauge the problem of criminal gangs in the country's fighting forces because the military refuses to report gang activity. This dereliction of duty could, the report said, "ultimately jeopardize the safety of other military members," as it did so tragically in the case of Johnson—and he was far from being the only one.

The unit of the military assigned to investigate criminal activity in the service, the CID, was an integral part of the cover-up, denying the existence of the problem from start to finish. "We recently conducted an Army-wide study, and we don't see a significant trend in this kind of activity, especially when you compare this with a million-man army," said its report into gang activity in the military, published at the same time as the FBI report.[53] CID's own report found that gang-related investigations went up from four to sixteen between 2003 and 2006, while incidents went up from eight to forty-four in the same period, in keeping with the enlargement of the force. But FBI gang investigator Jennifer Simon told *Stars and Stripes* that "it's no secret that gang members are prevalent in the armed forces, including internationally."[54] She said gang members had been documented on or near US military bases in Germany, Italy, Japan, South Korea, and Iraq. The discrepancy in the reporting of the problem caused huge tensions between the FBI and the military's investigative units, who seemed piqued that the federal authorities took their job so seriously. They were shocked that the FBI was failing to understand the manpower pressures the military was under. The resulting internecine war was bitter. On the back of the worrying FBI report, the military said the bureau was "overstating the problem, mixing historical and more recent events, and using unsupported hearsay type comments and statements from various undocumented experts."[55] In the aftermath a joint memorandum from the military investigative units was sent to the FBI "contesting parts of the assessment, asking for its withdrawal, and offering increased cooperation and coordination to obtain a more accurate estimate of the gang problem in the military." The FBI said no, and the military published its own report in riposte.

A military spokesman later asked about the problem entered the realm of fantasy: "In nearly every one of the cases that we looked into, it is a young man or woman who thought that the symbol looked cool," he said. "We have found some people even get gang tattoos not really knowing what they are, or at least that they have not had any gang affiliation in the past." It's a serious strain to believe that the significance of florid gang tattoos would be unknown to their owners: usually an indelible mark on the skin demands some research. But these dopey soldiers had company within the military in the form of recruiters, who seemed to know even less about what gang tattoos look like. It wasn't entirely their own fault: as the military investigators demonstrated so impeccably, commanders didn't see it as an issue and preferred to turn a blind eye in the face of pressure to maintain recruitment levels. On top of that, as the FBI pointed out, many "military recruiters are not properly trained to recognize gang affiliation and unknowingly recruit gang members, particularly if the applicant has no criminal record or visible tattoos."[56]

Hunter Glass, the gang investigator, adds: "If we weren't in the middle of fighting a war, yes, I think the military would have a lot more control over this issue, but with a war going on, I think it's very difficult to do." The military was also experiencing an intense financial squeeze from the Bush administration, which was impacting its ability to control the problem. "Forming multi-agency task forces and joint community groups is an effective way to combat the problem," says the FBI report. "However, decreases in funding and staffing to many task forces have created new challenges for civilian communities."[57] Recruiter conduct deteriorated at the same time. In a single year, from 2004 to 2005, the number of military recruiter violations increased by 50 percent as recruiters tried increasingly aggressive tactics and unscrupulously doctored documents. In the same period, the local CBS station in Denver, KCNC, did an important investigation into recruiter conduct when faced with a prospective soldier who claimed to be a gang member. The station's reporter asked his interlocutor in the recruitment center: "Does it matter that I was in a gang or anything?" to which the recruiter responded, "You may have had some gang activity in your past and everything . . . OK . . . but that in itself does not disqualify."[58] There were also numerous reports of recruiters trying to cover up the previous affiliations of gang-members-turned-soldiers. In 2005 a Latin Kings gang member was allegedly recruited into the army at a Brooklyn, New York, courthouse, while awaiting trial for assaulting a police officer. He was reportedly told to conceal his gang affiliation. The effects were perhaps predictable. Jennifer Simon, the FBI gang detective, added: "It's often in the military's best interest to keep these incidents quiet, given low recruitment numbers and recent negative publicity. The relaxation of recruiting standards, recruiter misconduct and the military's lack of enforcement have compounded the problem and allowed gang member presence in the military to proliferate."[59]

In this period, according to reports from soldiers and investigators, Baghdad had become a veritable canvas on which gang members sprayed their markings after the invasion. The Gangster Disciples, as well other heavyweights like Latin Kings and Vice Lords—groups fostered in the badlands of Chicago—had left their mark on armored vehicles, walls, barricades, and bathrooms. An Army Reserve sergeant, Jeffrey Stoleson, seeing this all around him and growing increasingly angry about it, decided to go out on a limb in an effort to alert the American public. Stoleson was deployed twice— first in Kuwait and Iraq in 2005–6, and then later again in Iraq—but he stayed away from a face-to-face confrontation with the gangs. "We all carried loaded weapons at all times and with these hot heads you never know who they may be trying to prove something to," he tells me. He adds that there were two types of gang members: some genuinely wanted to escape from the 'hood and the lifestyle and without the military had no chance. But the majority were training themselves for the war back at home. He says they were "using the methods taught in combat to take home and use against others who have no chance in hell of defending themselves." They weren't trying to hide it either, many posting up graffiti all over Iraq. "It was all over the place, the graffiti was blatant; they were not trying to hide the colors or gang affiliations or even tattoos. Most of the bases had gang graffiti on them from Kuwait to the border with Turkey. It was on Baghdad International Airport, the blast walls. It was a Who's Who of American street gangs, everything was there." Stoleson tried hard to get pictures of the graffiti, but when his senior officer realized he was intent on publicizing the problem "he made sure I was busy and not able to get them." Before he got to the airport to take the snaps they painted over the graffiti. "I mean it was covered with graffiti close to one mile long, twenty feet high." "Some was 'Hi Mom' and derogatory terms for other soldiers but most of it was gangs," he added. Stoleson was also hearing from his colleagues that graffiti was being sprayed on the streets of Baghdad by US troops from different bases to denote their domains of influence. "It was like their turf, you didn't go there after certain times of the day," he says. "Many feared for their safety." Some troops would even wear their gang colors in their military fatigues by coloring the inside pocket of their fatigues red or blue and when they passed each other they would pull them out to show allegiance.

As an upstanding soldier, Stoleson thought that if he raised this with his superiors they would take action or at least investigate. He was wrong. "I brought it up a couple times, but I was told to leave it alone, that they [gang members] were doing a good job et cetera," he says, adding, "but for who and what flag? Not the red, white and blue." Things got more serious when Stoleson started seeing military gear begin to go missing—mainly parts for weapons systems, mounts, optics, and small things that were easy to hide or ship. The command still weren't interested. "At first they blew it off and said to leave it alone, it's not your job," he says. But Stoleson had taken an oath to protect his country from terrorists domestic and foreign, so he went to the press. "When the CID got a hold of me after the story got out in the *Chicago Sun-Times*, the 2-Star General wanted my ass on a platter," he says. "Then it got messy." The military sent an agent from California who was a gang specialist for the San Bernardino Sheriff Department in California. Two agents sat Stoleson down and spent a whole day going through his documentation which included hundreds of pictures. "My captain came through and was amazed when the CID agents looked at him and said his sergeant was right: they had a problem and he had a set of balls for what he did."

But Stoleson wasn't treated like the hero he was; he was ostracized. "I was not allowed to do convoys for forty-five days because there were death threats up north on military bases on me," he says. "Nice from your own troops, eh?" The command sent him south into Kuwait instead, and on his first day there he saw gang graffiti nearby. "Then I went to a place we called Area 51 which was 90 percent covered with gang graffiti and after taking pictures only then did I call the CID agents and within two days it was closed." But soon the case was given to another CID agent. "He wasn't so agreeing with the pictures," says Stoleson. "Go figure," he adds, "it's not what they wanted to hear." The new CID agent called the commander of Stoleson's unit and told him he was coming over to inspect the soldiers in it in three days time. "That's like a cop telling a drug dealer 'hey, drug bust tomorrow at 3 p.m.,'" says Stoleson. The commander merely cleared out anyone suspicious and made sure others were on a mission. Soon after, the commander of the unit called Stoleson's captain and said that Stoleson's safety could no longer be guaranteed. It was a diversion tactic. "In fact, the unit had been brought under investigation several times already while in country for false documents relating to firefights, but they were sealed." When they finally let him go home, Stoleson was sent several memos from the Central Command stating that he was under threat of court-martial, loss of rank, and imprisonment if he did not realize that what he had seen and documented was classified and secret and he must never speak about it. "I even had a captain tell me he would see that I would be thrown out and disgraced and never be allowed to talk about it," he says. "I was told I would never be promoted, had my job threatened, my life, my daughter's life threatened. I got a price on my head on the streets." The pressure of the threats to his family eventually led to his divorce. "When they need info about it it's OK, then they call and expect me to give it. But of course, no way, I am non-cooperative; I am doing this for myself, not watered down so it is what they want to hear."

Stoleson is not optimistic about how this will end. "Now the cartels are in our military and have proven they can and will use their power," he says. "Just look at the murders recently at Fort Bliss, Texas, by troops . . . They say 10 percent of the military is gangs. I say 15 or a little more just because they are becoming a more educated bunch, not showing the tattoos and flying the colors . . . It's bad, don't even fool yourself," he continues. "Law enforcement isn't taking this any more serious than ever. The DOD has told us to leave the bikers alone, which are some of the most dangerous and fly full colors and are involved in white power groups." He adds, "There is no room for any gang member prior or present in the military. If they are allowed, the cancer of our streets here in the States may one day run the most violent army in the world." But the military only ever punished Stoleson for his bravery in speaking up. "Oh Jeff, they tried to destroy him," Hunter Glass tells me. "They wanted him gone, he was showing them up." They were nearly successful. When I last speak to Stoleson he tells me he has just been approved for admittance to the VA for nine weeks of treatment for PTSD.

Back in the US it was the same story of shooting the messenger. At Fort Sill the problem again raised its head when Specialist Gregory Darnell King, a reservist in the 177th Field Artillery Battalion, was arrested six times by local police for a variety of offenses, including drugs possession. He was seen showing the hand signs for the 107 Hoover Crips and was believed to be a member. The head of the police gang investigations team, Lieutenant Darnell Southerland, warned, "People don't want to face the truth but it's true. Fort Sill still has a problem with gangs. We see it every Friday and Saturday nights on the streets. But nobody wants to listen."[60] The army didn't want to know and shot the messenger again. Southerland, the brave whistle-blower, was "completely inaccurate and totally outdated," an army spokesman said.[61] They went further to say that none of their soldiers had been arrested on "gang-related charges" that year. It was the same tactic of plausible deniability that the military used in relation to white supremacists.

Even when cases did make it into the law courts, there was a strange aversion to convictions. Army Private Jamal Rashad Davis of the Eleventh Air Defense Brigade was alleged to have shot and killed nineteen-year-old Jurell Battles during a Christmas Day fight in northeast El Paso in 2004. Investigators believed that the murder was gang related because of Davis's close connections with the Folk Nation gang. Another man who had been shot in the incident identified Davis in a police line-up and the soldier received a general discharge from the army in February 2005, although the military denied this was related to the murder case. After his arrest, Davis's case took four years to move towards trial stage. But before that could happen, District Attorney Jaime Esparza dismissed the murder case in October 2009, citing lack of sufficient evidence to obtain a conviction. It was clear something had gone very wrong with the investigation, as there were no other suspects. John L. Williams, Davis's attorney, denied that his client had been associated with the Folk Nation, saying by way of extenuation, "My guy was in the military. He was a Louisiana choirboy and his stepdad is in law enforcement." Davis was sent back to college where he was studying engineering.

Rearing Its Head

With so little being done by the military and law enforcement, the situation started to spiral out of control. By early 2006 it was seriously impacting on the military's plans for basic domestic troop movements. When the army unveiled its plan to reposition a tranche of soldiers to El Paso, Texas, as part of an efficiency savings program, law enforcement officials feared that it "could trigger a battle the military has not trained for—a turf war between violent criminal gangs."[62] The military wanted to move between ten and twenty thousand troops, but in that group there was a large contingent suspected of belonging to the Folk Nation, the umbrella group for a collection of Chicago-based street gangs. The El Paso area, however, was already home to another sizeable and powerful criminal outfit by the name of Barrio Azteca, a Texas-based prison gang. The DOD was so concerned it set up a special office in El Paso with the sole remit of weeding out Folk Nation members from the new soldiers who arrived. An FBI agent confided with serious understatement: "Our understanding is that Folk Nation has a presence in the military." She predicted that about 800 people were linked to the gang in El Paso, of which about 80, including military personnel and members of their families, were actively committing crimes. "It is my understanding that the police department in Killeen [in Texas] has reported a gang problem where military-affiliated people are involved," she added. There were two problems that sounded ominous—the spread of gangs to the young in the area, and weapons training. "The intelligence that we have thus far indicates that they may try to recruit young people who have clean records and encourage them to keep their record clean to get into the military," she said. "They would get great weapons training and other types of training and access to weapons and arms, and be able to use that knowledge." The military denied it, with Nancy Hutchinson, public affairs officer for the Army Recruiting Battalion-Phoenix Headquarters that includes the El Paso area, saying simply that gang members or those with gang tattoos are barred from the military.

Although publicly there was a deafening silence from the military community, the murmurs from inside were increasing and filtering up to the lawmakers. In a Congress of 535 elected officials, just one lone Congressman, Representative Mike Thomson (D-CA) decided that enough was enough and introduced an amendment to the 2008 National Defense Authorization Bill which stated that the DOD would have to "prescribe regulations to prohibit the active participation of military personnel in street gangs."[63] The bill passed through the House and Senate with the amendment, but was eventually vetoed by Bush, one of twelve presidential vetoes during his time in power. Thomson's reasoning for sticking his head above the parapet was simple: he didn't believe the military was doing its job. "I've heard from police officers across the country that there are problems with gangs on posts," he said. "The FBI suggests there are problems not only in the states but on bases abroad. So somebody hasn't been serious enough."[64] It was clear who he was talking about. His aim, he said, was to make sure different agencies were sharing their information in order to close down the opportunities for gang members to enlist, calling the problem "a serious danger to society."[65] That danger was clear in the statement he posted with the amendment: "This is an important amendment that is a first step in solving a very serious problem on our military bases both here in the States and abroad; and it is a problem that, unfortunately, spills over into our communities. This is the issue of members of criminal street gangs joining the military and getting the training that they get in the military and now, unfortunately, on the battlefield, and then bringing that back into the community and deploying those tactics on the streets in our neighborhood."[66]

In 2009, another FBI report, this time focusing on the threat gangs posed to the US, registered the effect of the military's willingness to turn a blind eye: "Gang migration from larger cities to suburban and rural areas is an ongoing concern for law enforcement," it said. Its data showed that the percentage of law enforcement agencies in the United States reporting gang activity in their jurisdictions increased from 45 percent in 2004 to 58 percent in 2008. Gang membership was estimated conservatively at 1 million members in 2009, a 25 percent increase from 800,000 in 2005.[67] By 2007, the army reported seventy-nine separate gang incidents in the year, crimes which included drug dealing, homicide, and robbery—and these gangs were not just terrorizing each other. The report noted: "Military-trained gang members . . . present an emerging threat to law enforcement officers patrolling the streets of US cities."[68] For the gangs, this was always the desired endgame. Those serving in the desert may have paid lip-service to their love of US-style freedom and democracy, but in truth the military was a training camp for the skills they required to combat law enforcement agencies and their gangland enemies back home. The FBI said as much in its report: "Military training could ultimately result in more sophisticated and deadly gangs."[69] "Gangs are gaining strength across the United States," added Hunter Glass. "The numbers are increasing like crazy around the US and adding this extra fuel is just not going to help matters."[70] It was fuelling crime all over America, with 80 percent of offenses being committed by gang members in some communities.[71] An FBI agent confided that gangs "will hand pick [recruits], ask them to keep their record clear so that they can enlist in the military and then once they're in the military, they want them to try and gain access to weapons and explosives and basically try to filter that back to the street level."[72]

One potent warning about how this would end came early on, one evening in January 2005: A call came in to the local Ceres, California, police department from someone who claimed to be a store employee and requesting help from a single police officer at Sequoia Market. Soon after a second call came from the area with a report that a man was lurking and acting suspiciously with a gun. A short time later, three policemen showed up. Waiting for them was Andres Raya, a nineteen-year-old veteran who had spent seven months in Iraq in 2004 but hadn't seen any combat. On this night he was determined to make up for it, and had armed himself with a high-powered assault rifle for the task. When the policemen arrived, Raya started shooting. Trainee Chris Melton managed to take cover, but his colleague Sam Ryno was hit, sustaining what turned out to be career-ending injuries. The other policeman, Sergeant Howard Stevenson, then fired off eight rounds before taking bullets in the back and leg. Raya walked slowly towards him and unloaded two bullets into his head at point blank range. Later that evening Raya was killed in a firefight with another set of police officers. Taking out two armed police officers is no easy task and would likely not have been possible without Raya's military training. It was later revealed that before the attack Raya had bragged to his friends in the Marines that he would use the assault rifle because of its ability to pierce police body armor, knowledge he probably gained in Iraq. He also used a marine technique known as "cutting the pie" whereby he went on the attack instead of retreating. In the subsequent investigation, it was revealed he was member of the powerful Norteño organization, a group of Latino gangs out of northern California. A police report concluded: "Although—while in Iraq—the gang member had not experienced any combat, he used his military training to shoot out the windows of a nearby vehicle to use as a shield in his attack against officers."[73] Ceres Police Chief Art de Werk said: "It was so rare, an almost unheard-of, brazen attack."[74]

But this was 2005. America was about to change. The aftermath of the murder brought the already tense relationship between the police and the local Latin population to a new low as police conducted a series of "sweeps" for suspected gang members as well as drugs and weapons in Ceres and south Modesto. It fundamentally altered how law enforcement agencies viewed the threat from gangs on the streets of the US. They were now dealing with fully trained warriors. "Gang members have enlisted since the 1980s," said a police report.[75] "However, following the January 9, 2005 attack of two police officers, law enforcement authorities began paying closer attention to gang members in the military and discovering skills and knowledge in the tactics, and access to military weapons were also being used to bene-fit gang members." But law enforcement was helpless when confronted with a military establishment desperate for more wood to throw into the fire in the Middle East, so nothing was done to address the situation. By late 2009, the heavily armed gang problem had got so bad in Salinas, California, that city officials turned to the military for help. They started working with combat veterans and lecturers at the Naval Postgraduate School to devise a counterinsurgency operation likened by the veterans to those fought against insurgents on the streets of Mogadishu or Fallujah. In April 2010 the National Guard was called out to police the streets of Chicago. Local lawmakers said they were needed to "stabilize communities," just as had been done in the Middle East occupations.

The Cancer Spreads

Meanwhile, on the southern border of the US another problem was flaring up. In December 2006, Mexican President Felipe Calderón sent the nation's military to get a grip on the drug-related violence that was ripping apart towns on the northern border. The campaign's success over the ensuing years was muted to say the least: the number of people killed increased every year subsequently. In 2009 alone there were 6,500 drug-related murders in the country. To put that in perspective: after eight years of continuous war, 5,600 Americans had fallen in Iraq and Afghanistan.[76] Both are tragically high figures, but the links were rarely pointed out. One of the manifold problems that the proliferation of criminal gangs in the military has exacerbated in the US, and by extension Mexico, is the drug trade. The illegal drug industry is wholly administered by street gangs, which operate on both sides of the border to get drugs onto the streets of America and cash the gargantuan profits. The military environment is a godsend for such operations, for obvious reasons. The ability to move around, the relative protection afforded by being a soldier, and the ability to work in large concentrations all suit the needs of a drug trafficker. As the FBI cautioned in 2009, a "rising number of U.S.-based gangs are seemingly intent on developing working relationships with U.S.- and foreign-based drug trafficking organizations and other criminal organizations to gain direct access to foreign sources of illicit drugs."[77] It continued, "gangs have . . . been known to use active-duty service members to distribute drugs." The Justice Department reported that members of the Latin Kings gang in Midland, Texas, purchase cocaine from Mexican traffickers for between $16,000 and $18,000 a kilogram. It is then shipped on to Chicago where a kilogram may cost up to $30,000.[78] Elements in the US military are often used as a conduit. The situation became so serious that in 2010, Secretary of State Hillary Clinton said in Mexico City that gangs "are fighting against both of our governments" before pledging $1.6 billion in US aid for the Merida Initiative aimed at fighting drug cartels. She told the Mexican government: "This new agenda expands our focus beyond disrupting drug organizations" to include "strengthening a 21st Century border, and building strong, resilient communities."[79] She didn't mention the sterling work the US's own military has been doing in training the traffickers. One of these alleged military-trained cartel soldiers was eighteen-year-old Army Private Michael Jackson Apodaca, based at Fort Bliss, Texas, the center of a lot of the activity. In August 2009 he was charged with the murder of a lieutenant in the Juárez drug cartel, José Daniel Gonzalez Galeana, who was shot eight times in El Paso outside his luxurious $365,000 Mediterranean villa, complete with tile roof and swimming pool. Apodaca was allegedly hired alongside another man in the contract killing by a member of the same cartel.[80] The *LA Times* reported that the "killing was prompted by suspicions that Gonzalez was either an informant or had trade alliances amid the Juárez cartel's violent battle with rival drug gangs for control of Ciudad Juárez, just across the Rio Grande from El Paso."[81] A spokeswoman for Fort Bliss merely stated: "Anytime someone does something like this, and a soldier in our case, it's terrible."[82] But it wasn't terrible enough for the military to take a look in the mirror.

These same gangs were also trafficking drugs from Iraq and Afghanistan. "We'd stop convoys at the border, both military and civilian, and we would find heroin and hash and lots of cash," Stoleson tells me. "The biggest was around 750 kilos and $500k in cash." He says you could pick up a camel shoe of hash or heroin on the Iran border for $1,200 and transport it to the Syrian border, making up to $25,000 per shoe or kilo, and it was a big industry until the border controls were tightened up in 2006, when the threat of bombings in Kuwait became a reality (Stoleson was in Camp Navistar in Kuwait, which was just forty miles from Iran). "But we had a Latin King from New York getting pot shipped to him and dealing on base," he added. "I turned in a Latin King by noticing his [tattoos] and nothing happened." They were even planning trafficking from Latin America to the US while deployed. "I overheard two troops talking about working with [Mexican drug gang] Zetas to move product from his cousin in Colombia to the States," added Stoleson. His claims were given further credence in early 2012 when a drug ring "kill-team" composed of veterans and active-duty US military personnel was broken up by drug enforcement agents. The men involved—led by First Lieutenant Kevin Corley—were under the impression that the violent, mass-murdering Mexican drug cartel, the Zetas, had hired them. They were not naïve—it was becoming increasingly common, as the Drug Enforcement Administration (DEA) was only too well aware, hence the methodology of the sting operation. As *InSight Crime* magazine, which covers organized crime throughout the Americas, reported:

On March 24, First Lt. Kevin Corley arrived with a three-man team at a warehouse in the border city of Laredo, Texas, armed with two semiautomatic rifles, a combat knife and a .300-caliber bolt-action rifle equipped with a scope. The men believed they had been hired by the Zetas to carry out a contracted killing and raid of a rival drug trafficking group's storehouse, and had been called to receive the final details of the assignment.[83]

Corley had been conferring with DEA agents posing as Zetas for six months, and promised to carry out assassinations for them in the US, which are known in the business as "wet work." Aware of his privileged status as a US soldier, Corley had boasted to his would-be paymasters of the ease with which he could steal weapons from where he was posted in Colorado. It wasn't just bluster. He allegedly provided agents with "bulletproof vests, training manuals and other stolen military equipment." They were the same kind of products you could now find on sale on eBay courtesy of the US military. In America in 2012, none of this was out of the ordinary.

But inter-gang violence, while prevalent on the streets of Los Angeles and Chicago, has not erupted into full-scale war within the US military, mainly because gangs like the Bloods, Crips, and Gangster Disciples have pooled their resources and embarked on joint criminal enterprises, including but not limited to drug trafficking. The FBI reports that "rival gang members at Fort Bliss . . . have joined forces to commit assaults on civilian gang members."[84] One of those alleged to have been involved was Jerell Hill, an eighteen-year-old soldier who was arrested at Fort Sill, a military base in Oklahoma, in October 2007, and charged with attempted murder in connection with the shooting of five people in the Barclay neighborhood of his hometown, Baltimore. Investigators suspected Hill of being a member of the Pasadena Denver Lane gang, a local Bloods group, while the five shot—including a sixteen-year-old and a woman—allegedly had links to a rival gang called the Young Gorilla Family. Both gangs had a history of homicides which had brought the number of slayings in Baltimore to a stunning 240 by October of that year. Hill's father was incredulous, telling the press: "He had a little gang he hung out with . . . As far as calling them one of these Bloods or Crips, I have no idea about that."[85] But he need not have worried, as two days later the prosecutors dropped the case, saying it was "legally insufficient" but that Hill would remain a "person of interest."[86] Hill's parents claimed that he had returned to Oklahoma on September 11, long before the September 20 murder. But police drew attention to the fact he had only checked into Fort Sill on September 21. Police said they would continue to investigate his whereabouts in that interregnum. In the meantime, Hill was sent back to Fort Sill and returned to active duty.

Scott Barfield was a Defense Department gang detective at Fort Lewis in Washington state before he was ejected for raising the alarm in the media. "I have identified 320 soldiers as gang members from April 2002 to present," he said in 2006, before adding, "I think that's the tip of the iceberg." At a later stage he said, "a friend of mine is a recruiter. They are being told less than five tattoos is not an issue. More than five, you do a waiver saying it's not gang-related. You'll see soldiers with a six-pointed star with GD [Gangster Disciples] on the right forearm." An investigation by *Stars and Stripes*, the military journal, found that the number of gang-related incidents officially recorded by the army was small in 2007 at sixty, but that had nearly tripled from the year before. The 2007 report stated the extent of the problem at Fort Bliss: "Since 2004, the FBI and El Paso Police Department have identified over 40 military-affiliated Folk Nation gang members stationed at the Fort Bliss Army Installation in Texas who have been involved in drug distribution, robberies, assaults, weapons offenses, and a homicide, both on and off the installation." In May 2005, eight US soldiers were charged with participating in a widespread bribery and extortion conspiracy. FBI source information revealed that several military personnel stationed in Colombia had "transported forty-six kilograms of cocaine to El Paso."[87]

Weapons Training

While some gang members may enlist to escape their lifestyle, or as an alternative to incarceration (having been offered clemency in exchange for service), most enlist to receive weapons and combat training. One of the main dangers of the proliferation of gang members in the military is the access they gain to the top weapons in the world, along with the attendant training in how to use them. "While in the military, enlisted members are exposed to high-power weapons, such as machine guns and rocket launchers, and explosives, such as grenades and C-5—as well as body armor night-vision devices, gun parts, and ammunition," said the California Department of Justice in 2005.[88] It warned that "enlisted personnel are able to steal items by improperly documenting supply orders or by falsifying paperwork." Throughout the War on Terror there have been countless cases of gang members stealing weapons and selling them on, as well as using their military training to heighten their effectiveness when carrying out a crime. A concerned Milwaukee, Wisconsin, police detective complained to the *San Francisco Chronicle* that "gang members are going over to Iraq and sending weapons back." And sure enough in 2006, a former National Guard soldier was arraigned in federal court after being accused of bringing machine guns back to the US from Iraq to sell to a gun dealer in Georgia.[89] A Government Accountability Office (GAO) report found that stolen US military equipment, including body armor, night vision goggles, and gear to protect against nuclear or biochemical warfare, was being sold on Craigslist and eBay.[90] America was becoming a warzone. In El Paso, members of the city council decided they needed to tool up. They didn't want to take any risks and approved the purchase of 1,145 assault rifles for $750,000 in order to supply all their officers with the civilian version of the M-4 military rifle. Representative Steve Ortega of District 7 said there had to be precautions to help "a population coming back from an extremely violent environment integrating with the civilian population," adding "we want to make sure that the police department has all the resources it needs to make us the safest city in the nation."[91]

It was not hyperbole. In 2004, a fearless gang had begun a two month orgy of "commando-style" robberies in which they raided six banks in Maryland using fully automatic assault rifles, managing to cash in more than $350,000 and terrorize local citizens before being caught.[92] It was revealed subsequently that the military-style operations were in fact made possible by the weapons which had been bought for $5,000 from a friend of one of the gang members, recently returned from Iraq. The police kept the soldier's identity secret but said he was based at nearby Fort Meade. The weapons, which are "plentiful and cheap" in Iraq, according to the *Washington Post*, "were key to their strategy: using overwhelming firepower and body armor to frighten and intimidate bank employees and customers— and ward off police." It worked. In the middle of their crime spree, Kate Collins, a police officer, pursued the getaway van shortly after the gang robbed a Chevy Chase Bank branch in Temple Hills. The robbers fired their machine guns in the officer's direction as they fled the scene. "I felt my car shake," she said. Collins was alone in her vehicle, armed with only a 9mm handgun. It wasn't a fair match; by the end of the firefight her car had been hit forty-seven times. "I had a BB gun compared to them," she complained. The *Post* reported at the time: "Law enforcement officials expressed concern that more high-powered battle weapons could end up being used in crimes against U.S. citizens and police." A law enforcement official familiar with the case commented that winning prosecutions was a hard business before adding that screening for equipment sent back to the US by military members was nearly non-existent. In other words, there was little either law enforcement agencies or American civilians could do in the face of the onslaught. Baghdad had come to Temple Hills.

In 2008, as the Bush administration drew to a close, General David Petraeus, then commanding general in Iraq, went to Washington, DC, to testify in Congress about progress in the troubled country. The political and media world gathered hoping to hear hopeful signals from the four-star general, but right-wing Republican Representative Tom Tancredo shocked the room by raising what many lawmakers thought was an obscure topic. "The fact that gang members are being trained in our military is a growing cause for concern," he told Petraeus. "Our local law enforcement officers and gang units are now facing criminals who have obtained advanced weapons and training courtesy of the U.S. taxpayer." Then he began to show a hint of anger. "I find it very disconcerting that there are high-level military officials that are unaware of this growing problem. This is a serious issue that deserves serious attention from the Pentagon brass."[93] In response, Petraeus merely confirmed Tancredo's worst fears, saying that he was not aware of gang activity in Iraq before promising to look into it. Of course, he never did. In truth, the military brass could not have been unaware of what was happening all along—all they needed to do was pick up a local newspaper across the country. But they couldn't afford to slow down and instead of stemming the tide their program was only making it worse. The one regulation that had previously stopped the gangs' infiltration, the ban on felons and other persistent criminals, was falling away as well.

WAR CRIMINALS

My main preoccupation in life is wanting to kill Iraqis, whoever they are and wherever they are.

Steven D. Green, Iraq veteran and recipient
of a "moral waiver" to serve, 2006[94]

In broad daylight on March 12, 2006, one of most horrific of the reported atrocities by the US military in Iraq was underway in a house near Yusufiyah, a town just south of Baghdad. A group from the Black Heart Brigade of the 101st Airborne Division, famed for its courageous exploits during World War Two, had arrived at a family home fresh from a long drinking session of locally made whiskey, or what the soldiers called with disdain "hajji juice." The men were frustrated, some at the end of their tether, after promises that they would soon leave the Triangle of Death, an area renowned for its high levels of violence and chaos, were consistently broken by their commanders. The tension had been compounded in recent days by the death of a sergeant close to the group, killed by an IED. The house in question was in close proximity to the checkpoint manned by the soldiers, some of whom over the past months had had their eye on the fourteen-year-old daughter of the couple who lived there. Conversations often involved fantasies about raping her; that day, they resolved to do it. They were led by Private First Class Steven D. Green, who had already been showing increasing signs of mental breakdown and illness, telling a combat-stress adviser sometime before of his overriding desire to kill Iraqis. On that day, he was on guard at a traffic control point and had been on duty eighteen hours. He told the other soldiers: "I'm going to waste a bunch of dudes in a car." Not good enough, replied another soldier, James Barker, who told him: "I've got a better idea. We've all killed hajjis, but I've been here twice and I still never fucked one of these bitches."[95] The planned murders would actually only be the coda to a long day of crimes around checkpoints, which were a signature of the conflict. Earlier amid chaos at that same checkpoint, one soldier had opened fire, allegedly to restore order among a crowd, with one shot killing a woman in a pickup truck. "You fucking shot her in the head," exclaimed another soldier. The squad, according to one of its members, fabricated a cover story to explain the shooting. Army investigators found no evidence of wrongdoing.

It was in that frame of mind they arrived at the house that night and separated the girl, Abeer Qasim Hamza al-Janabi, from her family. Green went into the room where Abeer's parents were and shot them dead, along with their six-year-old daughter. Meanwhile, two other soldiers raped the young girl. When Green came back he raped her as well before using the family's own AK-47 to shoot the girl in the head. The soldiers then burnt the house to the ground with the bodies inside. For three months nothing happened as the military believed the lie that it had been the work of Iraqi insurgents. In the Iraq War logs, released by Wikileaks, it wasn't even recorded.[96] In Mahmudiyah—the nearest major town to Yusifiyah—on that day, there were no significant activity reports detailing what the soldiers had done. There was no report of a family's death in a burning house, or the charred corpse of a raped fourteen-year-old girl. It would have stayed that way, as many massacres of its kind undoubtedly have in Afghanistan and Iraq, except for the conscience of one of the soldiers in the battalion, Justin Watt. After a period of soul-searching he told officers that he had heard it was in fact soldiers in his own unit who had carried it out. Even then the military refused to believe him, not even taking precautions about the threat to his life from the soldiers who had learned that he had spoken up.

In the eventual trial of those guilty, the level of incompetence in the military became horrendously clear. Testimony during the trial of Green revealed that an army counselor had called the unit "mission incapable" and recommended that it stop taking on missions due to high levels of stress, anger, and diminished morale. That didn't happen, although before the allegations and criminal proceedings got underway, Green was discharged from the army with a "personality disorder." In the end, he was given five life sentences. The defense had argued that the military should have withdrawn Green long before the massacre, and they had a sterling case. About a year earlier, in January 2005, Green was a high school dropout with too much time on his hands and soon to land himself in jail. He was convicted on alcohol possession charges, which was his third misdemeanor conviction. After he got out he decided to enlist in the military, a course that would—because of those convictions—require special dispensation because of his criminal record. It also emerged that he had unpaid fines against his name, and court records showed it had instructed "he must contact the court immediately." Instead of doing so, Green was deployed to Iraq as part of the 101st Airborne Division, where he would go on to rape and murder. His journey from criminal to soldier was, however, becoming increasingly common.

Immoral Waivers

The Department of Justice cites losing your "right" to serve in the military as one consequence of a felony conviction, and those like Private Green with multiple civil convictions for what the army considers to be misdemeanor offenses also lose their automatic right to serve. But in both cases there is a system in place to give ex-cons a second chance. "Exceptions to the prohibition on military enlistment . . . may be authorized by the Secretary of the affected branch of the service in meritorious cases," says the guidance.[97] In military jargon these "meritorious cases" warrant what are called "moral waivers," by which a moral failing in the past may be overlooked and the individual allowed to serve their country depending on the circumstances "surrounding the criminal violations, the age of the person committing them, and personal interviews."[98] For obvious reasons—not least that of offering former criminals a second chance—the moral waiver system has its uses and is an old institution founded on the valuable principle that society shouldn't be closed to someone for a single transgression. The Pentagon puts it this way: "The waiver process recognizes that some young people have made mistakes, have overcome their past behavior, and have clearly demonstrated the potential for being productive, law-abiding citizens and members of the military."[99] But like most well-intentioned (and discretionary) pieces of military regulation, during the War on Terror it was exploited and stretched to the maximum by the Pentagon as it struggled to keep up troop numbers.

It took a report from the Palm Center at the University of California, Santa Barbara—a group committed to discussion of homosexuals in the military—to blow the lid on figures the military brass were trying hard to cover up. In 2007 it published information obtained through the Freedom of Information Act which led it to call the proliferation of ex-cons in the military a "major recruitment trend" which it said was "a cause, effect, or even correction of the military's apparent recruitment problem."[100] It found the number of convicted felons enlisting in the US military nearly doubled in two years, from 824 in 2004 to 1,605 in 2006. In that period a total of 4,230 convicted felons were enlisted in the military, including people guilty of rape and murder. On top of this, 43,977 soldiers signed up who had been found guilty of a serious misdemeanor, which includes assault. Another 58,561 had drug-related convictions, but all were handed a gun and sent off to the Middle East. "The fact that the military has allowed more than 100,000 people with such troubled pasts to join its ranks over the past three years illustrates the problem we're having meeting our military needs in this time of war," said Aaron Belkin, director of the Palm Center.[101]

But in the face of this dangerous trend, the media focus remained mostly on cases where felons were shown to be upstanding and trusted soldiers when given a chance—what I call the narrative of the "noble felon." The case of Osvaldo Hernandez, for example, drew national attention after he was allowed to serve in the Middle East, but then turned down for a job with the New York Police Department on his return home. His moral rectitude was good enough for an M-16 in Afghanistan, but not for the Upper East Side. In 2002, when he was twenty, he had been caught with an unlicensed loaded gun in his car and had served a year in prison. He was the lucky recipient of a moral waiver and deployed in 2007 with the Eighty-Second Airborne in Afghanistan, where he spent fifteen months mostly in Ghazni province. Despite returning with a trophy cabinet of accolades, including a Combat Infantry Badge, two Army Commendation Medals, and three Army Achievement Medals, this didn't help him in his application to join the NYPD, which does not have moral waivers like the military. "I just want to take my experience in the military and put it forth in New York City . . . I want to continue to do public service. I grew up in New York City, so that's just where I want to give back," he told the *New York Times*.[102] Luckily for Hernandez, this ridiculous contradiction between military and police regulation led to a public backlash and the then-Governor of New York, David A. Paterson, granting him a pardon for his felony. "Gov. Paterson did the right thing by pardoning Spec. Osvaldo Hernandez from a felony conviction that barred him from achieving the dream of becoming a cop," said the *New York Daily News* at the time.[103] Another case was that of Nasser Hempel, who signed up for the army in October 2006 after spending eleven years in a succession of maximum security prisons in Texas for a robbery he committed in 1991.[104] He was involved in two riots and twelve fist-fights in his first month in prison. Hearing about 9/11 from behind bars changed him and led him to want to sign up to defend his country. "I remember how helpless I felt being stuck behind millions of dollars of concrete and steel while America was under attack," he said. "For a guy who built his reputation on fear and violence in prison, that feeling I had that day was something I've never experienced. That's the day I realized the world was bigger than me."[105] Soon after he was an Army Reserve corporal serving in Baghdad, having received a moral waiver.

One Hundred Hadithas

During the War on Terror, however, not all felons managed to put their indiscretions behind them as the media and military liked to suggest. A raft of research has highlighted the detrimental effect allowing ex-cons to serve in the military has had on the institution itself and on the civilian community being policed by them. Aside from atrocities (like those in Yusufiyah) that were arguably a consequence of recruiting more ex-cons, research has shown that these recruitment practices engender a lack of stability and cohesion within the ranks. A report from the Center for Naval Analyses pointed to higher attrition rates for those with waivers, who were "quite a bit more likely" than those without to get a misconduct charge and be separated from service within their first two years.[106] It reported that "recruits with felony waivers have the highest chance of a misconduct separation."[107] A GAO report that studied attrition rates from 1990 to 1993 had already supported this conclusion, finding that recruits granted moral waivers are more likely to be discharged from the air force because of misconduct.[108] The consensus went even further. "Unsuitability is by far the most common reason for service member attrition," added a 2007 Palm Center report.[109] "Nearly all research on the relationship between offense history and unsuitability attrition points to the unsurprising conclusion that recruits with criminal backgrounds are more likely to be discharged prematurely than those without such backgrounds."

The Pentagon knew it couldn't slow down, but that didn't stop concerns from being expressed within the military community itself. There was a glaring problem with putting a gun in the hands of a convicted criminal and sending them off to a war where they would be expected to kill. John D. Hutson, dean and president of the Franklin Pierce Law Center in New Hampshire and former judge advocate general of the navy, cautioned: "If you are recruiting somebody who has demonstrated some sort of antisocial behavior and then you are a putting a gun in their hands, you have to be awfully careful about what you are doing. You are not putting a hammer in their hands, or asking them to sell used cars. You are potentially asking them to kill people."[110] Christine Wormuth, a senior fellow at the Center for Strategic and International Studies, acknowledged that criminal records are "absolutely an important indicator," before adding the caveat that "it won't mean 100 more Hadithas or cases of soldier abuse," referring to another massacre of civilians in Iraq. "The numbers seem pretty clear to me that we are lowering standards and it's difficult for me to see how that wouldn't have a negative impact on the quality of the force."[111]

Wormuth may have been right that linking atrocities in Afghanistan and Iraq to moral waivers is impossible to do with any certainty, but the anecdotal evidence indicates that the negative impact was shocking. On New Year's Eve 2006, Lance Corporal Delano Holmes, a twenty-two-year-old marine who had been in Iraq for only three months, was on sentry duty in Fallujah, then the country's most dangerous city and a focal point for opposition to the US occupation. His partner on watch that night was army Private Munther Jasem Muhammed Hassin, a soldier from an Iraqi army unit that was helping the US in their attempt to stabilize the city. A few hours into their shift, Private Hassin decided to light a cigarette, a popular pastime for most Iraqis. Lance Corporal Holmes objected, saying the lit end would alert snipers to their whereabouts, and told Hassin to put it out immediately. When his partner just laughed it off Holmes went ballistic, repeatedly stabbing Hassin with a thirteen-inch bayonet. According to the autopsy report, Hassin's body had seventeen stab wounds, twenty-six slashes and a face injury that had just about severed his nose.[112] A year later, in December 2007, a military jury at Camp Pendleton, California, found Holmes guilty of negligent homicide and of making a false statement. He was sentenced to only ten months in jail, effectively time served—in other words, he was a free man. At the court-martial, the prosecutors said Holmes had fired Hassin's AK-47 afterward to make the cold-blooded murder look like self-defense, a common military ruse. Newspaper reports of the trial said that Holmes's "eyes filled with tears so large that they could be seen falling on the lectern from across the room."[113] He told the jury he saw himself as a warrior and a Christian. "God gave me more than I could handle," he informed them. It would have been more accurate had he replaced "God" with "the US military." The military, however, would show further clemency two years later when an appeals court overturned the conviction. It was the last stage in a long line of betrayals by the US military which failed its Iraqi partner Hassin and cost him his life. For a start, Holmes should never have been in Iraq: he had a checkered mental and legal history that should have alerted his recruiters and superiors. At high school he had threatened to commit suicide and had to be hospitalized and was later accused of assault, trespassing, and disorderly conduct. As close as a few months before deployment he was linked to drug use twice. But defense attorneys said Holmes had been given a cocktail of drugs by military medical staff including Ambien, a sleep medication. According to the *Macon Telegraph*, a local newspaper that carried out extensive investigations, "military officials didn't publicly blame the war in Iraq, but some privately acknowledged it is why they accept individuals who previously would have been rejected." When asked how someone like Holmes could have been deployed to Iraq, Marine Captain Brett Miner, a prosecutor at the court-martial, said simply, "We're kind of short on bodies."

Fight Back

Concerned veterans' groups picked up on the waiver system and urged the military to offer different incentives to recruits to end the necessity for the practice—such as an updated version of the GI Bill, which had provided education training to World War Two veterans, or better health care for reservists. "These are safer strategies for attracting a solid core of defenders for our country," said Perry Jefferies, the veterans' outreach director for Iraq and Afghanistan Veterans of America. "The phrase 'moral waivers' euphemizes the real problem," he added, "which is that some of these new soldiers are dangerous criminals. It is hard to capture the true effect of a violent criminal mixed into a unit with no warning and then put under tremendous stress."[114] Worried veterans were gaining support within Congress, but as usual it was left to one courageous lawmaker to blaze a trail. On this issue it was Representative Henry A. Waxman, who in his position as chairman of the House Oversight and Government Reform Committee requested details from the Pentagon on the number of service members with felony convictions, information previously withheld from the public. The data showed that army waivers for felony convictions had more than doubled in a year, from 249 waivers in 2006 to 511 in 2007, while the marines' waivers increased from 208 to 350 in the same period.[115] In a letter to David Chu, the Under Secretary of Defense for Personnel and Readiness, Waxman wrote: "The data you provided the Committee shows that there was a rapid rise in 2007 in the number of waivers the Army and Marine Corps granted to recruits convicted of serious felonies, such as aggravated assault and burglary. Some recruits were even granted waivers for felony convictions involving sexual assault and terrorist threats." Two involved planned domestic bomb attacks.[116] These convictions also included eighty-seven waivers for those convicted of assault and maiming, sometimes with a dangerous weapon. The marines also gave a number of waivers to those convicted of rape, sexual assault, incest, and other sex crimes.[117] Another lawmaker with his finger on the pulse was Representative Marty Meehan, who along with Representative Waxman was trying to get more information from the Pentagon. "The data is crystal clear," he said. "Our armed forces are under incredible strain and the only way that they can fill their recruiting quotas is by lowering their standards. By lowering standards, we are endangering the rest of our armed forces and sending the wrong message to potential recruits across the country."[118]

This unraveling of the US military's moral fiber was a large factor in the rise in criminal acts *within* the military: during the War on Terror, for example, one in three female soldiers reported being victims of some form of sexual assault while in service, dwarfing the one in six women in the civilian world (a development to be explored in greater detail later in the chapter). The military was on the back foot trying to explain this one away. Army Lieutenant Colonel Jonathan Withington, a Pentagon spokesman, retaliated by saying that waivers "are used judiciously and granted only after a thorough review," adding, "The Department strives to maintain high standards ensuring that military recruits surpass the overall qualifications of the contemporary American youth population."[119] Others spun it as a civil rights issue. "The thing is, you've got to give people an opportunity to serve," said Lieutenant General James D. Thurman, the army's operations chief. "We are growing the Army fast, there are some waivers . . . it hasn't alarmed us yet."[120] For some recruiters and commanders it seems soldiers with criminal records were also viewed kindly because as proven "risk-takers" they were more likely to succeed in combat. "Gang members, ex-cons, extremists, they are all more 'war-like' than your average soldier, there's no doubt that's attractive to the military, it's definitely a factor," Hunter Glass told me. Douglas Smith of Army Recruiting Command also put forward the thesis that because there "are more and more young people getting caught up in the criminal justice system than in the past," the US military has had to become more lenient to compensate. This explanation should not be dismissed. The growing numbers of Americans put behind bars was a scandal in itself. In 2008, it was found that one in one hundred adult Americans was actually behind bars, as the prison population ballooned to 1.6 million, the highest in the country's history. It was particularly acute among those segments of the population which have traditionally proven the trustiest military fodder. One in every thirty-six Hispanics was behind bars, while one in nine black men between twenty and thirty-four was also locked up.[121] To the military brass, disenfranchising vast swathes of individuals from ethnic minorities didn't make any sense; now, the government wouldn't just lock you up, it would send you to war afterward. It was a straight path, made even smoother by the fact that a felony conviction in itself makes finding work very hard—a "death sentence" according to DC Congressional Delegate Eleanor Holmes Norton.[122] A newly open military became the best option for a generation of disenfranchised and desperate Americans—they could even sign up while still in prison. The situation was so farcical that by 2007 military recruiters went to the biannual jobs fair at Alexandria City Jail to try to sign up inmates close to release. "They offer a lot of opportunities for advancement, educational opportunities, vocational training, and so it's definitely a great opportunity for anyone interested," said a prison official.[123]

Criminal Denials

In 2007 there was a revealing exchange at a House Armed Services Committee hearing on army recruiting and retention. John McHugh (R-NY) was questioning the witness, Michael Dominguez, Deputy Under Secretary for Personnel and Readiness from the Department of Defense. "Just to kind of state it in a different way and put it on the record again, I would like to ask you gentlemen to state how you feel about the quality of the men and women overall that you are recruiting into the military today, and make a comment, if you will, about felons in terms of waivers if you have such a thing," asked McHugh. "I mean, generally when we talked about waivers, there is the medical waiver, there is the moral waiver, which by and large has to do with minor crimes, generally as a youth, whether it is an alcohol situation or some kind of truancy, vandalism, something like that. But are we admitting hardcore felons into the United States Army today? Did I miss something?"[124] There was a pause. Then Dominguez replied (erroneously): "We exclude members of hate groups and gangs and those kinds of things. We have very well established procedures to exclude those. We don't recruit murderers and rapists and that kind of violent criminal. What amounts to a felony in the United States of America varies from state to state." But the numbers speak for themselves. In 2005—when it missed recruitment numbers by the largest margin since 1979—the army took in 21,880 new soldiers, or 17 percent of recruits, on a waiver.[125] That's more than an entire infantry division. The situation had become so bad by 2007 that nearly one in five recruits entered the army courtesy of a waiver for a felony or misdemeanor, representing a 42 percent increase in the use of waivers since 2000. This was not normal. "They've been doing it forever, but the numbers were small," said University of Maryland military sociologist David Segal. "It's only with the current conflict in the past couple of years that the numbers have gotten so large."[126] Back in the hearing, General Bostick then took over in a support role, using the method of exculpation outlined earlier: appealing to the noble criminal. "Corporal Vaccaro, killed in Afghanistan, 10th Mountain Division—he smoked marijuana 20 to 30 times; he saved many, many soldiers and earned a Silver Star," he said. "Those are examples of the kind of soldiers that have been given a second chance, have demonstrated before that second chance opportunity that they had overcome any misgivings they had earlier in their life. So I feel very, very confident of it." He didn't mention Steven D. Green.

Despite continued military assurances that it was not a problem, they gave the game away when the financial crisis hit and their recruitment problems abated. In 2009 the military met its recruitment targets for the first time since 2004 and pledged to lock out those with criminal records once again. Brigadier General Joseph Anderson, deputy commander of the US Army Recruiting Command, said that the "adult major misconduct" waiver, given for felony offenses, was now closed, and additionally those with a history of juvenile criminal activity would not be allowed to recruit without a high school diploma.[127] It was an admission of guilt, but for many in Iraq and Afghanistan, like Genei Nasir al-Janabi, it was too late. In February 2008, Staff Sergeant Michael A. Hensley was put on trial after he had ordered the shooting of an unarmed civilian near Iskandariya, a city in central Iraq. Hensley claimed he had to issue the order because al-Janabi had discovered his unit's hiding place, but he was later found guilty of placing a rifle next to al-Janabi's body to buttress his claims that the unit had been under attack. It was a harrowing case. "I put him face down on the ground, with my knee in his back. He started to make a lot of noise. He started to cry . . . he was yelling, I was trying to shut him up," said Hensley in his testimony.[128] The incident came on the back of a hard campaign against the insurgency in Jarf Sakhr, thirty-five miles southwest of Baghdad. The defense attorney for Evan Vela—the soldier on trial for murder after having carried out Hensley's order—blamed the intense regimen for the tragedy, a fair criticism as we will see. "They have no superpowers," he said. "When pushed beyond human ability to absorb sleep deprivation, heat exhaustion, and post-traumatic stress disorder you can expect bad judgment." Hensley added that this was nothing out of the ordinary: "We had been losing a lot of people without doing anything . . . My sergeant major told me he wanted to produce more kills and I was the guy to make it happen."[129] The placing of an AK-47 next to the body was, as we have seen, common procedure. It was impossible to verify Hensley's claims about the episode, although his past should have alerted the military authorities. According to a family who lived in the same area as Hensley, they were so worried about his conduct nine months before his deployment that they secretly filmed him. They recounted how one morning they had awakened to screams to see Hensley threatening a woman inside a vehicle. He had pounded the car so hard that a police report said he "had bloody knuckles, and the windshield of the Jeep was broken."[130] Hensley pleaded no contest to the charges of disorderly conduct. Subsequently the eighteen-year-old who filmed the incident said: "He obviously wasn't stable, just from seeing him the 20 minutes I did."[131] The military was given a perfect excuse to bar his enlistment: Hensley had already served six months probation for a drunk driving conviction in Georgia. But they took him anyway.

The War on Women

The proliferation of serious criminals in the military was, as mentioned, among the reasons for the huge rise in crimes against female service personnel—particularly sexual abuse and rape—during the War on Terror. Andrea Neutzling was one unfortunate witness who left her decade of service in the US military during the War on Terror with deep mental and physical scars, the most painful of which were inflicted not by the enemy but by her comrades-in-arms. It wasn't meant to be like this. She had wanted to follow in her family's footsteps when she signed up for the US army in 1999: her great-grandfather had served in the Marine Corps in World War Two and Korea, while her uncle was in the navy and her dad an army veteran. It ran in the family, but she was the first woman to serve. "It was an important thing in that respect," she tells me. She signed on the dotted line when she was nineteen, but had started talking to recruiters when she was much younger. "I always knew it was what I wanted to do," she says.

Originally from a small town on the banks of the Ohio River, Neutzling was deployed to Camp Bucca in southern Iraq in the middle of 2005 as part of a military police unit where she would oversee the care of new Iraqi detainees. One day after work, still acclimatizing to her new surroundings, she waited for a friend to join her for a workout at the gym. "While I was waiting for him, two guys came up and started talking to me," she says. At the time she was living in an eight-woman tent while the group waited for their residency halls to be finished. "They were with the unit I was replacing so I went into the living quarters with them when they asked." The men lived in a so-called "pod," a small two-man room. "I went into there and I sat in there with the two and they were drinking Crown Royal, which is kinda like a whisky, you drink it with 7-Up or Sprite, but they shouldn't have been drinking alcohol. I'm not sure how they got it." Over the next twenty minutes they would brutally rape and physically assault her. "They grabbed a hold of me and told me that 'we're all gonna have some fun' and if I didn't go along with it they would be beat me and leave me naked in front the shopping facility on the base." Understandably terrified, Neutzling focused on trying to keep herself alive, choosing not to fight back. "It was two against one so I kinda did the whole self-preservation thing, I had kids I wanted to come home to." The men raped her repeatedly while verbally abusing her. "One guy was putting finger nails down my back and calling me a 'whore' and a 'fat pig' and that I should be grateful for all the attention I was getting from them." After the attack, the men told her to keep her mouth shut but didn't appear overly concerned about any consequences. "One of them pinched the inside of my thigh and told me that I should go and I shouldn't tell anybody about it."

Amazingly this wasn't the first time Neutzling had been sexually assaulted while in the military. In 2002, while serving in Korea, a drunk colleague had abused her outside a latrine. Back then, when she had told her commanders, they handed out the non-sentence of five days of base restriction for the man. For this reason, after the attack at Bucca, she was reticent about telling her commanders again. "Women knew it wouldn't be good for your career to make a fuss," she says. In Iraq, she didn't say anything to anybody for a week after the incident, until another woman in her unit said the men were showing a video of the rape and bragging about it. At that point she told her command. "The woman who told me was our armorer, she gave us our ammo and weapons, and when she told me that, I asked her if she wanted my ammo, because I would have shot them." The men were scheduled to leave in three weeks and they left on time, facing no charges—a situation that remains to this day. The battalion commanders told her explicitly that the reason was they "didn't want to leave anybody behind." If the men had been charged, they would have had to stay in Iraq or be sent to Kuwait, and been out of action for a long period the military could ill afford. In fact, the only person to get reprimanded was Neutzling herself, who was married at the time and later chastised by her commander for "committing adultery." He told her that since the military considered the incident a case of "forced consent," an oxymoronic term for a situation where the victim is drunk or goes along with the sexual activity for his or her own protection, he considered her behavior infidelity. Sympathy was equally lacking elsewhere. The chaplain merely told her it couldn't have been rape because she didn't act like a rape victim: she wasn't visibly upset or crying. "But if he had come during the first three days afterwards, I was sleeping with my M-16 locked and loaded," she says. The military's tactic of looking the other way worked: when no one wanted to do anything for her, she just tried to block it out by concentrating on work. "I busted my butt doing my job over there," she says. Often working twelve-hour days, she was instrumental in setting up important procedures for separating detainees, after she found Sunnis and Shias were being put in the same living quarters. But none of this was rewarded as it should have been, simply because she hadn't kept her mouth shut. At the end of her tour, the brass merely gave her a "certificate of achievement," a minor recognition of service. Others who had done much less work received Bronze Stars and Army Commendation medals. Neo-Nazis had often done a lot better.

Neutzling explicitly blamed the opening up of the military to criminals (alongside its failure to kick out service members guilty of misconduct) for the treatment she received. "When I first got in they didn't have those looser standards and the first time I saw any type of sexual harassment or anything I was based in Arizona for my job training," she says. "Some guy was done for sexual assault and they sent him up the river, they spoke to every female and he got dishonorable discharge." But this all changed after 9/11. "After that you could get waivers for pretty much anything, including sex crimes and other violent offenses." She is now part of a lawsuit against the Pentagon which was filed in early 2011 and includes seventeen other service members who were subjected to sexual assaults and rape while serving in the armed forces.[132] It names as defendants Defense Secretaries Donald Rumsfeld and Robert Gates, whom it blames for a culture of punishment against women who report sexual crimes and the failure to prosecute the offenders. The charge sheet does not include Rumsfeld's opening up of the military to assorted criminals—but it could have. The lead lawyer on the case, Susan Burke, said the scale of the problem became clear when the lawsuit was made public and hundreds of women (and men) contacted her with similar stories. "We received a significant outpouring of support from both women and men soldiers," she told me. "In addition, we have been approached by many more rape survivors."

The lawsuit blew the lid on what had become a huge problem for the US military. By 2009, one in three of the 20,000 active-duty women serving the US military had reported being the victim of a sexual assault while serving—double the rate for civilians. Since the Pentagon began tracking assaults in 2006 under pressure from Congress, the reporting rate has risen every year.[133] The situation was so bad during the most fraught years of the War on Terror that the Pentagon belatedly decided to apply a Band-Aid, creating the Sexual Assault Prevention and Response Office, or SAPRO. "What we saw during the first part of the Iraq war under Rumsfeld was that he loosened standards to what were serious crimes—rape, grand larceny—that would normally disqualify folks," says Greg Jacobs, policy director of the Service Women's Action Network, an organization focused on the assault and sexual abuse of women in the military. "They let a bunch in, which was a problem." In 2009 the Pentagon reported 3,230 incidents of sexual assault which represented an 11 percent increase from the previous year. In combat zones, specifically Iraq and Afghanistan, it was even worse—rising by 16 percent.[134] In fact, US women service members are today more likely to be raped by a fellow soldier than to be killed by enemy fire. No one knows how many Iraqi or Afghan women and girls have been subjected to similar atrocities, although cases like the rapes and murders in Yusufiyah suggest it was equally endemic, and went equally unpunished. We will never know the full truth.

A further problem for women service members is that the military handles assaults of this kind in a different way than civilian law does. Military discipline is set up to ensure good order in the ranks, not justice for victims. In other words, the military handles sexual assault like it's a matter of personal misconduct rather than a criminal offense. In New York, for example, rape is a Class B felony carrying a sentence of ten years in jail; in the military, however, you are in minority if you go to jail for rape. When the need for troops was most chronic this wiggle room allowed many rapists to escape punishment. Furthermore, the Pentagon itself estimates that as few as 13.5 percent of sexual assaults are reported and even those rarely end in prosecutions.[135] While 40 percent of sexual assault allegations in the civilian world are prosecuted, the number is just 8 percent in the military.[136] Pentagon policy also dictates that any physical evidence of a rape should be destroyed after five years, making it much harder for a service member who has been sexually assaulted to file a legal or benefit claim after they leave the military. Likewise, if the perpetrator commits another crime there's no record of the previous incident, giving them even less of an incentive to clean up their act. "Sexual assault is one of our nation's most underreported violent crimes, and is a problem worldwide. Unfortunately, our military is not immune to larger societal problems," Kaye Whitley, director of SAPRO, told me. "What is evident in the larger society is also reflected within the military." She did not mention how much worse it was for service members than for regular civilians.

Pressure from within the military as well as the latest lawsuit has had an effect on the debate in Washington, but it came far too late for thousands of women and men whose lives had already been needlessly wrecked. In April 2011 a bipartisan bill was introduced into Congress which will allow sexual abuse victims the automatic right to legal counsel, the right to a base transfer, the right to maintain confidentiality when speaking with commanders and medical staff, and will provide greater training in sexual assault prevention and response. Many asked why it had taken a decade to get to this point and why the link between the loosening of standards and the deterioration of the behavior of soldiers was still not being made, although it was clear to everyone that it was a major factor. The military had become the *perfect place* to be a criminal simply because in it normal legal constraints didn't apply. You could commit rape and know that there was very little chance of any penalty arising let alone a criminal prosecution. And it wasn't just rape. The military was turning a blind eye to a host of other prohibited and criminal activities as it tried to keep troop levels up, including the use of alcohol and illegal drugs, which are ostensibly banned in the military. "They didn't even get in trouble for having alcohol!" said Andrea Neutzling, exasperated at the complete impunity of the men who raped her. Unfortunately, this was not as surprising as she assumed.

CHAPTER TWO

Sick, Addicted, and Forsaken

SIPPIN' ON GIN AND HAJJI JUICE

Alcohol and drug use starts a cascade of worse problems. It's like throwing gasoline on fire.

Dr. Richard McCormick, retired director of mental
health for the state veterans affairs system in Ohio, 2008[1]

In early 2004 reports began to emerge of detainee abuse at Abu Ghraib prison, or Baghdad Correctional Facility as it was rechristened post-invasion. It was a notorious venue for torture and general barbarity during Saddam Hussein's twenty-five-year reign, and rumors were flying around that similar atrocities were now taking place under the auspices of the US military. It wasn't long before the mutterings were confirmed and photographs surfaced showing the physical and sexual abuse of the Iraqi detainees by grinning American troops. These included pictures of naked Iraqis piled on top of each other in a pyramid of human bodies, and of electrode treatment, among other horrors. It was a turning point in the public perception of a war we had been told was undertaken to defend human rights and democracy. The personal attempts by Donald Rumsfeld to cover it up, and his disregard for the Uniform Code of Military Justice that set the stage for the torture, likely signaled the first step towards his ignominious departure two years later. But in the long and heated debate that followed the revelations, one crucial topic was breezed over and barely considered. Many of the soldiers who had carried out the torture and humiliation of the Iraqi detainees had been drunk at the time. During its brief period under US control, Abu Ghraib had been turned into a swinging frat party with the free-flowing alcohol and ritual acts of humiliation that accompany such events on American campuses. The problem was known widely among the service members in the prison (and the military brass); in fact, weeks before the photographs were made public, commanders at Abu Ghraib had launched a crackdown on the alcohol abuse amid persistent rumors about intoxicated guards soliciting sex from Iraqi prostitutes. One army analyst at the time recalled a senior prison and interrogation officer bellowing at them: "There's a prostitution ring and a liquor smuggling ring . . . I'm going to pursue it and I hope there's no military intelligence people involved."[2]

His hopes on that score weren't realized, but the military's blushes were saved somewhat by a media blackout. In the flood of news coverage about the torture scandal, only one newspaper, the *Los Angeles Times*, gave serious coverage and investigative resources to the issue of alcohol abuse. In a 2004 article it reported that some officers thought alcohol consumption had been a contributing factor. At least one prisoner told investigators that they frequently smelled alcohol on the guards' breath in the cellblock where most of the abuses occurred.[3] Apparently there was even an Alcoholics Anonymous chapter at the prison. "I remember one soldier telling me he gave a [vendor] a twenty and he brought him back a bottle of alcohol," said one intelligence analyst at the prison. "They would try to bring it to you as a gift," added Lieutenant Antoine Brooks of the 870th MP Company. An investigation into abuses at the prison had cited two cases of military police officers being pulled up for alcohol consumption, but the incident was in May 2003, before Abu Ghraib was turned into an American detention center.

Since alcohol is strictly forbidden by the US military, how was this flagrant breaking of the rules allowed to go on for so long? How had this feted "liberation" turned into a frat party within a year? In truth, the obscenities at Abu Ghraib were merely the tip of a problem that penetrated deep into every level of the occupation forces during the War on Terror. The military could no longer afford—in monetary or manpower terms—to lay off or treat its most vulnerable soldiers, including alcoholics and drug addicts, and Iraqi and Afghan civilians often paid the price for their intoxication. Of course, that wasn't the message the military was putting out. In fact, looking at the discharge figures for alcohol and drug abuse during the most critical years of the War on Terror, they could be interpreted as a cause for celebration. Ostensibly, the US military enjoyed one of the most successful periods in its history in tackling alcoholism and substance abuse. According to figures obtained through the Freedom of Information Act, failure in the drug rehabilitation program resulting in discharge fell from 164 in 2002, the first full year of war, to a mere 51 in 2006. Failure in the alcoholism rehabilitation program fell from 271 in 2002 to 143 in 2006.[4] Aside from the military, there was one other group who saw this as a welcome progression: those agitating for greater rights *for addicts*. Robert J. Lindsey, of the National Council on Alcohol and Drug Dependence, told me, "military discrimination against alcohol and drugs users has certainly been an issue of huge concern in the past. There is absolutely no question that addiction to alcohol and drugs should be treated as a health problem not as a disciplinary one." But the War on Terror bought hope. "It's encouraging to see the numbers [of discharges] declining," he continued. "We hope that means more people are getting help." Although, he added, "It could mean they are more desperate for troops."

His second guess was the right one. Unfortunately for both the troops and the people being policed by them—who belonged to societies with deep sensitivities about alcohol—the discharge figures were a chimera: there was no sudden improvement in the treatment of addicted soldiers. What the figures revealed, rather, was a military that could just no longer afford to discharge them and increasingly failed to send them to the one place they might be able to get help. Medical professionals within the military were aware of this huge problem, even though the military continued to look the other way. "It's clear that we've got a lot of significant alcohol problems that are pervasive across the military," said Dr. Thomas R. Kosten, a psychiatrist at the Veterans Affairs Medical Center in Houston. "The treatment that they take for [combat stress] is the same treatment that they took after Vietnam . . . They turn to alcohol and drugs."[5] The increasing number of "moral waivers" provided to recruits for previous alcohol and drug offenses made the problem even more serious.

Through 2005 and 2006, when the need was at its greatest, military spending on programs to reduce alcohol abuse, alongside a few other addictions like smoking, dropped from $12.6 million to $7.74 million.[6] A staggering 39 percent decline. It was this dereliction of duty to serving men and women that aroused the interest of Senator Clair McCaskill (D-MO), one of the few lawmakers to pick up on the issue and bang heads. In 2007 she wrote a letter to General Peter Chiarelli, senior military assistant to the Secretary of State, asking him to investigate allegations that a tranche of 150 soldiers at Fort Leonard Wood, Missouri, were not able to get the counseling they needed and wanted because of staff shortages at the base. McCaskill didn't mince her words, saying the base's program had been "in a shambles" for years, before adding, "If it was that bad at Fort Leonard Wood, it very well could be an Army-wide problem."[7] Her hunch was right, and the army-wide problem was causing untold suffering for the service members fighting in the Middle East and around the world. "How is it that a program can so deteriorate at a time when drug use and alcohol abuse is known to be closely tied to PTSD, suicides, criminal behavior, divorce and domestic abuse, all of which have substantially increased in recent years in the Army?" McCaskill asked the general.[8] But it was two years—during the War on Terror not a shabby response time for a generally unresponsive military— before General Chiarelli eventually acted, sending a memo to army leaders in 2009 lamenting the lack of discharges as regulation permitted, before pressing commanders to address the shortage of qualified counselors to help the soldiers through their addictions. "Our soldiers need this resource and I expect you to provide it for them," he instructed. Until then the best the army could point to was the relatively puny growth of its Substance Abuse Program, the budget for which grew from $38 million to $51 million between 2004 and 2008.[9] It was peanuts.

Back home, alcohol use among the general US population was increasing as well, hitting 67 percent of citizens in 2010, its highest since 1985, according to a Gallup poll, with an increasing number of states allowing Sunday liquor sales and moving sales start-time to 6 a.m. It was even worse within the military. The Pentagon's own health study found that binge drinking surged by 30 percent from 2002 to 2005, prompting the conclusion that it "may signal an increasing pattern of heavy alcohol use in the Army."[10] More than a quarter of army servicemen said they often drank heavily, which was defined as five or more drinks in one session. It constituted the largest proportion of the military since (again) 1985.[11] One academic study in March 2009 found that of the 16,037 active-duty personnel surveyed, 43 percent reported binge drinking in the previous month, a rate very similar to that of college students.[12] One of the biggest problems for the military was the same as in Vietnam: easy access. In Iraq it was easy to get your hands on what the troops call "hajji juice" or "hajji hooch," the locally produced 90 percent proof whiskey that the soldiers who participated in the Mahmudiyah massacre were supping before embarking on their crimes. This is sometimes combined with amphetamines provided by medical staff to keep troops alert on missions. In Iraq, despite the pro forma ban, soldiers would squeeze ampoules of food coloring into bottles of clear liquor and transfer it to bottles of mouthwash. Army medics, in a mild dereliction of duty, had been known to fill IV bags with vodka in lieu of saline solution. By 2010, the US military itself was spending $602,189.90 per year on alcoholic beverages.[13]

Partying It Up

In a warzone, a culture of binge drinking is dangerous for the same obvious reason that drunk driving is dangerous: drunk people aren't in full control of what they are doing. As the UK *Daily Mail* reported in March 2007, "Figures forced from the Pentagon by the *New York Times* under the Freedom of Information Act make shocking reading:

240 of the 665 cases of military indiscipline in Iraq and Afghanistan involved drugs and alcohol. Seventy-three of those 240 cases were the most serious yet known from these two wars: murder, rape, robbery and assault."[14] Many of these cases were fatal for Iraqis and US service members. In May 2004, as Bush was infamously pronouncing mission accomplished in Iraq, Private Justin Lissis went on the rampage with a stolen Humvee and his M-16 rifle in a residential district in Balad after getting drunk on whiskey smuggled into the base by Iraqi contractors.[15] Just six months on, Private Chris Rolan of the Third Brigade was having a heated argument with a fellow US soldier after a heady cocktail of alcohol and ended up shooting him with his 9mm pistol.[16] And it wasn't just Iraq. In 2006, one of the many errant airstrikes carried out by NATO in Afghanistan killed seventy civilians after the strike had been called in on Germany's instructions but carried out by American pilots. When staff at NATO's Kabul headquarters were to be questioned on the event the command found that they could not be interviewed because they were "either drunk or too hungover."[17] General Stanley McChrystal subsequently banned alcohol at the base, laying into the forces for "partying it up" when it emerged that there was a serious scene there. He said they did not have "their heads in the right place" after the attack.[18] It's hard to know what is more worrying: that the strike may have been called in by people either hungover or drunk, or that they decided to go on a binge after taking out seventy civilians. Binge drinkers, one academic study worryingly found, "report being drunk while working and being called to work during off-duty hours and reporting to work drunk."[19] The idea they may have been drunk was implied when a spokesperson said: "General McChrystal is extremely focused on the mission and he feels that the folk who are here at the headquarters level need to be at the top of their game in terms of supporting the folks out in the field." One insider was more explicit. "Thursday nights are the big party nights, because Friday's a 'low-ops' day. They even open a bar in the garden at headquarters," they said. "There's a 'two can' rule but people ignore it and hit it pretty hard."

This was now starting to endanger even the safety of America's own diplomats as well, as allegations of drunken brawls and lewd behavior at the US embassy in Kabul led to another drink ban being imposed. An independent group sent a ten-page dossier to Secretary of State Clinton containing evidence that security guards at the embassy had been having "drunken parties involving prostitutes" and forms of "ritual humiliation associated with gang initiation".[20] The dossier included an email from a guard serving in Kabul describing guards and supervisors "peeing on people, eating potato chips out of [buttock] cracks, vodka shots out of [buttock] cracks (there is video of that one), broken doors after drnken [sic] brawls, threats and intimidation from those leaders participating in this activity."[21] In Tokyo, the US navy imposed a movement and alcohol ban after a Japanese taxi driver was found dead with a twenty-centimeter kitchen knife blade stuck in his neck in Yokosuka, just south of Tokyo, where the US has a naval base.[22] The culprit, Olatunbosun Ugbogu, was a Nigerian national and US sailor, one of the many foreign citizens enfranchised to fight by the War on Terror. Even animals weren't safe. Over at Baghdad Zoo, a drunk soldier shot and killed a Bengal tiger on one of the Thursday binge nights. "The soldiers arrived in the evening with food and beer, accompanied by a group of Iraqi police officers," head of the zoo, Adel Salman Musa, said of the incident. "One of the soldiers, who the Iraqi police said had drunk a lot, went into the cage against the advice of his colleagues and tried to feed the animal who severely hurt his arm," he added. The tiger, said the news agency, tore off the soldier's fingers and mauled his arm and another US soldier immediately fired at the animal and killed it. "The soldiers don't have the right to behave like that. That was the most precious and valuable animal in the whole zoo. It was fourteen years old and had been born here," Musa said.[23]

In a Birthday Cake

The problem with illicit drug use was even worse in US-occupied Afghanistan, the country with the biggest poppy harvests in the world, producing 9,000 metric tonnes of opium each year, which is chemically treated to make heroin. Production had not slowed down substantially during the occupation, and soldiers found they could buy heroin quicker than they could buy a bottle of water. There were even rumors that the US was not getting a handle on the drug production because it was too lucrative. General Mahmut Gareev, a former commander during the Soviet Union's war in Afghanistan, alleged that the US was paying for its occupation through the harvests, which could yield up to $50 billion a year.[24] Whatever the reason, US service members using heroin frequently went unpunished by the military. "They don't do anything to you," one soldier said. "Two from my unit were sent home after they got caught more than once." Asked what was done to them, he replied, "Nothing. They're still in the unit. Just got sent home."[25] It was so rife that a top military commander said he would be surprised if the army had not turned into a drug-dealing cartel. "I'd be astonished if we don't see soldiers who find ten kilograms of heroin and pack it up in a birthday cake and send it home to their mother," said General Barry McCaffrey, a former "drug czar" under President Clinton.[26]

Experts think it could be a decade before the true scope of heroin use in Iraq and Afghanistan is known. Dr. Jodie Trafton, a health-care specialist with the VA's Center for Health Care Evaluation, predicted that the scale of the problem will not be gaugeable until five or ten years after the wars are over and veterans enter the system in significant numbers. "We're just starting to get a lot of Gulf War veterans," she said. But the signs were definitely there. "I asked to buy heroin a dozen times during two trips a year apart and never heard the word 'no,'" said a filmmaker who had been to Afghanistan on numerous occasions. "I also saw ample evidence that soldiers were trading sensitive military equipment, like computer drives and bulletproof vests, for drugs."[27] The results were appalling for the many soldiers whose lives were ripped apart by addiction. The Veterans Health Administration counted over 3,000 veterans of the Iraq and Afghanistan wars as diagnosed with potential drug dependency from 2005 to 2007. This was a monumental rise on previous years. From 2002 through 2004 only 277 veterans were diagnosed with a drug dependency.[28] "It's a huge concern, it's a national concern," Lynn Pahland, a director in the Pentagon's Health Affairs office, said. "Any kind of drug use or health choice that leads to the impairment of a military person leads to the degradation of readiness."[29]

But the operational readiness of the force was strangely down at the bottom of the list of priorities. Veterans For America (VFA) member Jason Knobloch wrote, "Numerous studies have shown, as VFA has found over and over again, that heavy drinking and drug use are often attempts to self-medicate untreated psychological problems such as post-traumatic stress disorder. The programs to treat these conditions of both the military and the Veterans Administration are understaffed and underfunded."[30] In fact, the military was making it worse. The number of soldiers seeking help for substance abuse had climbed 25 percent in five years, according to *USA Today*, but the army's counseling program remained "significantly understaffed and struggling to meet the demand."[31] The army requires one drug counselor for every 2,000 soldiers, yet in late 2008 it was operating with one for every 3,100 soldiers.[32] It didn't come close to catering to the needs of the service members, many of whom were suffering from a variety of mental health problems and finding no help for them within official channels.

Guinea Pigs

It wasn't just that the military was ignoring the use of alcohol and drugs—in many cases it was promoting it. The streamlined, flexible, and understaffed US military that was Rumsfeld's dream meant that extra energy and service time had to be squeezed out of existing troops. To do this some were plied with cocktails of narcotics and stimulants. "The capability to resist the mental and physiological effects of sleep deprivation will fundamentally change current military concepts of 'operational tempo' and contemporary orders of battle for the military services," states a document from the Pentagon's Defense Advanced Research Projects Agency, or DARPA. "In short, the capability to operate effectively, without sleep, is no less than a twenty-first-century revolution in military affairs that results in operational dominance across the whole range of potential

U.S. military employments."[33] To achieve this operational dominance, amphetamines of all kinds were provided to the US air force—in street parlance, speed. The drug is traditionally used to treat narcolepsy or attention deficit disorder, but for the military's purposes it was perfect: it increased concentration, energy levels, and adrenalin. But there were psychological drawbacks, which appeared especially relevant to those using bomb-laden aircraft. According to *Wired* magazine, "serious potential side effects include psychotic behavior, depression, anxiety, fatigue, paranoia, aggression, violent behavior, confusion, insomnia, auditory hallucinations, mood disturbances and delusions."[34] The operational effect of this new "revolution" revealed itself early on in the Afghanistan war effort when in April 2002 a US aircraft dropped a 500-pound bomb on a group of Canadian soldiers at Tarnak Farms near Kandahar, Afghanistan, killing four and leaving eight injured. In the resulting investigations the two pilots claimed the air force's policy of handing out dextro-amphetamine, or Dexedrine, was responsible for the error, not them.[35]

Back at base, willing soldiers were welcome to another load of drugs to help them deal with the hell of war. As PTSD developed into a chronic problem, pills took the place of doctors in dealing with the mental health crisis among US troops. One soldier recounts going to talk to a military doctor about the trauma he was suffering as a result of the conflict. "Here's some medication," he was told, before being prescribed a cocktail of drugs: "Klonopin, for anxiety; Zoloft, for depression; and Ambien, to help him sleep."[36] Data from a mental health survey by the US army found that 12 percent of soldiers in Iraq and 15 percent in Afghanistan were taking some form of anti-depressant, anti-anxiety drug, or sleeping pill.[37] The army itself was more than happy to dispense them: it was much cheaper than increasing the number of medical professionals. By September 2007 prescriptions for narcotics for active-duty troops had reached 50,000 a month, up from 33,000 a month in October 2003.[38] In the midst of all this, it came as no surprise that an extensive drug smuggling network involving US soldiers was gradually developed. In 2008, a drug ring suspected of providing steroids to US service members in Iraq was busted in northern Italy. According to *ABC News*, briefed by government officials, "Dozens of active and former soldiers have abused their military uniforms and authority in a drug smuggling ring."[39] Their list included:

A U.S. army sergeant fighting the war on drugs in Colombia was recently sentenced to six years in prison for using military aircraft to smuggle cocaine into the United States. In April, an Air National Guard pilot and a sergeant used a C-5 Galaxy military transport plane to sneak nearly 300,000 Ecstasy pills from Germany into New York. In another case, three U.S. airmen were arrested in March for stealing military-issue bulletproof vests from Moody Air Force Base in Georgia and selling them to drug dealers for $100 each.[40]

It wasn't just rogue soldiers procuring ecstasy either. The military was in on it as well. In 2005 it moved to start prescribing the rave drug better known in the clubs and discos of big American cities to its soldiers. The scientists trailing the drug were said to be interested in the "emotional closeness" it creates among its users.[41] Two years later, the move to medicate PTSD away led to the so-called Psychological Kevlar Act, which was meant to formalize a program of research to help soldiers tackle the problem early on. Its stated purpose was to "implement a plan to incorporate preventive and early-intervention measures" to combat "post-traumatic stress disorder or other stress-related psychopathologies."[42] A drug called propranolol was the talk of the town at the time because if taken directly after a traumatic event it could apparently blunt the force of the experience on the brain. The brave new world was here. The Department of Veterans Affairs conducted its own tests on the drug's effect on PTSD symptom reduction and found that a single oral dose, compared to a placebo, immediately after reactivation of the PTSD-related memory of the traumatic event "significantly reduced physiological responses."[43]

It was all a bonanza for Big Pharma, which raked in billions of dollars of taxpayer money: in 2007 alone the DOD spent $3 billion on contracts for its ballooning pharmaceutical needs. The powerful Big Pharma lobby in turn pushed the military to continue drugging their soldiers and the military brass didn't demur: the pharmaceutical industry was becoming a full-fledged part of the military-industrial complex. It was a natural progression since their lobbying had already worked in wider society. In the general population over the previous decade, the number of Americans taking one or more prescription drugs had risen from 44 to 48 percent, while one 2009 drug-abuse survey found that 2.8 percent of the US population used prescription drugs in non-medical ways—up from 2.5 percent the year previous. The next front for the lobby was service members. "Armed with potent drugs and new technology, a dangerous breed of soldiers are being trained to fight America's future wars," warned one magazine at the time.[44] Soldiers were to be the guinea pigs for a burgeoning field of research. "Improved drug delivery systems and improved neurological understanding could make today's drugs seem rudimentary, giving soldiers a superhuman strength and awareness," wrote *Wired* magazine.[45] A report released by the intelligence unit of the DOD in 2008 contained a multitude of suggestions on how to manipulate the minds of soldiers using new research on brain functions. Perhaps the most sci-fi element of the report was its description of so-called "pharmacological landmines," using chemicals to incapacitate the enemy. But amazingly it wasn't the enemy that was being plied with dodgy drugs during the War on Terror, but US troops themselves. In 2008 an *ABC News* and *Washington Times* investigation revealed that the VA was testing the anti-smoking drug Chantix on veterans who knew nothing about its side effects until three months in.[46] The side effects were not innocuous either, including as they did psychosis and potential suicide. "Lab rat, guinea pig, disposable hero," said former US army sniper James Elliott when asked how he felt.

Even the military had gone too far this time, and they duly incurred the wrath of then presidential candidate Barack Obama who came out to denounce the testing. "It is outrageous and unacceptable that our government would irresponsibly endanger veterans who have already sacrificed so much for our country," he said. "Our veterans—particularly those suffering from mental health injuries—should have the very best health care and support in the world, they should never be needlessly exposed to drugs without proper notification of the dangers involved or effective monitoring of the side effects."[47] Obama was right that veterans deserved access to the best health care, but they would never receive it. Even back in the US—where much of the alcoholism and drug abuse played out in the most traumatic way among the families of veterans and those in their community—the military looked the other way. "We better be ready to offer compassion and treatment—not just a jail cell—when it comes to helping our brothers and sisters heal from the damages of war," said Tony Newman, communications director at the Drug Policy Alliance. "Let's hope that we support our current troops better than we supported the veterans who fought in Vietnam."[48] But they weren't treated any better—and only a brave few spoke out. "The war is now and the problems are now," said Richard A. McCormick, a senior scholar for public health at Case Western Reserve University in Cleveland, who served on a Pentagon task force.[49] "Every day there is a cohort of men and women being discharged who need services not one or two or five years from now. They need them now." While the military dithered on how to deal with an impending crisis, drug use was endemic. "Lots of soldiers coming back from Iraq have been using drugs," Specialist William Swenson, who was deployed to Iraq, told *ABC News*. "Right when we got back there were people using cocaine in the barracks, there were people smoking marijuana at strip clubs; one guy started shooting up."[50] The VA soon had the dubious distinction of being the world's largest provider of substance-abuse services, looking after 350,000 veterans per year, of which 30,000 needed treatment for opiate addiction.[51]

It wasn't helping the domestic US criminal justice system either, with troubled veterans spilling into the country's jails at unprecedented levels. "A small fraction wind up in prison for homicides or other major crimes. Far more, though, are involved in drunken bar fights, reckless driving and alcohol-fueled domestic violence. Whatever the particulars, their stories often spool out in unwitting victims, ruptured families, lost jobs and crushing debt,"[52] wrote the *New York Times*. The army claimed it was doing all it could, of course. That was its default position. "The Army takes alcohol and drug abuse very seriously and has tried for decades to deglamorize its use," said a spokesman.[53] "With the urgency of this war, we continue to tackle the problem with education, prevention and treatment." How seriously did it take the problem? In 2010 it put $2 million into starting up its "That Guy" website, which aimed to stop binge-drinking among veterans because it detracts from the "things they care about: family, friends, dating, sex, money and reputation."[54] It was completely inadequate: a single stitch to rescue an unraveling group of soldiers. By 2008 it was clear the situation was now a full-blown crisis destroying the emotional and psychological wellbeing of US service members across the board. A Pentagon investigation found that the psychological problems among troops were "daunting and growing" and betrayed a "fundamental weaknesses" in the military's approach. In reality it was out of control: nearly 40 percent of soldiers, half of all National Guard, and a third of Marines were reporting serious mental health issues.[55] Many were committing suicide.

COLLATERAL DAMAGE COMES HOME

I was in no condition to leave. I'm an infantryman. If I'm screwed up in my head, it could cost my life or the lives of the men with me.
   Michael De Vlieger, gunner with the 101st Airborne in Iraq, 2009[56]

In July 2007, Army Specialist Travis Virgadamo returned home on a "rest and relaxation" break to the serene mountain surroundings of Pahrump, Nevada, after an arduous tour of Iraq as violence in the country peaked. It was immediately obvious to his family and friends that he was in a bad way and had dipped into a severe depression while out in the desert. Back in the US he kept telling his grandmother about the horrendous things he had seen: images so distressing that he thought he could never go back. But in the military, refusing to go back into service can land you a prison sentence. Even so, Travis was thinking of going AWOL and fleeing to Canada, as many had done during the Vietnam War. His grandmother was more cautious and counseled him against it, advising that he tell the army to stop feeding him Prozac. "I told Travis when he was going back to Iraq in July to make sure to tell his doctor and chaplain that he wanted to go off," his grandmother said. "I had read that sometimes it had caused the opposite effect on young people. Instead of being an antidepressant, it caused them to commit suicide."[57] Travis simply told her, "Grandma, I did that, and they put me on something else. They changed my medicine, gave me a week of stress management."[58] There was no sympathy from the military: weeks later, with his leave time up, Travis was sent back to Iraq along with his Prozac. But his superiors obviously knew something was wrong as they placed him on suicide watch and removed the bolt from his rifle, rendering it useless. He was given more pedestrian desk jobs as he tried to sort out his head. If they had to send him back, it appeared a good course of action. But, inexplicably, Virgadamo was cleared for combat the following month, and on the night of August 30, 2007, was given his rifle bolt back. Three hours later he walked out of his barracks and shot himself in the head. The army told his family he had died from a "self-inflicted" gunshot wound, avoiding the word "suicide," now a dirty word for them. "I don't think he should have ever been sent there," his grandmother said in the aftermath. "Why would you deploy someone who was a danger to himself and maybe others? When they know, it's just unacceptable, pushing them out there."[59] In fact, Travis's whole time in the military had been extremely dangerous. Even though he had always wanted to be a soldier, it was in an emotional period after his father moved to the Philippines that he eventually decided to enlist. He was just seventeen years old. "He had a difficult time in boot camp," said his grandmother. "They sent him to anger-management classes. Feeling somewhat deserted by his father—he was so young." She added, "They had also put him in suicide watch in boot camp."[60]

Despite these serious signs of frailty, a year later Virgadamo was deployed to Iraq, with the Prozac he had been given by the military. The military belief in medicating away mental strife had many tragic consequences similar to that experienced by Travis. "Even though he was still on active duty (placing him under DOD jurisdiction), this incident only reinforces the fact that we need to place more emphasis on the mental health of service members in or returning from combat," said Shelley Berkley, a Representative in Congress from the State of Nevada, his home state.[61] The whole thing had uncomfortable echoes of Vietnam, where soldiers helped themselves to psychotropic drugs, while psychologists were singing the virtues of a myriad of different brain drugs to help troops concentrate, boost their energy, and ostensibly dull mental health problems. Medical opinion was, however, unambiguous about the dangers of pumping drugs into unstable soldiers: "There are risks in putting people back to battle with medicines in their bodies," said psychiatrist Judith Broder, founder of the Soldiers Project. Travis's grandmother agreed. "That is a suicidal medicine, especially with teens. I was livid. I just couldn't believe they put him on Prozac," she said.[62]

Unfriendly Fire

As medication became the primary and often only treatment for the psychological problems suffered by soldiers, more suicides followed. The Pentagon reported that in 2007, 115 US troops committed suicide: the highest toll since the military had tracked such figures.[63] The military rate was thirty times higher than for the general US population and it was getting worse year-by-year: by 2009 the number of suicide victims had reached 245. In June 2010 alone, 32 soldiers killed themselves, the highest number of military suicides in one month since the Vietnam era. Of those, 21 were on active duty, seven serving in Iraq or Afghanistan.[64] It was even worse for those who had been discharged. Three times as many young California veterans were killing themselves at home than California service members were dying in Iraq and Afghanistan combined. The Pentagon and VA don't count the dead after they come home, but an examination of coroners' reports showed that more than 1,000 veterans under thirty-five died in California between 2005 and 2008.[65] Despite these horrifying statistics, it took until 2009 before the mental health problems afflicting US troops were revealed to mainstream America by the military. In that year, an army report from Fort Carson was initiated after six 4th Brigade Team soldiers had been charged with murders on their return home from the Middle East. The substance abuse among some troops, pre-existing mental illness in recruits, and the failure of the army to provide help were major factors in the violence—a spate of crime that included the rape and murder of a nineteen-year-old girl and one soldier's murder of his child. All in Colorado, all in six months. "Those three [factors] in combination are a really toxic mix," said Lieutenant General Eric Schoomaker, Army Surgeon General.[66]

Soldiers involved in crimes related to homicide at Fort Carson were, the report said, "at risk for engaging in violent behavior based on a clustering of known risk factors for violence, namely prior criminal behavior and psychopathology," possibly with the "moral waivers" in mind. The investigation suggested a possible association between increasing levels of combat exposure and risk of violent outcomes. The Fort Carson report found that eleven of the suspects had been identified with drug or alcohol problems but only half of them had been sent for treatment, as army regulation stipulates they should have been. The army was immediately on the back foot, reverting to their standard evasion tactic, countering that there was no direct link between combat and crime, and reminding a news conference that in the vast majority of cases veterans don't commit crimes—a true but irrelevant point in the context of the shocking report. Major General Mark Graham, Fort Carson's commander, added that the report had resulted in more counseling and mental health training for returning soldiers. He also said the base was "stepping up efforts to ensure that soldiers who test positive for drug use or exhibit signs of problem drinking will get substance abuse counseling and treatment."[67] But it was a smoke-and-mirrors exercise to appease the media and lawmakers who were getting increasingly vocal. "The Army's support for our service men and women is falling short and we need to do better," Senator Michael Bennet (D-CO) said after the report was released. "This situation is unacceptable for our troops, untenable for military families and communities, and incompatible with our priorities as a nation."[68]

Away from its public promises, the military had been doing the opposite and knowingly sending mentally ill soldiers back into the warzone. In 2003, *United Press International* unearthed an Army

Medical Department after-action report which admitted that "variability in predeployment screening guidelines for mental health issues may have resulted in some soldiers with mental health diagnoses being inappropriately deployed"—those like Travis Virgadamo. The public impression was "that some soldiers develop problems in theater," it added, when in truth, "in some cases, they actually have pre-existing conditions."[69] The report was adamant that the army must change its practices or risk sending soldiers back into combat who had serious mental health problems. "Perhaps stricter predeployment screening is required to keep at-risk soldiers from deploying," it said; a move which could help "identifying soldiers that may become non-functional in theater due to mental health problems."[70] Pentagon policy is that members of the military must be mentally stable for at least three months before being deployed for active duty, but it wasn't being applied. The problem was amplified further by the longer and more-frequent tours of duty in the Middle East under the so-called "stop-loss" system—which describes the involuntary lengthening of tours. In 2007, the military had said its active-duty units would now serve in fifteen-month tours instead of the regular twelve months—a big demand. The prolonged periods away from family, friends, and normal life aggravated stress and anxiety. "This policy is a difficult but necessary interim step," said Secretary of Defense Robert Gates at the time.[71] "Our forces are stretched, there's no question about that." Broken would have been a better choice of word.

For those under occupation by the US military it was even more dangerous. In March 2012, a US soldier, on his fourth deployment in a decade, walked out of his base and went on a shooting spree in southern Afghanistan, murdering more than a dozen Afghan civilians, including nine children. "This is an assassination, an intentional killing of innocent civilians and cannot be forgiven," said Hamid Karzai, the president of Afghanistan, in the aftermath. It was the latest in a long line of repeated demands by Karzai for the US to put an end to the wanton murder of civilians. Then news came that US army staff sergeant Robert Bales, the thirty-eight-year-old suspect, was from Joint Base Lewis-McCord, in Washington state, which just four months earlier had convicted a member of an

Afghanistan "kill team" of murder via a military jury. Senator Patty Murray just the week before had been complaining about the military hospital overturning 285 diagnoses of PTSD.[72] "I heard something on Facebook about a soldier killing civilians," a corporal with the Fourth Stryker Brigade told the *New York Times*. "It's horrible, but I guess I've almost become numb to it."

PTSD was not a new phenomenon for the military, but sending soldiers still suffering from severe mental health problems back to the frontline in such large numbers was. "I'm concerned that people who are symptomatic are being sent back. That has not happened before in our country," complained Dr. Arthur S. Blank, Jr., a Yale-trained psychiatrist.[73] Senator Barbara Boxer (D-CA) helped create a Task Force on Mental Health in the DOD as the situation spiraled out of control. She mentioned "reports that doctors are being encouraged not to identify mental-health illness in our troops . . . I am asking for a lot of answers," she added. "If people are suffering from mental-health problems, they should not be sent on the battlefield."[74] The army's top mental health expert, Colonel Elspeth Ritchie, explicitly accepted that the reason so many mentally ill troops were being sent back was because of the demands on the military for more and more personnel. "The challenge for us," he said, "is that the Army has a mission to fight. And, as you know, recruiting has been a challenge. And so we have to weigh the needs of the mission, with the soldiers' personal needs."[75] In August of 2009, the US army announced a new $117 million program designed to expose its soldiers to "emotional resiliency" classes. The program aimed for so-called "Comprehensive Soldier Fitness," which, according to an army spokesman, was designed "to build resilience in soldiers, family members, and Army civilians by developing five dimensions of strength: physical, emotional, social, spiritual, and family."[76]

A rash of suicides was not the only worry; soldiers with mental health problems were more in danger than their healthy counterparts during combat, according to a US navy report from the Vietnam era. It had found that marines who'd been hospitalized between 1965 and 1972 for psychiatric reasons and then sent back into battle were more likely to be injured in combat.[77] And there were plenty of tragic examples to bear out this study during the War on Terror, such as Travis Virgadamo. Another was Michael De Vlieger, who went to Iraq in early 2006 as a gunner with the 101st Airborne. Soon after his arrival nine soldiers were killed when two Humvees in his platoon were blown up by a roadside bomb. Just a month later insurgents threw an antitank grenade under his Humvee and his knee shot through the door. He was sent to coalesce at Fort Kentucky but his personality had changed. He turned to drink and attacked his wife's dog. "I had lost so many friends and went through a near-death experience. I wasn't who I was when I left," he said. According to one report:

> He was updating his will and preparing to return to Iraq when he broke down. His wife, Christine, found him awake in the middle of the night, rocking while babbling incoherently. Frightened, Christine called his squad leader, who took him to the base emergency room. Doctors then sent him to a nearby private psychiatric hospital, where he stayed for 16 days, receiving medications to calm his panic and treat his blood pressure and depression. The doctors released him with four prescriptions.

But merely eighteen hours after his release from hospital, he was on a plane destined for Iraq after being told by a *non-commissioned officer* that he was needed back there. Decisions on whether to retain soldiers are taken by military commanders instead of qualified medical professionals, which puts the occupied populations at the mercy of thousands of unstable soldiers. De Vlieger later said, "I was in no condition to leave. I'm an infantryman. If I'm screwed up in my head, it could cost my life or the lives of the men with me." But he did manage to stay alive. A lot of troops suffering mental health problems and sent back into the firefight weren't so lucky. Private First Class Jason Scheuerman was stripped of his gun when he wrote his mother a suicide note from Iraq in 2005. He was later accused of inventing his mental health problems in an effort to be discharged and was warned that he could be disciplined. Three weeks later he was dead, after shooting himself in the head with the gun the army had returned to him. Needless to say, it is unknown how many Iraqi and Afghan civilians have been sacrificed to this policy.

Bradley Manning, the alleged US military source of the Wikileaks data, was another example of the mental health of recruits being ignored. He was in such a disturbed mental state before his deployment that he wet himself, threw furniture around, shouted at his commanding officer, and underwent regular psychiatric evaluations, according to the *Guardian*. Manning was a "mess of a child" who "should never have been put through a tour of duty in Iraq," said an officer from the Fort Leonard Wood military base in Missouri, where Manning trained in 2007.[78] He was sent anyway— a decision which came back to bite the US military. Chase Madar, the author of a recent book on Manning, told me, "He would never have been kept in the army if not for record-low recruitment levels in 2007 when he enlisted. Manning spent a few weeks in the 'reject barracks' at Fort Leonard Wood where he did basic training and that sounds like absolute hell, being confined with tons of criminals and young guys not right in the head." The only reason Manning made it on to active duty in Iraq, after repeated warnings about his fitness at all three of his stateside deployments (Fort Leonard Wood, Fort Huachuca, Fort Drum), was the army's "utter desperation for soldiers with IT and analytic skills during its historic low in recruitment." A portion of the chatlogs between Manning and Adrian Lamo, the hacker informant who turned him in, notes how the military, desperate for recruits, ran only minimal background checks on him. There is no mention of how he almost got discharged right away at basic training, which is no doubt a painful memory he'd rather not bring up:

(12:06:18 PM) info@adrianlamo.com: how did this not come up as an issue in your background check? I'm guessing you have an S and not a TS.

(12:06:29 PM) bradass87: TS/SCI

(12:06:47 PM) bradass87: i enlisted in 2007 ... height of iraq war, no-one double checked much

(12:07:06 PM) info@adrianlamo.com: Well, hell, if you made it in, maybe I should reconsider the offer I got from what used to be JTF-CNO.

(12:07:09 PM) bradass87: background checks are jokes anyway

(12:07:23 PM) info@adrianlamo.com: It's hit-or-miss.[79]

The Support

Throughout the War on Terror money was consistently pulled from programs set up to put homecoming soldiers back on the straight and narrow. A Pentagon survey in 2007 found that 38 percent of soldiers who returned from combat said they had experienced psychological problems, from depression to anger, but the same report disclosed there had been "dramatic decreases" in the number of health care professionals assigned to the military since the wars in Afghanistan and Iraq had begun.[80] With billions of dollars being expended on quashing the insurgencies the report concluded that the US military "currently lacks both funding and personnel to adequately support the psychological health of service members and their families."[81] At the time of the report's publication there were only 500 mental health professionals employed in an army of more than a million soldiers.

It was clear that caring for veterans was just too expensive for the Bush administration. In 2005, only two years into the war in Iraq, Bush was widely condemned for his budget for veterans' health care, which fell well short of maintaining the levels of the years before, bearing in mind the huge numbers of new soldiers returning from war.[82] In that year not only did Bush try to double the co-payment that veterans would pay for prescription drugs, but he also proposed a new flat $250 fee for some veterans to use the health care system. Even Senator Daniel K. Akaka (D-HI) warned at the time that this could force 192,000 veterans out of the health care system because of the price hike. Later in 2005 it was revealed that the Bush administration had left a $1 billion shortage for veterans' health care that had to be plugged by emergency supplemental funds voted for by Congress again.[83] In 2006, with discretionary spending apparently needing to be cut to deal with the massive deficit, the White House predicted a 16 percent cut in veterans' health care, despite the increasing numbers of veterans needing the services.[84] In that budget year Congress had to add another $2.7 billion emergency funding to the VA on top of Bush's budget.

The effect of turning veterans' health care from an absolute necessity, among the most important of government responsibilities, into an expendable commitment had painful consequences for those returning from combat. Ever-increasing numbers of soldiers were returning with mental health problems ranging from schizophrenia to PTSD, and one academic study estimated that in 2004, 1.8 million veterans were without health insurance, which amounts to about 12 percent of all uninsured people in the US.[85] From 2000, Bush's first year in office, to 2004, two years into his War on Terror, the number of uninsured veterans grew by 290,000.[86] Conditions were deteriorating for the medics as well: the air force lost 20 percent of its mental health workers from 2003 to 2005 while the army lost 8 percent in the same period.[87] By 2008, the Bush administration was even employing lawyers to fight a case that had been brought to insist that mental health should be included in health care provisions for veterans.[88] Unsurprisingly, Bush didn't mention this when speaking on Veterans Day in November 2008: "I am committed to making sure that today's veterans get all the health care and support they need from the federal government for agreeing to serve in a time of danger," he said just before he left office with the most squalid of records on the topic.[89] John McCain's plan was even worse than Bush's: he wanted to privatize veterans' health care, turning it into a market-oriented trust, which would have been devastated by the financial crisis. The Republicans' claim to be the party of the military (which they used to regularly beat the Democrats) was nothing but a sham from start to finish. To be fair, there was little improvement under the Obama administration as the president came under pressure in 2011 to ensure that veterans' benefits were delivered amid mounting criticism from different groups. During a Congressional hearing, Patty Murray, chairwoman of the Senate Veterans Affairs committee, chided the VA for reducing the number of eligible participants for a new benefit for critically injured veterans and their caregivers, and was deeply critical of the severe delays to the start of the program. "Families of wounded warriors are waiting for these benefits, and with each day of delay the strain from the sacrifices they make only grows," she said.[90]

Easy Picking

The best investigation into the problem was conducted at the height of the War on Terror by the Connecticut newspaper *The Hartford Courant*, but it had little impact as its revelations were largely ignored by the military. It opened with the story of Specialist Edward W. Brabazon, or "Crazy Eddie," of the 505th Parachute Infantry Regiment at Fort Bragg in North Carolina. "We were surprised they took him, with the kind of mental problems he had, but we figured the Army must know what they're doing," said his mother, Margaret. "We didn't think they'd send him into combat."[91] But send him they did, and less than three months into his second deployment, Brabazon shot himself in the head at a palace compound in Baghdad. "They talked about how he had a history of mental problems," Margaret said. "I said, 'No kidding. If you knew he had mental problems, then why was he there?'" The *Courant* concluded: "Despite a Congressional mandate to assess the mental health of every soldier sent to a combat zone," there was "a fractured pre-deployment screening process in which less than 1 percent of deploying soldiers ever see a mental health professional. It is a practice that has put unfit service members in harm's way, increasing their risk for suicide and post-traumatic stress disorder." Its analysis of data from the DOD found that one third of soldiers who killed themselves in Iraq did so within three months of being deemed mentally fit and sent into combat. Experts said that the vast majority of those who take their own lives are suffering from depression or bipolar disorder at the time, adding "it is doubtful soldiers would spontaneously develop a serious mental illness so quickly after deployment." But the required treatment was no longer available, and, even if diagnosed, soldiers would find themselves put back in harm's way with their minds still traumatized. In fact, the military was also actively working to send soldiers back because it was *too expensive* to treat them. A stunning investigation in the online magazine *Salon* revealed the lengths to which the military was prepared to go in order to stop medical staff diagnosing PTSD, on the grounds that the intensive care needed after such a diagnosis would be too pricey. It showed how a veteran from Iraq named only as "Sergeant X," who had been seeking treatment at Fort Carson for a brain injury and PTSD for more than a year, was misdiagnosed by military psychologist Douglas McNinch with an "anxiety disorder," not PTSD. The report outlined the case:

> Sgt. X believed his traumatic brain injury had been incurred in 2005–6 when his Bradley Fighting Vehicle buckled in an explosion in Iraq. While one of many he endured, this one knocked him out for 30 seconds. Mr McNinch told Sgt. X: "I will tell you something confidentially that I would have to deny if it were ever public. Not only myself, but all the clinicians up here are being pressured to not diagnose PTSD and diagnose [an unspecified] anxiety disorder [instead]." "Unfortunately," McNinch told Sgt. X, "yours has not been the only case . . . I and other [doctors] are under a lot of pressure to not diagnose PTSD. It's not fair. I think it's a horrible way to treat soldiers, but unfortunately, you know, now the V.A. is jumping on board, saying, 'Well, these people don't have PTSD,' and stuff like that." But this wasn't an isolated case. Two veterans groups had released an email from Norma Perez, a psychologist in Texas, directing staff at a Department of Veterans Affairs facility. "Given that we are having more and more compensation seeking veterans, I'd like to suggest that you refrain from giving a diagnosis of PTSD straight out," Perez wrote in the e-mail, suggesting the staff "consider a diagnosis of Adjustment Disorder."[92]

Sergeant X was brave enough to seek help for his problems, but not everyone was. Many soldiers were too scared to come forward because of what the military described as "stigma" in a macho military environment. "Stigma and lack of referral to the Army Substance Referral Program for required substance abuse screening were important barriers to soldiers," noted the Fort Carson report.[93] But this concern among the troops was more a concern about how seeking help would be viewed by their commanders. A 2007 survey found that three in five American soldiers felt that seeking help would damage their career prospects, with around half saying that they thought others would think less of them if they received help for mental health problems.[94] That kind of feeling doesn't develop in a vacuum: the fear of revealing mental problems to medical staff had been consciously fostered by a military unprepared to treat its soldiers. One study found that one in five soldiers who returned from the desert reported the effects of PTSD, but only half went on to receive treatment.

In a farcical public relations blitz, a delegation of Hollywood celebrities was dispatched to Baghdad in 2008 to tell the troops it was OK to feel mentally sick. The *Stop the Stigma* tour was organized by Sopranos star Joe Pantoliano, who had already founded the "No Kidding, Me Too!" group to break down taboos surrounding mental illness. As the group descended on Victory Base Complex, the troops were told by the psychologist accompanying the delegation that "the things that you experience, they are not military problems, they are human problems that happen to occur in the military . . . When you come home, educate us. We need to hear your stories." But the military knew their stories and was ignoring them. "I know the military is especially concerned; they've been willing to be very proactive and they obviously really care about their men and women, so it's an honor for us to be a part of this," added actress Lisa Jay, duped into believing the military propaganda.[95] To anyone watching the situation it was clear the military didn't care; it had stood by as the number of PTSD cases had risen exponentially. In 2008, the Rand Corporation released a report, based on surveys of veterans, estimating that of the 1.6 million American military personnel who had served in Afghanistan and Iraq, at least 300,000 were suffering from PTSD or major depression. Rand also estimated that as many as 320,000 may have suffered some form of brain damage from explosion blast waves, affecting their long-term cognitive capabilities.[96] The country at large was simply not ready to cope with this new influx. Back home, the number of Americans in the general population seeking treatment for mental health problems, including depression and bipolar disorder, had nearly doubled in the decade to 2006, from 19 million to 36 million. Spending on mental illnesses had skyrocketed in the same period, outstripping that for cancer and heart disease, reaching $58 billion in 2006.[97]

The Lifeline of Work and a Home

One of the toughest problems for veterans on their return to the US is finding a job, and frequent periods of unemployment are often a factor in the descent into depression and other problems. The unemployment rate for veterans hit 15 percent in 2011, nearly doubling over the previous five years, and leaving returning soldiers with much worse odds than the general population.[98] That the help available to unemployed veterans provided by the military was rudimentary became obvious to me when in 2007 I attended the third annual "Salute Our Heroes" veterans job fair in Manhattan, an initiative that aims to ease veterans' passage back into mainstream society after they retire from the military. An eclectic collection of organizations were in attendance, from financial companies to universities, all of which said they were on the lookout for prospective employees. William Offutt, the Special Assistant of the Veterans Employment and Training Service, told me: "The event is important because it is promoting and prioritizing a big section of the population that deserve recognition. When employers are looking for the best they need to be able to find it, and veterans constitute a highly skilled workforce." But it became clear that no one was actually offering any jobs. It was another public relations exercise. Sal Manze, sixty-six, was a Vietnam veteran and advertised the fact on his baseball cap as he sauntered around the floor of the hall. He fought for two years from 1965 to 1966. "They don't interview on the spot," he told me. "Most of the companies are just giving out information rather than offering jobs. I think if they were able to hire immediately it would be great, but as it is it's just frustrating." Now he was working a $7-an-hour seasonal job as a sales associate at Macy's. "They say age doesn't come into it but it's just not true," he said. "But how can you prove it? Go to the interview with a lawyer?" Others felt similarly. "I want to get into technology now," said Tyrone Webb, twenty-nine, and a veteran of nearly five years in the US navy. "I used to be an aviation engineer, working on the engines of aircraft. The problem is getting a job with a bad discharge from service is very difficult." Webb was given a dishonorable discharge after his mother contracted cancer and he became disheartened when he was not allowed to visit her and lost focus on the job. "I started being late and just not caring. I was discharged soon after and they gave me Reentry Code 4 on my [discharge form] and so it is impossible to get a job when it says 'other than honorable discharge' on my documents." Since he left the military in June 2006 he has worked mainly in retail sales and phone surveys, and is currently working in a restaurant. "I am angry," he said. "I have a lot on my plate, I think about children but I can't have any because of my situation, I can't even think about girlfriends."

It wasn't just the US military helping to ruin active-duty soldiers and veterans through neglect: the private sector contributed too, in its own exploitative way. During the War on Terror, huge numbers of veterans became a target for unscrupulous loaning companies. It emerged that leading banks and lending agencies in the US were failing to adhere to laws governing loan conditions to active-duty and retired soldiers. In 2011, one of the biggest banks in the world, JP Morgan Chase, was forced to announce a raft of new programs for military personnel after three veterans filed a lawsuit against the bank for overcharging interest payments on mortgages.[99] Under the Servicemembers Civil Relief Act, which dates back to 1940 but was updated in 2003, interest payments for soldiers cannot rise above 6 percent. Lenders are also barred from foreclosing on mortgages of service members while they are on active duty. "The mistakes we made on military foreclosures are a painful aberration," said Jamie Dimon, chief executive of JP Morgan, in the aftermath of a Congressional hearing. "We deeply apologize to our military customers and their families for these mistakes." JP Morgan then set their interest rate cap for service members at 4 percent.

But it was evident, despite the crocodile tears, that exploitation of the veteran community was no aberration for financial institutions. "I just think JP Morgan ignored it, they didn't care about it, they didn't want to know about it," Bob Filner, a Congressman from California and ranking member on the House Veterans Affairs Committee, told me. "And I think the other banks are doing the same thing." Veterans are a particularly vulnerable group, he added. "They get too discouraged and they feel powerless, so they can't fight back." Filner had been approached by mid-level staff at JP Morgan, Bank of America, and Wells Fargo who told him the lawsuit was part of something much bigger. And leading veterans' groups supported these claims. "There's been a constant stream of veterans complaining of overcharging and problems with banks," Selena Coppa, who dealt with veterans' financial difficulties for Iraq Veterans Against the War, told me. "This is an industry-wide issue, it's not solely limited to JP Morgan. Too many financial institutions see service members as numbers in ledger that they can exploit because of their unique vulnerability." When in the military, service members can be hit with a criminal charge for being overly indebted, which causes some to accept bad practices. "Let's say you are being exploited by a bank: in the civilian world you would dispute that, you wouldn't pay it," Coppa said. "But if you're in the military even if it's an unfair charge they are forced to pay under threat of jail under military law." It was even tougher for those veterans with PTSD who lived so close to wire anyway, meaning that one small economic injustice could be devastating. Many winded up being evicted. "I had a friend of mine, she was incorrectly charged for a late fee, they refused to grant her time to pay it, especially, vets suffer from PTSD [and] have difficultly navigating bureaucracy," said Coppa. "There is also the problem with the veteran population that they are very proud, which makes it difficult for them to come forward and talk about it"—and easy for unscrupulous creditors to prey on them: aware of the vulnerability of service members, loan-shark-type schemes are often set up around military bases.

The situation got much worse as the financial crisis hit in 2008 and the number of foreclosed veterans rose significantly. "I've noticed this being a problem for the last few years," Joe Sharpe, economic director at The American Legion, the largest veterans' group in the US, told me. "This had included vets having a problem paying mortgages while they are deployed. It's a shock once they return to discover their home mortgage has tripled or been foreclosed." According to Sharp it has even affected the operational readiness of the force. "I remember it came to a head recently, it became such a problem that unit commanders were concerned they couldn't deploy large numbers of soldiers because they were in financial trouble." Soldiers have the added problem that when they are away, they are not aware of what's happening at home. Thanks to the extended deployment periods they also had less time or opportunity to respond to legal issues. Because of this, default judgments were often entered against them unfairly. "I think lives were destroyed. I said the banks could be guilty of homicide," Bob Filner added. "We are at an all time high for the number of people committing suicide on active duty—higher than Vietnam. Financial stress is the second leading cause. Now who knows how many people did that because not just JP Morgan, but Bank of America and Wells Fargo didn't do what they should have. If they were fore-closed on illegally, and the wife left them, and he felt he couldn't support his family, I have no doubt that if we looked into the record closely we would find that." The Department of Veterans Affairs does offer its own mortgage scheme which has better terms, but not all service members chose to use it because it is incredibly complicated. The VA told me they helped 66,000 veterans fight foreclosure in 2010 through interceding with the lender (but there were 20,000 more who sought help but could not forestall the loss of their homes). "What has happened is that the vets with VA home-loans have fared best," says Joe Sharpe. "Those that did not get VA home-loans are the ones that are getting in trouble." Those with VA loans have, indeed, demonstrated the lowest serious delin-quency and foreclosure rates, but even the VA admit that their loan scheme is very difficult for veterans to use because its terms are so opaque. "We recognize it is a complex law," Michael Frueh, VA spokesman, told me by way of an explanation.

Unsurprisingly, in this climate, homelessness among returning veterans remained extremely high during the War on Terror. The most extensive survey of the problem, published by the Housing and Urban Development Department (HUD) and VA, found that nearly 76,000 veterans were sleeping rough on any given night in 2009.[100] On top of that, nearly 140,000 veterans spent at least one night in a shelter during the same year. Some of those are older soldiers, but the study also found that 11,300 younger veterans, aged eighteen to thirty, were in shelters at some point during 2009. Nearly all of them had served in Iraq or Afghanistan. Ronte Foster was one of them. When he came home in late 2004, he had changed radically. His wife no longer recognized the affectionate family man she had married and waved off to Iraq just a year earlier. He was drinking every day, taking a cocktail of drugs, and erupting in fits of anger as he tried to self-medicate his way through the PTSD he didn't even know he had. She stood it for six months, eager to salvage their eight-year marriage, but then she broke, no longer able to put up with the consequences for her and their two young children. "She told me to leave and at that point I had so much trauma in my head, I just had to get away," Ronte tells me. He had been deployed to Tikrit, hometown of the erstwhile Iraqi dictator Saddam Hussein, and had duly witnessed one of the bloodiest and most chaotic periods of the war. "The unit that I went with, we saw a lot of roadside bombs and a lot of RPG's, you saw that on a daily basis," he says. He was also involved in fire-fights which led to deaths that still haunt him. "I had to do some things I didn't want to do," he says. "There was this one incident where some insurgents tried to rush the gate of the base, I was there at Camp Anaconda and we killed one and three were captured, it's still with me." When he left his family in Danville, Virginia, he went as far as possible, running from the war and the memories that were still fixed in his head. He relocated to Los Angeles and slept in the car and at friend's places. "I would get very depressed, I felt this intense isolation," he says. "I realize now that I was experiencing a lot of the PTSD symptoms, I had a hard time remembering things and concentrating for any period of time." Ronte got lucky and was taken in by a Salvation Army shelter where he became a resident floor manager.

But seven years on from his return from Iraq, Foster is still not housed in permanent accommodation. "It's not perfect but I'm much luckier than other people I know of." He has no job and cannot afford his own food.

There are thousands of veterans of the wars in Iraq and Afghanistan with similar tales, but these are stories it is painful for America to hear. In 2011, however, the budget deficit and the search for programs to cut put the problem firmly back on the agenda. The HUD-Veterans Affairs Supportive Housing program, or HUD-VASH, is a flagship scheme working to help homeless veterans by issuing vouchers which can be used to pay for accommodation. Since 2008, it has issued around 30,000 vouchers and by 2011 the program had placed 21,000 veterans in permanent accommodation. But in the Republicans' proposed budget for the fiscal year 2011 it was completely eliminated, which caused outcry amongst Democrats and in a veteran community that had already been subjected to outrageous cuts to its health facilities by the GOP during the Bush era. The Republicans' "decision to slash funding for housing assistance to thousands of homeless veterans shows a total lack of humanity," said Barbara Boxer, a Democratic Senator from California.[101] After a compromise, the program was salvaged, but the department only got about 7,000 vouchers, less than the typical 10,000, after the Republicans bargained them down.[102] With veterans continuing to stream home, most analysts said this was far from enough and left community-based organizations to pick up the pieces. One of those community-based groups, US VETS, runs the shelter that Ronte Foster now lives in. The organization was started in 1993 in response to chronic levels of homelessness among the veteran population and it now has 2,000 beds in five states, making it the largest non-governmental provider in the country. "There is a lot of PTSD around because it is an all-volunteer [military] and they are doing everything they can to keep soldiers," said Steve Peck, chief executive. "They are going on multiple deployments . . . which is exacerbating the problem. The DOD is aware of the problem and they are doing something, but it's a lot bigger than they can handle." The lack of funds for medical and psychological treatment made the situation worse. When soldiers are discharged they are not required to go back to the VA for treatment, and it is estimated more than half were not accessing the treatment they need. Even those who did seek help were often told by the VA that there was a three or four month waiting list, which for someone with PTSD can be extremely difficult. By 2010, veterans were committing suicide at the rate of eighteen per day, many of them after serving in Iraq and Afghanistan.[103]

The military's use of soldiers outside of the regular army, as they strived to keep up troop levels, had a particularly negative impact. "What makes this different from Vietnam is that half of troops to Iraq and Afghanistan are reservists and national guardsman," John Driscoll, chief executive of the Coalition for Homeless Veterans, told me. For reservists the pressures from combat and training are particularly stressful because they lack the experience of their regular army peers. This is compounded when they come home, as they do not go through the typical transition program to help them adjust. "Anyone in a combat role knows you need decompression time, you need transition time to get your issues back in order," added Driscoll, himself a veteran. "During that time you have spent away from home you have changed. The way you communicate is different, so when you add to that extreme economic pressure from the housing crisis and economic slump it's not a pretty picture."

At the same time that it was exploiting veterans, corporate America was enjoying the fruits of the markets these same veterans had prized open for them in the Middle East. As the US began the withdrawal of its remaining 40,000 troops from Iraq at the end of 2011, US officials were trying desperately to shore up the position of the American business community. With domestic economic growth slowing fast (and hurting veterans), US companies were increasingly keen to exploit the potential of Iraq's post-war recovery. One example was 360 Architecture, a Kansas City–based design company, which was busy drawing up plans for a glitzy $800-million sports complex in the southern oil center of Basra. With the 2013 Gulf Games scheduled to be held in Iraq, the public-relations-conscious government was looking to build a stadium and facilities for athletes. "It will be like an Olympic training ground for Iraqi national athletes of all sports," John Radtke, 360's project director, told me excitedly. But there were surely better things to spend Iraq's new oil money on. How about schools? In 2008, only 50 percent of primary school age children were attending school, down from 80 percent in 2005. Or foodstuffs? By 2007, 28 percent of Iraqi children were malnourished. But such concerns didn't interest the State Department, which in the same period hosted a forum focused on "promoting commercial opportunities in Iraq" with representatives from nearly thirty major American companies—including Goldman Sachs and Monsanto. They joined Hillary Clinton, secretary of state, alongside other senior US and Iraqi officials to discuss economic opportunities in the "new Iraq." "Basically, the bottom line is we want to send a message that Iraq is open for business," a senior US official told me. "The US government will do whatever it can to get them into the market." Around that time, Caterpillar, the Illinois-based construction equipment and natural-gas turbine manufacturer, won part of a $6.3 billion contract to build fifty new power plants in Iraq as the country sought to increase its electricity output; while Lockheed Martin, the arms manufacturer, announced that it had a deal in the pipeline with Iraq and Oman for the sale of eighteen F-16 fighter jets, to be ready by 2012. The Maryland-based company said it expected up to one hundred additional orders from Iraq by the end of the decade.[104] America's veterans—and the large numbers of Iraqis mired in poverty—would see none of the profits.

rrest Fogarty, neo-Nazi who served in Iraq as a part of the military police from 2004 to 2005. [Matt
nnard, March 2008]

Fogarty in Iraq on the album cover of his neo-Nazi band Attack.
[Given to Matt Kennard by Fogarty, March 2008]

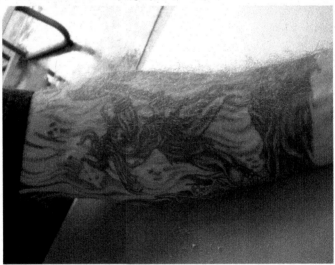

The Viking with axe tattoo riding up Fogarty's forearm. [Matt Kennard, March 2008]

Specialist James Douglas Ross, who served in Iraq as a military intelligence officer (Eighty-Second Airborne Division) in his barracks room. [Photo provided by Hunter Glass]

James Douglas Ross's boots, complete with swastika treads. [Photo provided by Hunter Glass]

...ss in his room in Iraq, holding fully automatic rifle. He was eventually caught mailing a submachine gun ...ck to his father in the US. The three-triangle tattoo on the top of his left arm is a Norse sign used by white ...premacists. [Photo provided by Jeffrey Stoleson]

Neo-Nazi soldier in Iraq does Hitler salute on extremist social network NewSaxon. [Obtained by M Kennard, 2008]

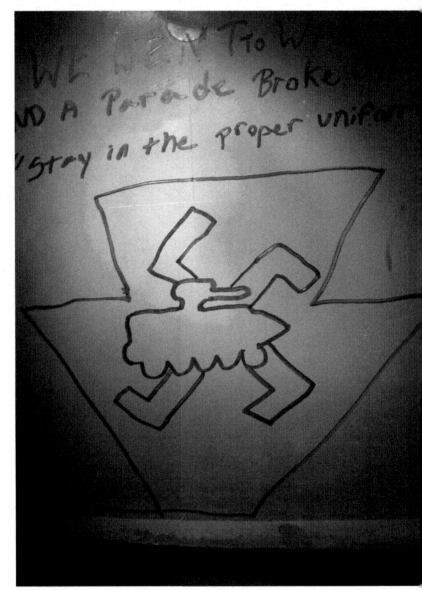

Neo-Nazi graffiti put up outside Camp Taji in Iraq. [Picture by Jeffrey Stoleson]

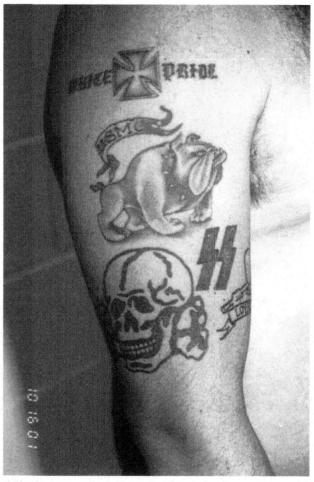

Skinhead marine with neo-Nazi tattoos who left military with honorable discharge and later went to federal prison after committing a hate crime in Montana. [Photo provided by T. J. Leyden]

Private in an engineer battalion at Fort Bragg with a tattoo of the logo of Hammerskins, a group described as the "most violent and best-organized" skinhead outfit in the US. The soldier told investigators he "didn't know" the tattoo was racist and was allowed to stay in the military. [Photo provided by Hunter Glass]

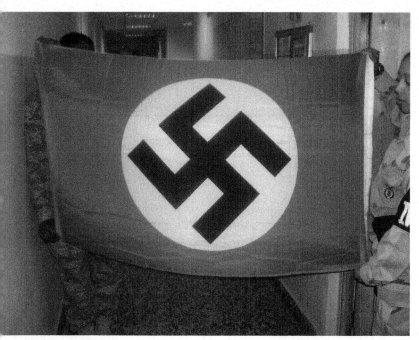

neo-Nazi swastika flag confiscated from billeting in Iraq in 2008 by military police. [Provided by Hunter Glass]

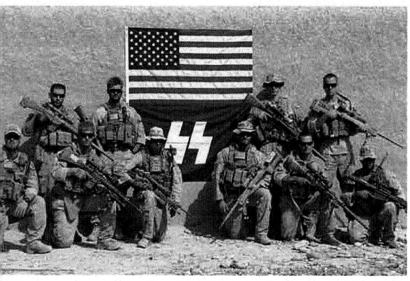

US Marine scout sniper unit posing with neo-Nazi SS lightning bolts flag in Sangin, Afghanistan. [Widely available on the internet]

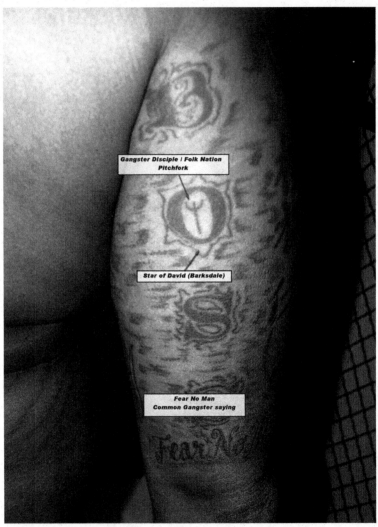

Gang-tattooed arm of former airman Rico Williams, the leader of the gang that beat fellow soldier Juwan Johnson to death during his initiation into the Gangster Disciples while on active duty in Germany. [Photo provided by Hunter Glass]

rmy cooks based at Fort Lewis, Washington, show their "west-side" gang allegiance. [Photo provided by ınter Glass]

Two soldiers in their barracks on Fort Bragg, both members of the Gangster Disciples, a Chicago gang. The soldier on the right is throwing the pitchforks sign of the GD; the other is throwing the rival Latin Kings gang sign downwards in a show of disrespect. [Photo provided by Jeffrey Stoleson]

Sergeant Jeffrey Stoleson sitting in front of a blast wall at Forward Operating Base Scania, two hours south [of] Baghdad, 2006. Graffiti is for Diablos 69, a subgroup of the Norteños gang, based on the west coast of the [US]. [Photo from Jeffrey Stoleson]

Stoleson at Forward Operating Base Scania in 2006. Graffiti reads "El Moco," the moniker of the individ[ual] that did the tag, while below is the name of Mexican gang La Eme (*By the Wings*), one of largest drug deal[ers] and smugglers in the US. [Photo provided by Stoleson]

Photo taken in Taji, Iraq, shows graffiti of outlaw motorcycle group 69ers, out of Brooklyn, New York, displaying their "1 per cent" patch on a tank. [Photo by Jeffrey Stoleson]

Photo taken in 2009 outside Forward Operating Base Anaconda, outside Balad, Iraq. The letters "BK" on the military vehicle denote "Blood Killas," a tag put up by the Bloods' rivals, usually the Crips. [Photo provided by Jeffery Stoleson]

Tank yard in Taji, Iraq, 2010. Graffiti on tank spells out Sactown Norte, a criminal gang out of Sacramento, California. [Photo provided Jeffery Stoleson]

Gang warfare in Iraq. The Mexican prison gang Sur 13 put a line through the tag of a rival gang and replaced it with their own insignia. [Picture from Jeffrey Stoleson]

CHAPTER THREE

Plump, Young, Dumb—
and Ready to Serve

THE BAGHDAD BULGE

Obesity is not just a public health issue. It's also a national security concern as well. We're not physically fit to defend ourselves.
Dr. Carlos Crespo, associate professor of social and
preventive medicine at the University at Buffalo, 2002[1]

America is getting fatter. It has been for decades. But only during the years of the War on Terror did the country's obesity problem become a full-on, deadly serious national security issue. Nothing was more likely to put Al-Qaeda at ease than the thought of a waddling phalanx rumbling towards them in Iraq or Afghanistan, but as the wars got underway, that's what happened as standards in the US military relating to body fat and fitness were relaxed: as the recruiting pool shrank, the waistlines of soldiers got bigger. The US soldier in the War on Terror weighed thirty-seven pounds, or 25 percent, more than his ancestor in the Civil War,[2] and obesity was by far the most common medical reason why prospective soldiers were refused entry into the military. And the situation was getting dramatically worse. In 1993 about 23 percent of prospective recruits would have been overweight—a pretty significant tranche. By 2006 this had increased to just over 27 percent, or more than a quarter of potential recruits. In the same period, obesity countrywide had increased from

2.8 percent to 6.8 percent. "We're not physically fit to defend ourselves," complained Dr. Carlos Crespo, a University of Buffalo professor. "As a society, we need to be physically prepared to respond to natural disasters, acts of terrorism, or any other emergency."[3]

The military gauges the physical fitness of its recruits using a measure called the body mass index, or BMI, which measures body fat as a percentage of overall weight. The BMI of a prospective soldier must not be more than 26 percent for a man and 32 percent for a woman. "An increasing number of young adults in the general population do not meet the current weight-for-height standards," lamented one military report. Among eighteen-year-olds who applied for military service in 2006, 35 percent of males and 28 percent of females had a BMI above 25, it added.[4] "I'd say that out of every 10 applicants that come in, probably three we couldn't take—they are obese," said Sergeant Darryl Bogan, a recruiter in Columbia, South Carolina. "We are getting heavier as a nation as far as our young people are concerned."[5]

Until 1960 there were no regulations on obesity; when soldiers were weighed it was to find out if they had enough not *too much* weight.[6] But that was before America ballooned. "There is no question soldiers are getting bigger—just look at photos of soldiers from the 50s," said Lieutenant Colonel Karl Friedl, the army's director of operational medical research, adding that that difference is a reflection of general weight gain among the whole population.[7] But something had to change. "The fatter America gets, the more lenient the military is going to get with their regulations," he added. Even before the war in Iraq was launched the Pentagon knew what a stickler this could prove. "If at some future time the federal guidelines are adopted, the impact will be to shift a sizeable group of personnel from a category of meeting weight standards to a category of being overweight," a leaked Pentagon report said.[8] "Such a change would have negative implications for perceptions of readiness of the forces." But readiness was of less importance than maintaining the force. And some believed it was purely a perception thing: did it actually matter? "The military, of course, has standards for appearances: you don't want a bunch of fat guys marching in your parade. But how critical is it? It is of significance, but in critical terms, that significance is marginal," said Arthur Frank, a medical director at George Washington University.[9]

Untightening the Belt

The most obvious way around the problem was the use of "medical waivers" to make exceptions for overweight recruits. In 2006, medical waivers constituted about 30 percent of all army waivers and 25 percent of those for the marines.[10] But this still wasn't enough, and in 2004 the military began a string of programs aimed at recruiting the fat of America into its fighting force. First, the army set up a program with the Olympian title of Assessment of Recruit Motivation and Strength, or ARMS, which was designed to cut some slack for recruits who didn't quite meet the army regulations on body fat. It became a sort of "automatic waiver" for recruits who had body-fat percentages up to 30 percent for men and 36 percent for women. Like being back in gym class, the recruits who fell in the upper margins of this criterion would be made to do a different "Harvard step" test exercise to other recruits, one which involved stepping onto a platform 120 times per minute, followed by a number of push-ups. If you made it through, there was no need to worry about being overweight, you were deemed army good and had a full year to get yourself in shape. One lucky beneficiary was Kyle Kimball who in 2006 wanted to follow in the footsteps of his father and enlist in the marines. The problem was that he weighed 250 pounds, about 35 pounds over the cut-off for a marine of his height. But he went to Westover Joint Air Reserve Base in Chicopee, Massachusetts, and became one of the first to take advantage of the ARMS scheme, taking fitness tests as a way around his weight problems. "I can get there," he told the *Boston Globe*, "I know I can lose the weight."[11]

On top of that, $6 million of federal money was granted to the Troop Recruit Improvement (TRIM) program run by the Nutrition Research Council, the aim of which was to "improve recruit readiness and fitness by determining and combating the causes of childhood and adolescent obesity."[12] Dr. Andrew Young, Chief of the Military Nutrition Division in Natick, Massachusetts, was an adviser on the TRIM project. "We definitely have seen that soldiers are not immune to the obesigenic environmental factors of this country and the rest of the world," he told me. "The military now recognizes that some of the soldiers in the army and probably other services are having trouble maintaining healthy body weight." Young claimed further that obesity is rising in the army. "The goal for us is to design intervention programs for soldiers to use in coping with problems of obesity," he added. "The environmental pressures are growing—more and more soldiers have duties that are not as active—not all soldiers have very physically demanding jobs, some have a relatively small physical component. The environment promotes fat gain unless we are aggressive to counteract those pressures."

During a 2009 visit to the army's largest training installation, General Bostick said a slim-down camp could be part of the new Army Prep School at Fort Jackson in South Carolina, which was giving prospective soldiers the qualifications they needed in order to serve. "We are looking at the Army Prep School as a place where we might send some that have weight issues," he said.[13] Bostick argued that although many of the young people who want to join the army have a hard time understanding the importance of a healthy diet and daily exercise, they could nevertheless get themselves up to the required military standards with guidance. "It took them 18 years to get to where they are at, so it's very difficult for them to lose the kind of weight that they need to on their own," he said. "[The military] are doing this because they are desperate," added Lawrence J. Korb, a former Pentagon chief of personnel during the Reagan administration. The desperation was starting to show in July 2008, when the Healthy Eating and Lifestyle Training Headquarters (HEALTH), an online program that designed troops a personal weight-loss program, was set up at Fort Bragg. It wasn't just a beefy army, either. The air force—or "chair force" as it was rechristened—had its own ideas and started its own Fit to Fight program in 2004. "I want to make very clear that my focus is not on passing a fitness test once a year," General Jumper said. "More important, we are changing the culture of the Air Force. This is about our preparedness to deploy and fight. It's about warriors. It's about instilling an expectation that makes fitness a daily standard—an essential part of your service."[14] The program required commanders to institute some sort of daily fitness routine. Lieutenant Colonel Friedl, however, as an expert in weight issues, believed all this wasn't enough. "It's a shame to lose somebody that you've invested a lot of money in and it's their career as well simply because they can't meet these standards and for lack of providing some kind of specialized assistance that might have made all the difference." But the specialized assistance was too expensive; it was easier to let the troops' waistlines expand.

Obesity Within the Military

Once in the military, there is ample opportunity for soldiers to pile on weight, as they sit around at checkpoints all day, or eat continually from boredom. The army has regulations to deal with this—or at least it should have. Every soldier is expected to stay in shape and pass biannual fitness tests, including screening for weight. If they fail that, they are put on to the "weight control" program, which has a strict regimen of exercise and dietary requirements. It's not good for your career either: you can't be promoted while on the program. The marines had their own version of this with the Body Composition Program—if a marine failed to get back in shape while in the program they risked discharge from the military. In 2008, however, an investigation revealed that only about one in three marines found to be overweight was actually enrolled in a BCP.[15] As these programs were neglected things predictably got worse. "In the past decade among active military members in general, the percent of military members who experienced medical encounters for overweight/obesity has steadily increased; and since 2003, rates of increase have generally accelerated," said a 2009 Pentagon report.[16] But despite the increasing number of "medical encounters," the military has discharged ever fewer service members for not meeting weight standards. In 1998, 2,224 soldiers were discharged from the army for not meeting the standards. In 2006 that figure had fallen to 589—a 74 percent drop in eight years.[17] This was not, of course, because the military's anti-fat programs had suddenly become much more effective. "These statistics should be seen against the background of the army trying very hard to maintain its overall numbers," Dr. Russell Pate, professor of health sciences at the University of South Carolina and a military adviser on obesity, told me. In his opinion, "They've been granting waivers to the weight exclusion program in the interest of meeting targets."

Some saw the proliferation of fat soldiers in a more positive light. Indeed, in the eyes of one group, it was a seminal moment: "I think it's great that they finally understand our value in society," Lynn McAfee, of the Council on Size and Weight Discrimination, told me. "Now they finally understand that everyone can play a part in defending our country . . . It's absurd that as desperate as we are now for soldiers," she continued, "we're still kicking out people of worth and people of value because of how they look. But I'd like to think this is a turning point." But the notion that overweight people swaddled in many pounds of Kevlar might not be fit for wandering around a desert in 30-degree Celsius heat has more to do with common sense than discrimination. McAfee had supporters in the US military brass though, who (as usual) denied there was a problem or anything to worry about. Nathan M. Banks, Sr., a spokesman for the army, dismissed the charges out of hand, telling me: "Soldiers realize how important it is to stay in shape. Especially in time of war, the heat in Iraq can get up in the 100s, soldiers carry body armor that weighs over 60 pounds." This explanation isn't bolstered by the statistics: from 2005 to 2006, there was a drop from 801 to 589 in the number of discharges for obesity.[18]

Despite the military refusing to kick out its tubby service members, there were still attempts by soldiers themselves to use it as a means to avoid fighting. Failing your fitness test is a way to avoid exercises or combat, one that doesn't carry the heavy burden of going AWOL. "There is a problem in the Army with overweight soldiers and malingering," said Specialist Oittis D. Allen in a letter to the *Army Times*. "These soldiers are claiming to be hurt so they don't have to participate in physical exercises, and they don't work like the rest of the soldiers. The doctor will write them a temporary excuse to malinger; the doctor will not sign off on a permanent profile knowing their only medical problem is they are overweight." The whole process was broken. "The Army regulation for overweight soldiers is to give them a certain amount of time to lose the weight or be discharged, but the chain of command is finding ways to overlook the situation," he continued. "In my company, I have seen several cases of soldiers being promoted even though they can't pass the Army Physical Fitness Test, along with passing weight and tape standards. I'm getting tired of the system being unequal. I and other soldiers are putting out 100 percent for the Army to get the mission accomplished, while the obese soldiers get everything given to them."[19]

Back home from the warzone, veterans had more given to them with yet another new overweight initiative by the VA (created in 2006), called Managing Overweight Veterans Everywhere, or MOVE. The program sought to help veterans escape their obesity or prevent them from falling into it when they return home and was piloted at James A. Haley Veterans Hospital, Tampa, Florida, where it was coordinated by nurse Norma Figueroa who oversaw about 400 veterans. "The veteran population is mostly obese and so we as a team decided the best thing to do was to help with prevention," she told me. "I don't know anybody who has been kicked out for being overweight," she added, "because it's not happening. They provided a program, but they let them all stay."

Medical Concern

This oversight was hugely damaging. The Pentagon themselves admit that being overweight "is a significant military medical concern because it is associated with decreased military operational effectiveness."[20] This includes the obvious fact that a lack of physical fitness and a few extra rolls of flab are going to make you less of a force on the battlefield, but it also puts a strain on the military medical services as overweight recruits are more likely to develop chronic health effects. "One of the implications is that having a significant number that are overweight there is a higher incidence of negative outcomes, limitations on work performance, but also to the profusion of veteran health care," says Dr. Pate. "There is the impact on physical performance; it's true that, to take a simple example, if we have 150lb person who has normal percent body fat today but five years later has 20lb [excess] that is going to have negative impact on performance, he will run slower, lift his body weight fewer times, in terms of combat military specialities which are done based on physical performance it's certainly true that you would expect negative impact on performance . . . I think the overriding issue," he continued, "is that in the broad sweep having significant numbers in military who are overweight is a concern in terms of soldier performance and both soldier and veteran health overall."

The Pentagon officially blamed the proliferation of video games and fast food for military chubbiness, but they must take at least part of the blame insofar as they allowed fast food joints to take over from mess halls as places for soldiers to eat in Kabul and Baghdad. In Baghdad's Green Zone there were outlets for Pizza Hut, Subway, Cinnabon, Burger King, and Taco Bell. There was also the Post Exchange, a military supermarket selling T-bone steaks and other goodies. Standing outside Burger King a journalist caught a group of soldiers contemplating a second Whopper burger. "Not me, man," said Specialist Joe Lorenzo. "I put on so much goddam weight, who knows if my wife will recognize me when I get home?"[21] It was made worse as operations were handed over to local Iraqi troops, leaving US service members with less and less to do—apart from eat. "You make the best of the situation," said Private Jonathan Roane. "We used to eat to fight. It's not like that anymore."[22] Their British allies were not much better. In a 2009 memo, Major Brian Dupree said: "The numbers of personnel unable to deploy and concerns about obesity throughout the army are clearly linked to current attitudes towards physical training," adding that "operational effectiveness" was being undermined.[23] It was even putting lives at risk. A British inquiry in 2007 revealed that Private Jason Smith had died of heat stroke in Iraq after concerns about his weight. It found he was "at the higher level of obese" at 17 stones and his BMI was dangerously high at 34, the implication being that it precipitated his death.[24]

INTELLIGENCE OPS

If you come from a poor family, you are more likely to drop out of high school. And if you drop out and stay out of high school, you are more likely to be poor.

Neve Grant, NPR, 2006[25]

On a sunny morning in August 2009 the ribbon was cut at the inaugural Patriot Academy on a National Guard installation in Butlerville, Indiana. It was the first institution of its kind in the US and pulled in a crowd of high-powered political figures from around the state. Indiana Democratic Representative Barron Hill and Indiana Lieutenant Governor Becky Skillman stood watching the theatrics, including a flyover by Blackhawk helicopters and other celebrations to mark the opening. There were reasons to be cheerful: the Patriot Academy would be the first military entity charged with giving a high school diploma to "at-risk youth" who wanted to serve in the National Guard but couldn't because they had dropped out of education, which was a bar to enlistment.[26] There was a heady feeling in the air as those giving speeches attested to the importance of this generous new educational experience. "The Patriot Academy can be described in two words: second chance," said Colonel Perry Sarver Jr., the Academy's commandant. "These soldiers are here because they have unfinished business, and they are getting a second chance to right a wrong. These young men have started down a path that will change their lives forever."

The project was the brainchild of Lieutenant General Clyde A. Vaughn, the former director of the Army National Guard, who had been troubled by the number of young Americans still not fit for service in the military. Why not provide high-school-age youth the opportunity to earn a diploma as an active-duty soldier, thereby bypassing the bar on enlistment for high school dropouts? It was "an investment in our most precious resource," he said, an opportunity to help the youth of America *at the same time as* defending American's freedoms. At the Patriot Academy, the students would receive full-time military pay and benefits while they were training. The first class beginning their journey on that afternoon was just forty-six students with a staff of thirty, but there were big ambitions for the program. Two years later it had expanded to 250 students and by 2011 reached 500. For its soldier students, the Academy was the real deal: it had secured Indiana educational accreditation which meant that their qualification would be a bona fide high school diploma, so graduating soldiers would be classed in the military hierarchy as so-called tier 1, opening up the full range of opportunities throughout their career in the armed forces.

There were a few requirements for enrollment: recruits had to be between seventeen and twenty years old and within ten credit hours of high school graduation. But those successfully picked would spend a period in basic training, then nine months at the academy before moving to a school which focused specifically on the military occupation (meaning job *not country*) in which they were interested. Giving those who had not had a good start in life a second chance while at the same time swelling the army's ranks did sound like a good idea, and there were the usual euphoric reports from the media: "Only months ago, four dozen high-school dropouts from around the country faced a bleak future and limited opportunities in the work force. Now they are soldiers at the Patriot Academy, on their way to earning their high-school diplomas and credits towards a college degree," wrote one military reporter. The new soldier students seemed chipper, too: "I'm going to be a Fire Support Specialist," Private Michael Meadows, nineteen, of Daleville, Indiana, told *US Fed News*. "But I have to get my diploma here first before I can go to Advanced Individual Training. I've been looking forward to this."[27] But of course it was not an altruistic Pentagon program (they tend not to exist). The Pentagon wanted and needed recruits and was prepared to hold young people's hopes for an education hostage to service in the War on Terror. This new program marked a full-scale militarization of the recruits' education, with no real pretence otherwise. When the nine-month program was finished the soldier students would be obliged to commit to eight years of service with the National Guard, which had been increasingly involved in the occupations of Afghanistan and Iraq. "The Army

National Guard has had a significant evolution in the last eight years," said Raymond Carpenter, acting director of the National Guard, in Congressional testimony. "Units mobilized and deployed from different states and territories provided support to overseas contingency operations and to the Homeland Defense mission."[28] In other words, they were sure to have to fight. The parents of the new students seemed aware of the inevitability that their loved ones would see combat. "War abroad, or war on the streets," said one mom, giving an apt description of the choice facing young, poor Americans. "At least he'll be fighting for something," the dad added.[29] The National Guard was to be the Trojan horse used to penetrate the wider community, which had still not *completely* sacrificed its young for the war effort. The Guard had a sterling record in this regard, one lauded by military bigwigs. Army Brigadier General Maria Britt, commanding general of the Georgia Army National Guard, speaking at the DOD's Worldwide Education Symposium about the Guard's youth and voluntary education programs, noted, "The Guard has a proud tradition of initiating and funding education programs that reach out to non-military adults, youth and . . . schools," adding, "We do this because we want to be good stewards in the communities that we serve."[30] In truth, it had nothing to do with being good stewards. The Patriot Academy was another way to blackmail the poor who have been failed by the mainstream education system only to be failed again once in service.

Despite all this, the Academy was no doubt a serious enticement. One of the new soldier students put it like this: "Just the fact that I could get a high school diploma rather than a GED sounded better to me. It just makes me feel and sound like I've completed my school. Like our sergeant major once told us, we're not going to get this chance again. If you get the opportunity to come to the Patriot Academy to have your second chance, you actually get paid to go to school and learn new things."[31] Amid all the rhetoric about "second chances," Iraq and Afghanistan weren't mentioned in the prospectus. And reports on the initial student body left no doubt about the ethnic demographic the military were targeting. "The current class at the Academy is a mix of Americans from a wide group of ethnic and racial backgrounds," reported the army's official news service, before quoting Private Rigoberto Rodriguez, who grew up in El Paso, Texas: "Being a minority with other minorities helps me to feel at home," he said.[32]

Student Soldiers

It wasn't surprising the military should focus on this pool of potential recruits; perhaps the only shock was that it took until 2009 to inaugurate the Academy. High school dropouts posed one of the major obstacles to the recruitment of America's youth. A report by a non-profit group composed of retired military figures entitled *Ready, Willing, and Unable To Serve* spelled out the problem, contending that 75 percent of eighteen- to twenty-four-year olds do not qualify for service, adding "many young Americans who want to join cannot."[33] The three most common barriers for potential recruits were, it said, failure to graduate high school, a criminal record, and physical fitness issues, including obesity. The criminal record had been dealt with by "moral waivers" and the obesity problem dealt with by "medical waivers," but restrictions on non-graduates would be more difficult to sidestep. Approximately one out of four young Americans lacks a high school diploma and like any military, the US needed "high-competent individuals who can operate high-tech machinery and computer machinery," soldiers who can "work in teams" with "excellent judgment." "That cannot be acquired just in basic training," the report concluded, so dropping the standards on educational attainment would not be so easy to do without seriously affecting operational readiness. The other option, of course, was that education would have to improve. But would it take the need for more fodder for the War on Terror to convince the political elite to raise educational standards? The report believed it had to: "The most proven investment to help kids graduate from high school starts early: high quality early education for at-risk kids." It never happened.

Over the previous decades the US public school system had been steadily degraded and exam results continued to be appalling relative to other developed countries. The National Assessment of

Education Progress reported in 2007 that 69 percent of the nation's eighth graders scored below proficiency level in math, and 70 percent scored below proficiency level in reading.[34] A study of high school dropout rates found it hit a trough at 20 percent in the late 1960s and then increased just 4–5 percentage points afterward, and in terms of black and Hispanic students, it found "no evidence of convergence in minority-majority graduation rates over the past 35 years,"[35] while high school dropouts were disproportionately from poorer families. As one journalist put it, "If you come from a poor family, you are more likely to drop out of high school. And if you drop out and stay out of high school, you are more likely to be poor."[36] Of course, the government didn't embark on a splurge of spending on the education system. This was the perfect demographic to reenfranchise into the military: Black, Hispanic, poor, and with a high probability of being unemployed. It would be an extension of the existing demographics of the fighting force: according to research, recruits from families with annual incomes below $60,000 are over-represented in the military, while those families earning more are under-represented.[37] The military now dangled a carrot: we'll give you a proper education if you agree to become war fodder afterward.

During the War on Terror, George W. Bush's educational reforms were further impacting the public schooling system through increasing standardization and lack of funds. "There is a dark side to the educational reforms initiated under the Bush administration and now used in a number of school systems throughout the country," wrote educational theorist Henry Giroux:

> As the logic of the market and "the crime complex" frame the field of social relations in schools, students are subjected to three particularly offensive policies, defended by school authorities and politicians under the rubric of school safety. First, students are increasingly subjected to zero-tolerance policies that are used primarily to punish, repress and exclude them. Second, they are increasingly absorbed into a "crime complex" in which security staff, using harsh disciplinary practices, now displace the normative functions teachers once provided both in and outside of the classroom. Third, more and more

schools are breaking down the space between education and juvenile delinquency, substituting penal pedagogies for critical learning and replacing a school culture that fosters a discourse of possibility with a culture of fear and social control.[38]

It sounded remarkably like boot camp. Giroux continued, "Any youth of color in urban school systems, because of harsh zero-tolerance policies, are not just being suspended or expelled from school. They are being ushered into the dark precincts of juvenile detention centers, adult courts and prison." During the War on Terror another "dark precinct" opened up: *the military.*

Typical of this move from the streets to the warzone was another National Guard program called the Youth ChalleNGe, which describes itself as a "preventive rather than remedial" at-risk youth program that specifically targets participants who are "unemployed, drug-free and law-free high-school dropouts, 16 to 18 years of age."[39] The twenty-two-week program, which takes place in camps, most of which are on military bases, is followed by a year-long mentoring relationship with someone from each youth's community. "By taking them away from their neighborhoods, we're giving them a safe place to get their act together," one colonel assured the critics. "These youths have been told they are failures. Here they find that if they straighten up, others will believe in them."[40] But it wasn't about providing disadvantaged youths with a safe place. It was about militarizing their education and sending them to the most *dangerous* places in the world—Iraq and Afghanistan. Even though it claimed it was not a military recruitment program, during the War on Terror 15 to 20 percent of Youth ChalleNGe graduates entered the armed services or the National Guard.[41]

There was another way still for non-graduates to get into the military: the general equivalency degree, or GED, which can afford recruits a waiver if they score well enough on the military's entrance exam.[42] The army accepts about 15 percent of recruits without a high school diploma if they have a GED. Alive to this loophole, the military instituted another program in 2008, the so-called GED Plus, to give more of America's youth the requisite qualifications they needed to go and fight. It opened its first prep school for the purpose, targeted, of course, at tough inner city areas. The program involved a harsh regimen with an intense academic component starting at 5 a.m. "An hour of marching drills and military discipline is thrown in for good measure," reported AP.[43] The militarization of education was complete. The whole concept was, again, framed in terms of "helping these lazy layabouts," the rhetoric sounding like something out of *Full Metal Jacket* rather than a caring teaching environment. "It's a tough, structured day. Some of them have sat on the couch for eighteen years, but I haven't heard any howling yet," social studies instructor John Solis said. Apparently Solis preferred high school grads because of their "tenacity," but, he added, "the reality of current graduation rates has the army pressed to find an alternative."

With the GED behind them, the class goes through to basic training, which often includes combat training. Those entering prep school have to agree to a two- to four-year commitment, just like a regular recruit. "We have two missions: get the GED and prepare them physically and mentally for basic training," said the school's commander, Captain Brian Gaddis. "These kids may have quit at some point, but the big thing is, a lot of people have quit on them," Gaddis added. "We are not going to allow them to quit." The prison-like conditions were successful in getting recruits. In 2007 the GED Plus Program trained 709 soldiers, with a 73 percent success rate. In the next two years, 2,400 soldiers had a 95 percent success rate, significantly higher than the 69 percent national average success rate in the civilian GED program.[44] Things looked so good that in 2009, $18 million was ploughed into a new GED Plus educational complex on a National Guard campus in Arkansas.[45]

It all had a strong echo of the Vietnam era. Defense Secretary Robert McNamara had started his Project 100,000 in 1966, which was designed to get 100,000 men into the military who had failed the qualifying exam even at the lowered standards. McNamara presented the move as one that would improve the lot of America's "subterranean poor": exactly the same as the War on Terror narrative. "The poor of America . . . have not had the opportunity to earn their fair share of this nation's abundance," McNamara said, "but they can be given an opportunity to serve in their country's defense and they can be given an opportunity to return to civilian life with skills and aptitudes which for them and their families will reverse the downward spiral of decay." But it was a complete lie. As one historian describes it:

> Never well known, Project 100,000 has virtually disappeared from histories of the Johnson presidency. It was conceived, in fact, as a significant component of the administration's "war on poverty," part of the Great Society, a liberal effort to uplift the poor, and it was instituted with high-minded rhetoric about offering the poor an opportunity to serve. Its result, however, was to send many poor, terribly confused, and woefully uneducated boys to risk death in Vietnam.[46]

Likewise with Iraq and Afghanistan. "Project 100,000 and the abandonment of all but the most minimal mental requirements for military service were crucial institutional mechanisms in lowering the class composition of the US military."[47] Likewise again.

Even with the military working hard to give recruits the requisite qualifications in exchange for service, it still wasn't enough. Eventually they began to stretch the existing standards, allowing greater numbers of those with no qualifications at all to sign on the dotted line. "The DOD's benchmark standard calls for at least 90 percent of troops to be high school graduates," writes one academic. "Meeting those benchmarks has been a hallmark of the all-volunteer military since the end of conscription in 1973," and since the mid-1980s there had been a strict cap on recruits with no high school diploma. But this was to change. In 2005, the number of recruits with no military experience and with high school diplomas was 83.5 percent; a year later it had dropped to 73.1 percent.[48] "The overall quality of the force today is lower than it was a year ago," complained David R. Segal, director of the Center for Research on Military Organization at the University of Maryland. "It means they can anticipate more problem situations with recruits in the training cycle."[49] The army found another way to avoid admitting its problems through the handsomely named Tier Two Attrition Scheme, or

TTAS, which would not count non-graduate recruits against the 10 percent cap if they were projected to have lower or similar attrition rates to graduates. "Compared with the costs of digging deeper into the relatively expensive [high school diploma graduates] recruiting market, the Army's ability to recruit more high-quality [non high school diploma graduates] could save millions of dollars in recruiting resources," said an army assessment.[50] It was merely a way to massage the figures. As *Military* magazine put it:

> The Army announced that 81 percent of its non-prior service recruits for 2006 were high school graduates. That was disturbingly below the 90 percent Department of Defense standard for every service. But the proportion of high school graduates would have been reported as 74.3 percent if the Army had to count the 5900 TTAS enlistees high school dropouts. The number instead is ignored. In March, Defense officials gave the Army permission to sign up 8000 TTAS recruits a year to ease increasingly difficult recruiting challenges.[51]

Despite all this, the military had the full support of lawmakers as they went about enlisting the poor and vulnerable young men and women of America. "I'm not totally naïve, but I have faith in recruiters," said Representative Joe Wilson, (R-SC). "There may be higher dropout rates. But a lot of times they're extending opportunities to minorities who wouldn't have opportunities otherwise."[52] The opportunities offered to minorities came, of course, at the expense of their service in war and the very real threat to their lives. What did it say about America that its ethnic minorities could only get the chance to better themselves by putting their bodies in the line of fire?

Intelligence Testing

Another way for the military to measure the brain power of recruits is the armed forces qualification test, or AFQT, which every prospective soldier has to take in an effort to weed out the slowest. For decades, the military had spent a lot of money and time developing psychometric tests because it believed in a strict correlation between operational performance and mental attainment. The testing was formalized as far back as 1968 and taken up by all branches of the military in 1976, but it didn't start rejecting low-scoring applicants until the mid-1980s. By the time of the War on Terror it was ingrained in the military recruitment process. The AFQT is a multiple-choice questionnaire very similar to an IQ test, or what psychologists call "G"—covering abilities from arithmetical reasoning to paragraph comprehension. From these results the recruits are put into five categories, running from Category 1, the best performing, to Category 5, the worst. Army regulation shut out anyone who scored in the lowest category, and strictly restricted Category 4 to two percent of the intake. By 2004, Category 4 recruits still only accounted for 0.6 percent of new recruits. But a year later, with the military desperate, a new DOD directive allowed in up to 4 percent of recruits from Category 4. Before long, that percentage had reached double figures.[53] The military was literally getting dumber. The *New York Times* reported that recruiters were even being *told* to accept more Category 4 recruits. "A recruiter in Washington, who insisted on anonymity to protect his career, said that at the time, he was concerned about whether these recruits could handle the increasingly high-technology tools of combat," its report noted. "Another recruiter, in New York, who insisted on anonymity for the same reason, said this month that the Army seemed to care less about quality than about filling the holes left by soldiers who decline to re-enlist . . . It's about one thing: numbers," added the recruiter.[54]

For some, letting in recruits with low IQs was actually more equitable as it is an extremely controversial metric, not least for its common use by racists to give a dubious scientific basis for their prejudices. In the US, for example, Hispanics and African Americans score lower than whites on IQ tests, as was demonstrated by the infamous *Bell Curve* book in 1994.[55] But serious psychologists put this discrepancy down to the differing educational standards that exist between ethnic groups. The average black IQ is 85, below the 92 that is the 30th percentile cut-off point for joining the military, for example. There was compelling evidence that strict IQ testing was discriminating against young black wannabe soldiers. But there was also evidence supporting the military's claim that IQ has a direct impact on operational performance as well as monetary cost. The differential in how quickly recruits leave the military (attrition rates) provides one clear example. Army studies demonstrate about 80 percent of those with diplomas complete their first three-year term of enlistment compared to only half of those with a GED.[56] "Recruits with a high school diploma are also valued since years of research and experience show that high school diploma graduates are more likely to complete their initial 3 [years of service]," said one directive.[57] The higher dropout rate for GED soldiers means they must be replaced, which "drives up military spending because of the need to spend money recruiting, outfitting, and training new troops," reports *Time* magazine. The cost of signing up a new, fresh recruit rose from $15,000 to $21,000 in five years to 2008.[58] Further to that, the military has been concerned about levels of attrition in the first years of service because it is, they say, "disruptive, degrades unit performance, and wastes valuable training and recruiting resources."[59] This *seems* like an argument for recruiting those who are most likely to adapt to military life and stay the course. The army explicitly accepted that "the high school diploma has been a reliable indicator of 'stick-to-itiveness.'"[60] But it didn't stop recruits getting in without one: the military simply couldn't slow down. A study by Rand concluded that the diploma was also an important indicator of operational performance, which was a more serious concern. Still the military didn't move. "Generally, studies conducted in this area have supported the assertion that higher-quality personnel, in this case personnel with a higher AFQT score, appear to be more productive and to exhibit generally higher performance," it noted.[61] Two other studies supported that conclusion. One from 1986 tried to answer the question, "Are smart [gun] tankers better?" by using their firing scores at a standardized course, and found that there was a strict correlation between accuracy and AFQT scores; for example, an increase of score from Category 4 to Category 3 led to an improvement of over 20 percentage points in performance. This was a serious business. It goes without saying that a bad shot in the War on

Terror could mean the difference between a dead and a living civilian, or even an American soldier being hit by "friendly fire." How many died as a result of this no one really knows, but there were large numbers of "friendly fire" casualties in the War on Terror. And then there was the money component: stray bombs cost.

None of this appeared to matter. The grand plan was in many ways coming together. High school dropouts composed 41 percent of the prison population in US, which, together with the new acceptance to ex-cons, was opening up the military to thousands more people. But, in truth, why stop at dropouts? They had already started recruiting in prisons; why not get into the high schools as well?

CHILD SOLDIERS

There is not a way out.
Military recruiter to seventeen-year-old Irving Gonzalez, 2008[62]

When Irving Gonzalez was seventeen years old he signed a nonbinding agreement with the local military recruiter in Texas saying he would join the military after his final exams at high school. He didn't worry about it too much at the time. He was concentrating on his finals and one of the provisos of the so-called delayed enlistment program, or DEP, was that he could pull out at any time before the start of basic training. At the end of school, it turned out, pulling out was what he wanted to do. He had other ideas about what he wanted to do with his life which didn't involve service. But it wouldn't prove as easy as it should have. When he informed the recruiter who had signed him up, Sergeant Glenn Marquette from Greenspoint Recruiting Station in Houston, of his decision, Sergeant Marquette went apoplectic. Gonzalez, alongside his friend Eric Martinez, who had signed the same document, were subjected to a tirade of threats and lies from Marquette who told them that their lives would to-all-intents-and-purposes be finished if they decided to spurn the military. Although intimidated, Gonzalez felt something was not quite right and was smart enough to start recording the conversations he was having with Marquette, later releasing them to a local television network. The recording gave a depressing glimpse into the kind of recruiter-conduct towards America's children that became *de rigueur* during the War on Terror. "The main thing is, I want out. I don't want to be in it. I don't want to go to the army," Gonzalez told the recruiter in one conversation, to which the reply was that he would have to come into the recruiting station and see the company commander. Marquette then added, "There is not a way out. You signed a binding contract," which was a barefaced lie. Later, the recruiter went further with the threats: "I'll tell you what happens to you, OK? This is what will happen. You want to go to school? You will not get no loans, because all college loans are federal and government loans. So you'll be black-marked from that. As soon as you get pulled over for a speeding ticket or anything with the law, they're gonna see that you're a deserter. Then they're going to apprehend you, take you to jail . . . All that lovey-dovey 'I want to go to college' and all this? Guess what. You just threw it out the window, because you just screwed your life."

To a young, impressionable child this attack-dog routine was usually successful. His friend, Eric, was a case in point. "As things went further, I decided not to go [into training]. And when I told [the recruiter] that, she said I had no choice and that I had to go, so I believed her," he recalled. He told his mom who hatched a plan to say he had gone to San Antonio and was uncontactable. But even that didn't work. When his mom went to talk to Sergeant Marquette and told him that Eric had changed his mind and didn't want to go, he lied to her, too. "Marquette said that I had to go, and if I didn't, that I'd have a warrant for my arrest and I wouldn't be able to get no government loans or nothing like that. So, my mom doesn't really know anything about it, so she believed it, and she told me," he said. Fortunately, Gonzalez managed to contact Eric and tell him that he didn't have to go, that the recruiter was breaking the law, and that he could change his mind. It may have saved his life. Because of the smarts of Gonzalez, the boys didn't have to go to the deserts of the Middle East; but how many kids have been misled and told they have no choice is unknown. These two boys had family and friends strong enough to support them. Not everyone was so lucky. "Whenever we were thinking upon not joining, they started calling us and telling us that we didn't have a choice, you know, that we could say all we want, we don't have a choice to go or not, if we want to or not," Gonzalez recalled. To most kids this would have been a terrifying routine, but its success in getting kids into the military meant it remained a common one. A *New York Times* report revealed that the army investigated 1,118 "recruiting improprieties" in 2006 ranging from coercing young people to lying to them. The army substantiated 320 of these.[63]

American high schools were always seen as a "target-rich environment" for any recruiter, for obvious reasons: the kids are often not aware of their rights and are easily manipulated by monetary inducements. The US Army Recruiting Command is explicit about how recruiters are expected to operate in the nation's centers of learning and it's not pretty. "Without a strong high school program you cannot have a strong grad recruiting program," says the School Recruiting Army Handbook.[64] It's important to play to their aspirations and dreams, it continues. "For some students it is clear that college is not an option, at least for now. Let them know how the Army can fulfill their college aspirations. This is a key decision point and one you must pursue without fail." The tactics are blatantly underhand and manipulative. "Know your student influencers," it says. "Students such as class officers, newspaper and yearbook editors, and athletes can help build interest in the Army among the student body. Keep them informed. Tell them about the excellent educational benefits and the opportunities available in America's Army." It adds, "Always remember, the first to contact will be the first to contract." Recruiters are assigned target high schools and instructed to offer their friendly services—such as basketball or track coaches. "Deliver donuts and coffee for the faculty once a month," recruiters are told, and "participate" in Black History Month and Hispanic Heritage Month, two of the most popular recruitment demographics for the military coincidentally. "Encourage college-capable individuals to defer their college until they have served in the Army," it advises. If they ever do get to university, recruiters are instructed to get them as freshman while they are still vulnerable:

"Focus on the freshman class [there] because they will have the highest dropout rate. They often lack both the direction and funds to fully pursue their education." In the perverse logic of the recruiters it suits to have less federal funds for college fees, the military often being the only other option.

During the War on Terror, the resources poured into recruiting impressionable young people skyrocketed, with 1,000 new recruiters added in one year to bring high school kids round to the military's way of thinking.[65] The Junior Reserve Officer Training Corps, or JROTC, expanded across the nation, and no child was free from their solicitations, even eleven-year-olds were taking part in the programs. Furthermore, in 2007 a Congressional cap of 3,500 for the programs was lifted which spawned a massive increase in the number of operations.[66] According to Congressional testimony in 2000 from the chiefs of staff of the various armed services, 30 to 50 percent of these cadets eventually enlist. The number would be higher still during the war years.[67] In the War on Terror, school became boot camp as one in ten high school students in Chicago wore a military uniform to school and took classes on shooting guns from retired veterans.[68] It was a process of shaping the minds of the young, planting seeds of war for fruit that would be readily pluckable when the kids reached the age of eighteen, ready to serve.

One of the main incentives offered was money—a lot of money from the perspective of a sixteen-year-old. In 2005, the army moved to raise the average bonus given to recruits when they signed on the dotted line from $14,000 to $17,000, with the possibility of as much as $30,000 for hard-to-fill vacancies.[69] Another of the military's slogans was "Join the Armed Forces, get a free education,"[70] an offer many of America's poorest kids couldn't turn down, even though it was not true. It's why Phylicia Coley, a tenth-grader with an A average, said she was thinking about enlisting. "That's the most important consideration," she said. "I want to be a psychiatrist. I want to go to a good school." In 2008, the GI Bill provided soldiers in the service for three years or more with an average $6,600 per year in educational benefits, with a maximum of $39,636 for four years. But tuition, room and board, and fees at most universities cost a lot more: in the majority of cases, the GI Bill benefits don't even cover half the costs of attending college full-time. But that's not what the recruiter told Coley. "He said the Army pays for everything," she said after being briefed by him. There were other means of reeling in high school students as well, one being getting them to take the Armed Services Vocational Aptitude Battery, or ASVAB. The military describes it as a must if "you're serious about joining the military," or if the Pentagon is serious about you joining the military.[71] It's a timed multi-aptitude test, which is taken at over 14,000 schools and military institutions nationwide. Career counselors are the main conduit through which the students come across it, and they are encouraged to promote it. There's even a *Dummies Guide* to the test to help students get a good score. The test is supposed to give the military a better idea of where the student would be best placed in the military: "These tests will give you an idea of how you'll score, and identify areas that need improvement," the military says. "Don't skimp on preparing for this test. It's your future. Get the most out of it."[72]

No Child Left Unrecruited

The penetration of the military into the nation's bastions of learning had been gathering pace for decades. In 1996, in the middle of Bill Clinton's tenure, the Solomon Amendment, named for its sponsor, US Representative Gerald B. H. Solomon, permitted the denial of federal funding to any educational institution which refused to allow military recruiters to go about their business on campus. This increased level of aggressive recruitment was facilitated and supported by one of George W. Bush's flagship pieces of legislation. In 2001 the No Child Left Behind Act was signed into law with great fanfare and bipartisan support. The act was supposed to enforce a more standardized testing regimen, but deep into its thousands of pages was a directive that would prove to be of huge help to recruiters looking to pester high school students to sign up. Though it drew no comment from the media at the time, which probably didn't have time to read the whole thing, the Act stipulated: "each local educational agency receiving assistance under this Act shall provide, on a request made by military recruiters or an institution of higher education, access to secondary school students names, addresses, and telephone listings."[73] In other words, high schools would now be obliged to hand over the phone numbers of all their pupils (no matter how young) to military recruiters, so a process of grooming them for service in the US military could get underway. It represented the manipulation of US youth at its worst. Before the age of eighteen, young people were not trusted to vote, to make legal or medical decisions, among others, but now they were ready to be solicited for the job of putting their life on the line.

There was a little-known proviso which did concede that a "secondary school student or the parent of the student may request that the student's name, address, and telephone listing . . . not be released without prior written parental consent." But in the end this turned out to be a hugely misleading, as only parents with a thorough knowledge of the Act—unsurprisingly, not many—were aware of the clause. Investigative journalist David Goodman did the most serious research into the effects of this policy.[74] He found that the Pentagon had gathered the names of 34 million young people, what they called "the largest repository of 16-25-year-old youth data in the country," in something they called the JAMRS database, or the Joint Advertising Market Research & Studies program run by the DOD. Worryingly, the data has also been retrieved by private data firms, such as the Student Marketing Group and American Student List, who were paid up to $600,000 by the Pentagon every year to aggregate young people's purchasing choices.

The result was a full-scale militarization of high schools throughout America. A concerned BBC report profiled Sergeant Larry Arnold, a career soldier "with a charming line of fast-paced chatter" who "circulates through the town like a salesman."[75] The victims of his sales routine were the youth of Kokomo, Indiana—population 46,000—many of whom receive "cold calls" from the sergeant in order to get them to enlist. "He uses lists of student that federal law requires the schools to provide to military recruiters," the article notes, without referencing the offending No Child Left Behind Act.

Therefore "it is not uncommon for students to get calls from every branch of the service." Sgt. Arnold said that army recruiters will make 300 calls a day, adding, "Pressure is always there. It's the army, it's your mission, and they drill that into you every day." There was one case which particularly caught the eye:

> Sgt 1st Class Arnold met 17-year-old Matthew, a quiet boy who may or may not be able to graduate from high school in the spring of 2007. He was not certain. If that was not enough cause for concern, Matthew's mother also confided that her son was taking two medications a day for Attention Deficit Hyperactivity Disorder (ADHD). Despite that clearly disqualifying medical condition, Sgt 1st Class Arnold admitted he was tempted to sign him up anyway.

The US military was acting like an African militia with grooming for service extended to kids as young as eleven in some cases. In the process, they were breaking the law. A report, *Soldiers of Misfortune*, by the American Civil Liberties Union (ACLU) found that the US government was actually in contravention of an international protocol prohibiting the recruitment of children into military service when they are under eighteen years old.[76] It also noted that the US military disproportionately targets poor and minority public school students, but its findings were dutifully ignored after being submitted to the UN Committee on the Rights of the Child. Maybe that was because the US is one of only two countries (the other is Somalia) to have never ratified the Convention on the Rights of the Child. Even so, the Senate puts the age minimum for recruitment at seventeen, but the report found that recruiters "regularly target" younger children, "heavily recruiting on high school campuses, in school lunchrooms, and in classes." The ACLU surveyed 1,000 children aged from fourteen to seventeen who were enrolled in New York City high schools as part of the report. One in five of the respondents said that class time had been given over to military recruiters, and 35 percent said that military recruiters had access to multiple locations in the schools where they could meet students. The ACLU contended that in their desperation the Pentagon had used the JROTC, which has access to thousands of junior high schools, middle schools, and high schools across the country, to systematically target children. Military recruiters use "exaggerated promises of financial rewards for enlistment, which undermines the voluntariness of their enlistment," the report noted. It detailed the use of "coercion, deception, and even sexual abuse" by recruiters. Punishment for such transgressions was rare. "The United States military's procedures for recruiting students plainly violate international standards and fail to protect youth from abusive and aggressive recruitment tactics," said Jennifer Turner of the ACLU Human Rights Project. African child soldiers, meet African American child soldiers.

Virtual War

The tireless effort to bring children into the orbit of the military was gathering pace even outside of schools, with underhand manipulation the order of the day. In 2009, Students for a Democratic Society found military recruiters scouting out Summerfest, the largest music festival in Milwaukee. They hadn't been an easy spot at first, as this time they were moonlighting as professional models, a developing tactic from the military that preyed on the sexual desires of pubescent America. Recruitment brass had enlisted the help of Encore Nationwide, providers of promotional models, to seduce America's young into service. Sex was soon supplemented by video games. There was a concerted effort to "make war fun," a job taken on by the army's first official marketing officer, Edward Walters, a thirty-eight-year-old West Point graduate and former marketing man for Kraft Foods. One of his first initiatives got underway in August 2008, in the form of the first and only Army Experience Center in Philadelphia (cost $12 million), a new variation on the recruitment office theme—this time providing arcade video games and a merchandise shop to reel the kids in. A 14,500-square-foot "virtual educational facility," it offered all the experiences of war played out in on-screen games and simulated exercises. Little kids could sit in a Humvee and think longingly of the deserts of the Middle East. The target demographic was hinted at by its location close to a popular entertainment complex and indoor skate park. Even so, the army maintained that it was not a recruitment center, although the twenty soldiers working in the facility were trained recruiters.[77]

Walters told the press that the army store was a "new kind of recruitment office . . . We're moving away from normal recruiting offices and desks to places where men and women can experience military service," he said, adding, "We've been doing that with innovative techniques like interaction with real soldiers and high-tech virtual experiences." In 2006, advertising agency McCann Erickson was enlisted to dream up a $200 million campaign with the "Army Strong" slogan to bring in even more kids.[78] "Traditional marketing has been challenging," Walters told the *New York Post* for its article entitled "An Army of Fun." "When you're just focused on TV and the Web, it's hard to get the full message out there." [79] In June 2010, however, it was revealed that the Center was to close down—a strange course of events considering the cost and its relative success: a newspaper report said that at least 236 recruits had joined the army through the Center and it had been attended by 40,000 people.[80] The organizers of resistance to the Center, who set up a website "Shut Down the Army Experience Center," claimed victory and said it had planned a protest just before the scheduled closing date.[81] Unbelievably, the military claimed that the installation was not intended to be permanent, but that its technology would be replicated around the country. The use of video games to glorify military combat, sanitizing its perception among the young, had, in fact, been a long-term strategy. In 2002, the Army Game Project had been released for download from the internet, allowing players to "fire on a rifle range, run an obstacle course, attend sniper school, train in urban combat and parachute from a C-17 transport."[82] It soon had eight million players worldwide. It was a serious operation to build, created primarily by the Modeling, Virtual Environment and Simulation Institute at the Naval Postgraduate School in Monterey, California. Help was also at hand from the bright lights of Hollywood, as Star Wars creator George Lucas's company, Skywalker Sound, provided them with sound effects from the *Terminator 2* movie. Soon after, an army office was opened with a staff of fifteen full-time video-game designers. The army proceeded to release the Virtual Army Experience, which it boasted was "based on actual missions" in its promotional video complete with images of Iraq. The game was the standard murder-fest, in which the player hunts down and kills the enemy, while, for instance, on patrol in Iraq. One journalist called it "a shoot-em-up, get-the-bad guys kind of affair."[83] It was the ultimate entertainment, except this time it was used to sign up kids for real war.

The Wikileaks release of the "Collateral Murder" video, showing a US attack on unarmed children and journalists in Iraq, brought the side effects of this video-game rendering of war painfully home. The language of the soldiers heard in the video revealed a complete dehumanization of the Iraqis on the ground, with words like "nice" being used to describe the massacre. The blame must rest partly with the army's use of video games to sell itself, which has numbed its young soldiers to the reality of war and destruction. It wasn't as if no one knew what effect it would have. In other domains, the idea that America's kids should be exposed to such unbridled violence was frowned upon. US lawmakers were clear: violence in video games is a corrosive force. A bill unveiled in December 2005 by Democrats Hillary Clinton and Joseph Lieberman proposed taking punitive measure against any business that sells or rents video games with an "adults-only" rating to anyone under age seventeen.[84] But things were different when it came to a military that kids were increasingly reluctant to join. For them, there was literally no escape from "adults-only" violence. In 2009, it was revealed that "Explorer" scouts, aged fourteen to twenty-one, were being dressed up in combat gear, given air guns, and taught to take on "counter-terrorist" duties and other law enforcement and military roles. "This is about being a true-blooded American guy and girl. It fits right in with the honor and bravery of the Boy Scouts," said A. J. Lowenthal, a tough-talking sheriff's deputy and Explorer leader in Imperial, California.[85] This glorification of violence and combat had a deleterious effect on the nation's youth. In 2006, at the height of the recruitment drive, police in cities around the country blamed a spike in violent crime on increasing levels of juveniles involved in armed robbery, assaults, and other serious crimes.

Minneapolis police estimated that juveniles would account for 63 percent of all suspects in violent and property offenses, an increase of 45 percent from 2002, just four years earlier.[86]

Parent Fight-back

The militarization of schools and childhood didn't pass without heroic protest from a coalition of parents, students, and teachers, understandably upset at society's colonization by the Pentagon. In June 2005 the *New York Times* ran a feature titled "Growing Problem for Military Recruiters: Parents," citing a DOD survey which had found that only 25 percent of parents would recommend military service to their children in late 2004, down from 42 percent just a year earlier. The situation was so bad one recruiter said: "I had one father say if he saw me on his doorstep I better have some protection on me," before adding, "We see a lot of hostility."[87] Organized counter-recruitment parents teamed up with more established groups like the Central Committee for Conscientious Objection in order to make sure as many students as possible filled out the requisite forms needed to stop their details being handed over to recruiters. One was Tina Weishaus, president of the Highland Park Middle School/High School Parent Teacher Organization in New Jersey. "The recruiters really harangue people, and this is what parents are trying to avoid," she said.[88] Local lawmakers also got in on the act. In Arcata and Eureka, the county councils voted for a Youth Protection Act which prohibited the recruitment of anyone under eigtheen within city limits, before it was ruled "unconstitutional" by a federal appeals court.[89]

Students themselves were revolting. In the largely black and Hispanic New York City neighborhood of Bushwick, the kids led the fight-back against the constant harrying and intrusion into their schools. One recent graduate of a Bushwick high school, Tamara Henderson, told a story that has been replicated across the US. She remembered recruiters hanging around the school "at least once a week," asking for students' names and approaching them in the hallways with flyers. "I feel like they are just targeting blacks and Latino students," she said, echoing the recruiter's handbook.

"We should be having college recruiters in our schools to present options to continue our education. Instead we are left with military recruiters, feeding us lies and empty promises."[90] This led community members to start working with local schools to counter the takeover. In 2003, the Bushwick School for Social Justice (BSSJ) was set up to work on campaigns and education, including counter-recruitment drives. Make the Road was another Bushwick-based activist collective that has organized street theater protests outside one of the two recruitment stations in the area. In one, kids dressed up in orange jumpsuits and had black hoods on to protest the 2005 Haditha massacre in which 24 Iraqi civilians were murdered. "We offer youth-led workshops on military myths, counter-recruitment and the cost of war. We also work collaboratively with other organizations on a city-wide level to fight recruitment in schools and on the streets," said Sarah Landes, education coordinator of Make the Road. But they had a problem: if they stopped allowing military recruiters in their schools, vital funding would be cut. "Schools with high poverty populations get Title III federal funding, which we cannot do without, nor do we have the choice to not accept it," said Mark Rush, BSSJ Assistant Principal. But they could distribute forms to students to prevent the school from being forced to turn over students' contact information to recruiters, as mandated by No Child Left Behind. It was an amazingly successful fight back. "I believe in our five years only two students have signed up," said Rush.

That success was ruefully noted by the military brass, who, not understanding why their drive was not working, turned on the young themselves. A 2007 navy presentation put the blame for the decline in enlistment on the reluctance of so-called "millennials" to sign on the dotted line. After detailing the falling numbers of recruits, it went on to decode youth lingo for the benefit of the audience—like "OMG," for "oh my god"—before asserting that "this is not just about a generation gap, this is an alien life force." The youth of America had apparently become "narcissistic praise monkeys" who "can get disgruntled if not praised for simply 'showing up' at work."[91] "The military is no longer on kids' radar," it laments, with many preferring college. Recruiters, therefore, had to try harder to exploit that educational dream. The report refers to an unnamed teenager who had said, "(If I join the Navy) I'd miss out on having the excuse of being a college kid and being irresponsible." But, in truth, it was the Iraq war that had turned the "millennials" anti-military, with 32 percent claiming it had made them "less patriotic," and 67 percent contending they are "less likely to join the military." It was a testament to the independence of the nation's youth in the face of relentless pressure and propaganda from authority figures. With this "over-praised" generation resisting being manipulated into service in the War on Terror in the numbers needed, the military turned to a more pliant, war-weary generation: their grandparents.

GRANDPA GOES TO WAR

Virtually every one of them is called Mom, Dad, Grandma, Grandpa, but they bring a special flair to every soldier in that group.
Colonel Kevin A. Shwedo, Army Accessions Command, 2006[92]

Charles P. Gaffney, Jr. had already been a soldier. In the mid-1980s, after quitting his job as an automobile specialist, he spent six years in the army, most of it in Germany, doing what he believed was his patriotic duty as an American citizen. When he discharged himself years later, he was looking for a fresh start. He moved to Las Vegas to pursue a post-military life, getting a job with a local Porsche dealership. At the time, serving in the armed forces again didn't occur to him—America had no direct threats and he had served his time with honor. But that would change on September 11, 2001. Like thousands of others, watching the destruction wreaked on the country he loved sent the lust to serve running through his veins again. In the years immediately following, however, he didn't reenlist: he now had twin baby daughters to take care of, and in any case his age prohibited him from joining up. He couldn't even contemplate the decision. Until January 2006, that is, when the situation changed. As the military scrambled for troops, the army raised its maximum age for recruitment into the service from thirty-five to forty. Gaffney was forty years old, just within the new limits. It seemed the perfect opportunity for the M-4 assault-rifle expert to get back to fighting for his country, so in August 2006 he entered the Arizona Army National Guard, a position that in less extraordinary times might not have meant combat. But this was the War on Terror, and Gaffney soon became one of the hundreds of thousands of reserve soldiers shipped off for a tour in Iraq, which finished at the end of 2007. "I won't say I was upset he was going back, but I didn't want him to," his dad said later. Gaffney still had the same passion for the cause he had back in the eighties. "He told me it was for people's rights around the world, for them to say what they want to say without other people beating them down," his dad added.[93]

In keeping with the extended deployments of these years, Gaffney was redeployed in 2008 with the 101st Airborne Division, this time to Afghanistan. It would be his last trip. He never saw his baby girls again. On Christmas Eve of that year, just a few months after he arrived in the country, he was slain at his combat outpost in Paktika province in eastern Afghanistan after it came under sustained enemy rocket fire. He was forty-two years old, another American warrior who couldn't put down his gun. He had believed the rhetoric of the War on Terror and sacrificed himself to bring democracy and freedom to foreign peoples and to protect his daughters. His memorial service at East Lawn was a poignant occasion, attended by more than 200 people who wanted to pay their respects and honor the fallen soldier who had received both the Bronze Star and the Purple Heart. The service finished with a three-volley rifle salute and one report noted "some attending the service sobbed quietly."[94] "We want to ensure that the sacrifice this soldier made will never be forgotten," said Lieutenant Colonel Thomas Kunk, rear detachment commander of the 101st Airborne. "This soldier had other choices, but chose the Army, because he believed his service to our country was important."[95]

Gaffney was a hero to many, but countless others would follow the same path. When the age increase to forty didn't work, six months later it was pushed up further to forty-two. In the six months following the first regulation change, the army recruited 300 soldiers over thirty-five years old, but only five of those were aged forty or older, one of which was Gaffney.[96] Over the whole year, the army enlisted 653 soldiers aged thirty-five or older—without them it would have missed its target of 80,000 recruits for that year.[97] The military paid lip service to the *benefits* of having older recruits but omitted to mention that it was chronic troop shortages that brought about the regulation change rather than some sort of eureka moment. "A few years ago, we had a marathon runner with a master's degree who spoke Russian, and he wanted to join the Army," said a Pentagon spokesman. "We said no because he was 40. Where is the sense in that?"[98] The army was now, apparently, on the lookout for recruits with more refined qualities (contradicted somewhat by their penchant for criminals and extremists). "What we're gaining in terms of experience and maturity and desire is phenomenal," assured Colonel Kevin A. Shwedo, a director at Army Accessions Command, which oversees recruiting. "Virtually every one of them is called Mom, Dad, Grandma, Grandpa, but they bring a special flair to every soldier in that group."[99] He wasn't joking, either. In 2001, the military had established another enfranchisement program in which retired military personnel could be pulled out of their summer homes on Cape Cod and sent back into active-duty in support of "contingency operations." The so-called Retiree Recall initiative was, specifically, to "close gaps in hard-to-fill specialities."[100] But by 2009 nearly 3,000 veterans had passed through the program, while nearly 750 served in the Middle East—more than 1,000 were in the service in the same year.[101]

While a gray-haired Clint Eastwood may be capable of looking poised on screen, gun in hand, it was unclear if that could be duplicated in the real world. The military was intent on finding out. Grandpa now had a chance to stop telling his Gulf War I stories to the grandkids and join Gulf War II. Even a Vietnam veteran—Steven Hutchison, who retired from the army in 1988 as a member of the 101st Airborne division and was decorated with a Bronze Star and a Meritorious Service Medal—was among the first retiree recalls. In a familiar story, the events of 9/11 had pushed this soldier, who had experienced the Tet Offensive in 1968, to serve again. At the time, his wife dissuaded him, arguing that he had done enough to serve his country already. But she died of breast cancer in 2006, after being helped through her illness by her doting husband. In the heat of the trauma, Hutchinson had nothing left to stop him and signed up again at the age of fifty-nine. The military sent him on a tour of Afghanistan, initially in a non-combat role. When he came back to the US he arrived at Fort Riley to meet his new unit and some were shocked at his age. "I thought 40-something, maybe 50," said Staff Sergeant Rivas Nestor, who was seven years old when Hutchison retired from the military. Nevertheless, his unit was sent to Iraq as part of the First Infantry Division. Less than a month shy of his sixty-first birthday Major Hutchison was killed by a roadside bomb that exploded next to his vehicle near Umm Qasr. He was the oldest American soldier to die in Iraq.

Despite their apparent enthusiasm for bringing in the oldies, the army did stop the practice briefly after reaching the numbers it wanted through the "Grow the Army" program, which cost \$15.1 billion in 2009, more than double the previous year.[102] But in September 2009 a message went out from Vice Chief of Staff, General Peter Chiarelli, *reinstating* the program "due to the recent approval of a temporary increase in active component end strength."[103] President Obama was now seeking to increase army strength by 22,000 over three years. The change allowed retirees on duty to apply for a one-year extension at the end of their current tour, and it opened the program to new applicants. "Retirees up to 70 years old can apply for a one-year tour, with the chance of renewal, through the program," the military promised. It was, however, understandable why the army had stopped the programs when recruiting figures were better. The older recruits were leaving the army at *nearly double the rate* of their younger peers: among the recruits signed up when the age restriction was raised, 11.4 percent from the thirty-five-and-up category left the army before serving a full year, a marked increase from the 6.5 percent among the rest of the recruits.[104] Older soldiers also found it harder to handle the rigors of combat. The army claimed publicly that it did not segregate older recruits in basic training or consider age when deploying them to different areas, but training exercises were undoubtedly a problem. "The type of training they receive is pretty much geared in one direction and focused on 18 and 20 year olds just coming in," Sergeant First Class Chris Patterson said. "When the older Soldier comes in, we don't know the kind of person we are getting. They bring to bear some experiences we haven't had. And we also have to take their physical strengths and abilities into consideration." This created problems for operational performance. The military knew it would have to change certain procedures to deal with this batch of older recruits: immediately they moved to lower the physical benchmark for them. On recruitment, a seventeen-year-old, for example, would be expected to do forty-seven sit-ups and thirty-five push-ups. For a forty-one-year-old this was a little easier with just twenty-nine sit-ups and twenty-four push-ups needed to prove themselves Army Good.

Unfortunately, bullets and IEDs don't discriminate in the same way. "Our training program has to ensure that every soldier is going to be able to outmaneuver, outfight, and win on today's battlefield," claimed Colonel Shwedo. But the truth was that older recruits like Gaffney and Hutchinson were at much greater risk of death and injury. In June 2010 it was reported that 566, or 12.1 percent, of the deaths in the War on Terror had been suffered by over-thirty-fives, a figure which dwarfed their representation in the fighting force.[105] The problem of PTSD was also more chronic in older soldiers: the older brain is not able to follow the rules of engagement as easily and is more questioning, which makes it more susceptible to traumas. It wasn't just battlefield problems either. The older recruits were at much greater risk of dying from the host of ailments associated with mature years. "Military service is a young person's profession. The physical in the first six months of service can be particularly stressful for older people," said David Segal, director of the Center for Research on Military Organization.[106] But the military refused to kick people out who couldn't hack it. One older soldier to pay the ultimate price was Staff Sergeant William Chaney, another veteran of the Vietnam War. He died of a blood clot aged fifty-nine, after surgery for a medical condition and appendix problem that had necessitated his evacuation from Iraq. He had signed up thinking that Iraq would help him get over the bitterness he still felt over Vietnam and the military's failure to take care of him. "When he came back [from Vietnam], he had trouble joining the [Veterans of Foreign Wars] because they said he hadn't fought in a real war," his wife Carol Chaney said. "He wanted to be an air traffic controller, what he was trained to do in Vietnam, but he was told that training was not transferable back at home. That left him a little bitter."[107] The military rubbed salt in the wounds when he died by not even informing his wife of what had happened. She discovered his passing when she called to check on him in hospital. "It is the most horrendous experience," she said. "I hope no other family has to go through this."

A Family Affair

From 2000 to 2006, the number of new soldiers over thirty soared by 92 percent nationally.[108] It turned the American military experience into a family affair, as parents joined up with their kids and were shipped off to the Middle East *together*. Margie Black, a forty-one-year-old grandmother from West Columbia, Texas, signed up with her twenty-one-year-old daughter. Russell Dilling, forty-two, of San Antonio, graduated with his nineteen-year-old son, Robert. Dilling said he had arrived at Fort Jackson at 11 p.m.—one hour before his forty-second birthday—the army's cut-off. "It's been tough physically, but my company has been pretty supportive," he said.[109] Older recruits joined up for a variety of reasons, from desperation to patriotism to boredom. "I was comfortable in civilian life and did that 9-to-5 thing all the time for a long time. I was just in a rut," said thirty-nine-year-old Private First Class Randy Covington. "When they changed the age, it seemed like the opportunity came back for me."[110] "When I'd see a soldier walk down the street when I was a small child, they'd look so disciplined, so sure," said Private Aletha North-Williams, a forty-one-year-old mother of two from Houston. "I wanted that for myself, and it has always stuck in my soul."[111] Politicians, however, rationalized the program by pointing to the changing demographics of the nation. "In part, this decision is an indication of how difficult the recruiting environment is right now," admitted Representative Vic Snyder (D-AR), the ranking member on the Subcommittee on Military Personnel of the House Armed Services Committee. "But [it] is also part of a changing society, a healthier and longer-living society, and Army standards ought to reflect that." He *had* a point. A federal report in 2008 found life expectancy for Americans continued to increase and older Americans were in better health than previous generations. As the baby-boom generation entered middle and old age it *was* changing American demographics. In 2006, an estimated 37 million people in the US—12 percent of the population—were sixty-five and older, and this was forecast to reach 20 percent by 2030.[112] "We're finding there's a lot of people out there that wanted to join, and age was their only disqualifier," said Leslie Ann Sully, a spokeswoman for the army's local recruiting battalion near Fort Jackson.[113]

There was a lot of talk about baby-boomers being a burden on the health-care and pension systems during the War on Terror, but many were now fighting America's wars and when the financial crisis hit in 2008 it created a new army of unemployed oldies. Not surprisingly all branches of the military met recruitment targets in 2008 and Pentagon officials publicly attributed the military's new popularity to the layoffs that hit America's biggest companies, pushing the national unemployment rate above 7 percent soon after. In the aftermath of the crisis, many older people lost their jobs, livelihoods, and self-respect in the middle of their lives—stuck supporting a family on unemployment insurance (if they were lucky). The newly open military became an obvious place to go. Basic military pay for the first four months of active duty was just over $15,500 a year, but more when benefits were included.[114] This was quite an attractive pay deal for those slung on the unemployment heap. "It's a guaranteed job, as long as you go to work every day," boasted Captain Jared Auchey, company commander of the Army Experience Center in Philadelphia, who estimated that one in ten of the enlistments are over thirty-five. "There are no layoffs in the Army," he added, not mentioning there are other ways to be "laid off" on the battlefield.[115] Staff Sergeant Arron Barnes spouted the familiar military line that older recruits tended to bring technical skills and maturity. Then he revealed the real reason for their desire to join: desperation. "They contribute at a higher level because they have no other place to go," he said. "This is their life." A new generation of desperate people whose lives had been torn apart by a financial crisis that was not their fault was now turning to the one place that promised redemption. Profiled by the *New York Times*, Specialist John D. Butts, thirty-eight, was emblematic of the recession-recruit:

> An aspiring writer who was a house painter outside Philadelphia for two decades, he lost his steady paycheck last November after the housing market crashed. A part-time job at Blockbuster did not pay his rent, and when his landlord threatened to evict him, his girlfriend (now his wife) and her three teenage children, he decided radical action was required. He called an Army recruiter he had met recently and signed up for a three-year stint. Despite years as a dedicated beer drinker and smoker, Specialist Butts made it through basic here at Fort Sill and is now training with an artillery unit that may head to South Korea this year. A tour in Afghanistan could be in the cards, he says.

It was the same place Private Gaffney had been sent to die.

CHAPTER FOUR

Outsiders

GREEN CARD SOLDIERS

The only for sure way of gaining citizenship through military service in the United States armed services is to die.

Marco Amador, filmmaker, 2010[1]

In late March 2003, the month the invasion of Iraq got underway, America received news of its first battlefield casualties. It was a stark wake-up call for the country and brought home the tragic human costs of war. "The violence of the war against Iraq made its way to small towns . . . when residents learned that one of the first military victims was someone they knew," wrote the *Atlanta Journal-Constitution* at the time.[2] The soldiers fell while carrying out one of the early objectives of the invasion plan—to secure the port city Umm Qasr in the south of Iraq. In older times a sleepy fishing village, it had been turned into a military port after the Iraqi Revolution of 1958 because of its strategic proximity to Iran and Kuwait. US Marines advanced from Kuwait as the invasion got underway, taking the port surprisingly quickly. But they then had to spend days securing it against what a British commander called "heavy resistance." "We were told Umm Qasr wasn't too bad, then we get reports of dug-in Iraqi infantry, it was hair-raising," said one platoon sergeant, Marc Montez.[3] One of the soldiers in his platoon who was trying to hold back Iraqi resistance was Lance Corporal José Antonio Gutierrez, First Marine Division, who had arrived in Kuwait just two months before aboard the USS *Rushmore*. In a major firefight on March 21, he became America's first combat casualty in the war, shot fatally in the chest by a fellow soldier, in a so-called "friendly fire" incident.

Except Lance Corporal Gutierrez wasn't an American casualty at all—the twenty-four-year-old was, in fact, Guatemalan, an orphan who had travelled 2,000 miles and crossed two borders illegally for his crack at the American dream. In death, there was no one in small-town America to mourn him, and his dream of becoming a US citizen was realized only posthumously. He had given his life for a country that was not even his own, a sacrifice made even more poignant considering the tragic history of US military involvement in his native country—which had destroyed his own family. Gutierrez was born in the small Guatemalan village of Escuintla at the height of the country's brutal civil war, which had raged from 1960 to the middle of the 1990s, and for which the US government and military establishment were in large part responsible. Before 1944, the Guatemalan elite composed 2 percent of the population but had control of more than 60 percent of the land, according to historian Walter LaFeber.[4] "The poorest 50 percent of the population owned only 3 percent of the land but depended on [it] for their food," while half the population were indigenous and earned less than $100 a year while being subjected to brutal and harsh discrimination by the ruling elite.[5] The country's corrupt dictatorship was overthrown in 1944 by a student-led middle-class revolt and in 1951 the progressive social democrat Jacobo Arbenz Guzman came to power in democratic elections. He planned and enacted a huge redistribution program that gave land back to the previously disenfranchised poor and Indian population. In doing so, he particularly upset the United Fruit Company, a US-based multinational company that controlled a large proportion of the region's fruit production and transport.

For the then incumbent in the White House, President Dwight Eisenhower, this was confirmation that Guatemala was close to teaming up with the Soviets. He soon ordered the CIA to train Guatemalan exiles to get rid of Arbenz and Guatemalan democracy. Though not at this stage actually affiliated to the USSR, "the frightened Guatemalan government gratefully accepted a shipload of armaments from the Soviet bloc." Eisenhower needed no other pretext and ordered the CIA-backed exiles from their bases in Honduras and Nicaragua to start attacking Guatemala. This was supported by American-operated planes that dropped dynamite onto Guatemala City, its capital. Arbenz had no choice but to flee and the exiled leader, General Carlos Castillo Armas, took control. The remnants of the reform movement were put before a firing squad and the pre-revolution order was reinstated, clearing the way for decades of brutality and oppression. Philip C. Roettinger, a US Marine colonel who was instrumental in liquidating Guatamalan democracy, wrote in 1986 that his actions "turned out to be a terrible mistake . . . Our 'success' led to 31 years of repressive military rule and the deaths of more than 100,000 Guatemalans."[6] It was actually a lot more. In February 1999 the Truth and Reconciliation Commission established to investigate the atrocities during the civil war squarely blamed the genocide of the Indian population on the right-wing military dictatorship, which was supported by the US. American military advisers and the CIA had also helped design the "scorched earth" campaign in which 440 villages disappeared from map. When the killing finally abated in the 1990s, 200,000 people had been killed or disappeared. "The United States must not repeat that mistake," President Bill Clinton said simply in the aftermath.[7] A few years later, in the attack on Iraq, they *would* repeat it, and Gutierrez would pay for the "mistake" a second time.

In the late 1970s amid countless hideous massacres of the Indian population in the countryside, Gutierrez's Mayan parents had been forced to flee to Guatemala City which was being flooded with people seeking a safe haven. Their son, José, was the embodiment of this broken and abused society: when both his parents died, he was forced to live by his wits on the streets, one of 300,000 street kids that shame the country to this day. At eight or nine, and undernourished, he was saved by Casa Alianza, a UK charity that takes in street kids. He was lucky: many of his friends on the streets would die before they reached their teens. But inside he was "bleeding with loneliness and sadness," said Patrick Atkinson, the director of the orphanage. When he arrived at Casa, he was still looking for his mother who had died. No one had told him that when people die they don't come back, and as he got older his yearning for a family led him to search desperately for his sister. "He was always talking about his sister but couldn't find her, he didn't know where to look," said his mentor at Casa. Eventually, with the help of a social worker, he tracked her down; but José dreamed of a bigger family and of becoming an architect so he could build a house for himself that no one could throw him out of. These dreams couldn't, he gradually recognized, be achieved in Guatemala. At fourteen, he told his friends there was nothing left for him in the country and he wanted to leave. They tried to dissuade him from the perilous journey north to the US that so often ends in death or prison for thousands of Latinos. But early one morning, he caught the bus to the Mexican border and waited until dawn to wade through a river into Mexico before catching a freight train north, the start of a journey that would take him 2,000 miles and put him between the wheels of fourteen different trains. Along the way he worked on food plantations to stay alive. At the US–Mexico border it took three attempts to get over, but he was smart and pretended to be Mexican, avoiding deportation back to Guatemala. In the back of his mind was his beloved sister, Engracia, who had promised to follow him north if he was successful. On arrival in the US, he was soon picked up by immigration authorities who let him stay after he told them he was sixteen and applied for asylum. He was put with foster parents, themselves Latin American immigrants, but still made sure to send $20 or $30 back to his sister from small jobs he did while he went to high school and community college.[8]

After being taken in by a number of foster families, in September 2002 he enlisted. "I remember when he came in . . . I had to interview them, find out a little about them," his platoon sergeant said later. "One question on there is 'Why did you join the Marine Corps?' And I distinctly remember his [answer], because I read it a couple of times and it said that, the reason he joined the Marine Corps was to give something back to the US, to give something back to the country that took him in basically. And that struck me pretty hard, like wow you know he's not joining for any other reason than to give back to the US, to the country." José's decision actually had much more to do with the desperation brought on by the end of high school and with it the foster child program. He was on his own—again. At the same time, his grades weren't sufficient to get him a scholarship to study architecture, his lifelong dream. He was enticed by the prospect of citizenship and the benefits offered by military service. "He wanted education, to be an architect, to write a book," said his social worker. "He said, 'I feel like I'm running out of time and I want to do it all, so if I get my education paid for by the government I can do a lot of things.'" The military was offering all sorts of inducements at this point, so he enlisted as a rifleman in the First Marine Division, based at Camp Pendleton, California. He had got the family he had always yearned for (in the form of the military), but less than a year later he was dead—apparently consumed with love for the US. Well, such was the story the military wanted to put out, and the media was happy to oblige in repeating the fairytale of the "patriotic foreigner." "Fallen Marine wanted to give back to adopted country"[9] ran the headline on CNN when he died. It was a lie. As a proud Latino, José didn't even want to learn English. "He was proud of being from Guatemala and he said he never wanted to be an American," said his social worker in the US. "José wasn't being himself. He was playing a role in order to reach his goal," added his mentor. But he was useful to the military in death. "The story that was told by the US embassy, by the US military, was a classic war propaganda story," said a close friend. "Once again using and exploiting [José] for their own ends. And you read this boy came to the States illegally at 14, wants to be an American, wants to be a Marine. You know what? False. Completely untrue. Why would they lie like that when the boy's story is so powerful for who he is?" José's dreams of becoming an architect and getting an education had actually never included military service. "He hadn't planned to do it," said his foster brother in the US. "He never intended to go into the marines. That's the last thing that would have occurred to him. What he wanted was to become an architect or professional soccer player. That's what he always talked about. I once told him I wanted to join the marines. He said, 'You're crazy. Don't do that. They're nuts.' It wasn't his thing. But after he graduated from high school he couldn't see any future for himself. He did it out of sheer desperation. What else could he have done?" He wrote to his sister frequently while deployed. One letter began: "Dear sister, things are different here, everything has to be done fast and be decided right away. In Guatemala I had no discipline and much less respect but now my life is based on discipline and respect. Life is so different, friendships get lost, people don't remember each other, they live to work, time goes by, my life has changed, but for you I'll always be the boy you knew as a child and met again as an adult, the one who can laugh and cry, who has known bad times and is trying to forget them. Write to me, send me a picture, a few lines at least, love you, don't forget that, pray for me and that we'll see each other again soon, stay out of trouble. José Gutierrez."

In death his coffin was draped in the Stars and Stripes, but his friends at Casa Alianza wanted to bury him at their Ciudad Vieja cemetery, which is where all the street kids killed by the police and security services are laid to rest. The US embassy told his sister that they already had a plot sorted in a more high-end cemetery and she didn't demur. "He's laying where he doesn't belong, he wasn't part of that reality, a cemetery with mausoleums as big as houses, houses that he never knew on the streets," said his mentor. "He's lying there all alone, cut off from us." It was the final insult.

Although José's story is singular and attracted a lot of media attention because he was the first soldier to die in Iraq, the War on Terror would see many other foreign nationals perish while serving a country which was not their own. As the Pentagon scoured the domestic population for recruits, it struck home that America—the land of immigrants—could look elsewhere. Its allies continued to use foreign fighters to swell their ranks, from the British Gurkhas to the French Foreign Legion, while the private military contractors populating the frontlines were enlisting recruits from all over the world. So why not the US military? Immigrants with permanent status, or "Green Cards," had been able to sign up for the military for decades, but the number enticed to do so shot up during the wars in Afghanistan and Iraq, as the carrot of citizenship was held out in front of their noses. The rules stipulated that only immigrants legally in the US (i.e. with a residency visa) for two years were eligible to sign up. However, while in 2001 the number of immigrants who became US citizens while in the military was just 750, by 2005 that figure had jumped by 500 percent to 4,600.[10] The changing demographics of the US population added to the pressure. The foreign-born population of the US was the largest in the history of the country, up to 11.7 percent of the population in 2003, a significant increase from the 9.3 percent registered in 1995.[11] These people were often younger, and more vulnerable. "Immigrants will fuel much of the growth in America's youth population," said a report by the Center for Naval Analyses (CNA), a federally funded research and development center for the navy and the Marine Corps. About a third of the world's population was under fifteen, with the vast majority living in developing countries. "Because many will have difficulty finding work in their native countries, large numbers of young adults emigrate—either alone or with families—with many choosing the United States as their destination. Of the 16 million foreign-born people who came to the United States between 1990 and 2002, almost a quarter were under age 21." It was the perfect pool of new recruits and the CNA recommended mining the legal immigrant community more heavily. "One overlooked source of military manpower is immigrants and their families," it noted. "In fact," the organization concluded, "much of the growth in the recruitment-eligible population will come from immigration." It was the new American Dream.

In July 2002, George W. Bush issued an executive order which shortened the period that non-citizen soldiers would have to wait for citizenship from the usual three years to just one. He greased the path to military service further by waiving naturalization fees and allowing recruits to take the oath of citizenship at US embassies and consulates abroad rather than in the US itself. The incentives worked. "We've had a record surge of applications," said a spokesman for US Citizenship and Immigration Services, before lauding the ease with which immigrants could "apply for citizenship immediately, the day they are sworn in as members of the military."[12] In 2004, the US immigration agency started to conduct the first overseas military naturalization ceremonies since the Korean War. During 2005, 1,006 foreign-born soldiers became citizens outside the United States. As of May 2010, there were 16,966 non-citizens on active duty.[13] For the Bush administration, it was the perfect solution: the introduction of more immigrants would kill two birds with one stone, "as a way to address a critical need for the Pentagon, while fully absorbing some of the roughly one million immigrants that enter the United States legally each year."[14] Instead of providing a sanctuary or granting them amnesty, the Bush administration would use service in the military as a bargaining chip. It worked: there has been an extraordinary increase in the number of immigrant soldiers who have gone on to become naturalized citizens. From 9/11 to the end of 2009, 52,000 foreign-born soldiers had become full-fledged US citizens, more than one hundred of them posthumously after being killed in combat.[15] But while it served a purpose for the military, they weren't overly kind in their treatment of the immigrant soldiers. There was an important proviso that a Green Card soldier who obtains US citizenship through service in the military can have that revoked if they receive an "other than honorable" discharge before completing five years of service. With the prevalence of drug and alcohol abuses—alongside the traumas of untreated PTSD—running through the service, this proviso was invoked widely and impacted countless immigrant families. After returning from the Middle East with their family's futures in mind, some committed crimes and were put in jail, then, on release, deported. It sparked outrage among some lawmakers. Representative Bob Filner (D-CA), chairman of the House Veterans Affairs Committee, was a proponent of changing this part of the law so that immigrants who had put themselves in danger in war could avoid deportation. "You come back from Iraq or Afghanistan today, you have put yourself on the line for this country," said Filner. "An incredible number of kids come back with an injury or illness that puts them in trouble with the law. To simply have these people deported is not a good way to thank them for their service."[16] Dardar Paye was one of those who served the US proudly for many years, after coming to the country aged thirteen from the strife of Liberia. He joined the army in 1998 and went on to serve in the first Gulf War and then in Kosovo. In 2008, a decade after he signed up, he was convicted of six weapons-related offenses and went to federal prison. On being released, he faced deportation. "When I was in Kuwait, in Kosovo, I was like everyone else who was there, putting their lives on the line," said Paye, who was an armored vehicle crewman in the army. "Now I feel like they just used me for what they wanted, and now they're throwing me away." (While waiting on his appeal, Paye was tragically murdered, his body found in the boot of a car with multiple gunshot wounds.) Everything had become much harder for immigrants with the passing of the 1996 Illegal Immigrant Reform and Immigrant Responsibility Act, which added crimes such as drug possession for sale to the list of serious offenses that could lead to deportation of a legal immigrant. "Drugs, anger management, weapons charges, that's what a lot of vets are getting caught for, and there is no relief," said Margaret Stock, a recently retired army reservist and immigration attorney who taught at the United States Military Academy at West Point. "The 1996 law really put the nails in their coffin," she added.

Nightmare Act

On top of revoking citizenship once granted, the Bush administration was not short on ideas of how to send legal immigrants out to the desert in the first place. In 2007, the so-called Dream Act went before Congress, ostensibly as a way to provide immigrants with further means to citizenship, but, like all legislation in the period, including the No Child Left Behind Act, it had a military element. There was a crucial provision that would allow immigrants to achieve citizenship through either a two-year stint at a community college or military service for the same time period. With many immigrants unable to pay for the even the bare necessities, the chances of them being able to fork out for a two-year course seemed unlikely, as was the case for Gutierrez. Military service was the only other option. The Act also made extreme provisions for giving a Green Card to undocumented high-school students who agreed to serve in the military. It was eventually defeated in Congress, and then resubmitted without the community service option, before being defeated again in December 2010. The group Vamos Unidos, which represents Latino youth in the Bronx, New York, one of the main areas of recruitment activity, were particularly critical of the Dream Act's provisions. "We demand that we return to our original DREAM ACT that had a community service option instead of a military one," the group said. "The military has been losing their numbers due to the multiple wars the US has begun. The DREAM ACT would hand us over on a platter to fight these unjust wars. The DREAM ACT has been warped over the years to draft Latino youth into the military, as they need more and more soldiers to fight their wars." The group called it a *de facto* draft.[17] At the time, influential military analysts and think tanks were beginning to voice support for allowing *any* foreigners who wanted to enter the military to become Americans, in a full-scale "barbarization" of the military. ("Barbarization" is the term used to describe the later Roman military when it started allowing outsiders, or "barbarians," to fight in their army.) "Now is the time to consider a new chapter in the annals of American immigration," wrote two of the biggest enthusiasts, Max Boot and Michael O'Hanlon, in the *Washington Post*. "By inviting foreigners to join the U.S. armed forces in exchange for a promise of citizenship after a four-year tour of duty, we could continue to attract some of the world's most enterprising, selfless and talented individuals."[18] Not only that, it would go some way to treating the problem of the millions of undocumented workers already in the US (and the million that enter every year)—a kind of amnesty with the caveat of military service. Who cares if they have to risk their lives to achieve their dream? In fact, Boot and O'Hanlon wanted to go even further: "We could provide a new path towards assimilation for undocumented immigrants who are already here but lack the prerequisite for enlistment—a green card. And we could solve the No. 1 problem facing the Army and Marine Corps: the fact that these services need to grow to meet current commitments yet cannot easily do so . . . given the current recruiting environment." The *de facto* draft, in other words.

The cheerleaders for this new policy pointed to history for support (not Roman history, however). This kind of approach, they argued, had deep roots in the history of America's armed forces, which was partially true. In one of the country's most celebrated military victories—the Revolutionary War—German and French soldiers fought alongside the colonists to expel the British. In the Civil War about 20 percent of fighters were foreigners freshly arrived in the US, and English was "barely spoken" in some units. But that was 150 years ago. During the War on Terror, America was undergoing one of its most fervent anti-immigrant, jingoistic phases since the early 1980s, which didn't sit too well with granting citizenship to thousands of immigrants. In November 2005 the Bush administration had announced it was to build a "virtual fence" along the Mexico–US border as part of a multibillion dollar effort to keep illegal immigrants out, incorporating a range of high-tech devices, including radar. The militarization of the Mexican border—likely pitting Mexican immigrants willing to serve against those trying to get across—went on unabated, while five years later, Arizona passed the most regressive immigration laws since Jim Crow: obliging police to query the immigration status of people whom they suspect are in the US illegally—i.e. brown, Latino-looking people. Boot and O'Hanlon were aware of this surge of jingoism, but told the racists not to worry. Everyone one was a winner—apart from those like José Gutierrez. "Nativists need not fear that this would lead to a flood of foreigners," they wrote. "Say we decide to recruit 50,000 foreigners a year for the next three years. That sounds like a lot, but it represents less than 10 percent of the total number coming to the United States anyway—and less than 10 percent of our active-duty armed forces. This would not radically change the demographics of our society or our military, but it would make a big difference in the size of the rotation base for our ongoing missions." In other words, white people can still rule the roost *and* we get fodder for our wars of aggression. It also made sense money-wise. The CNA found that non-citizens were "far more likely" to complete their enlistment obligations successfully than their US-born comrades. "Non-citizen service members have a long track record of military success," it noted. Thirty-six month attrition rates for non-citizens are between 9 and 20 percentage points lower than those for white citizens.[19]

Illegal Immigrants, Illegal Recruiters

Quietly, after the defeat of the Dream Act, something more insidious was passed in its stead: a law which gives the Pentagon power to bring immigrants into the US if it is deemed (in that beautiful piece of bureaucratic ambiguity) "vital to national security." Although this law hasn't been applied frequently, its has the potential to be widely used. The military had already started looking beyond the legal immigrants within its borders, casting its gaze to Mexico and the millions of desperately poor young men who dreamed of making it to the US. As early as 2003, the US embassy had to release a statement reiterating official policy that "undocumented or illegal immigrants cannot serve in the U.S. armed forces," after a US military recruiter was found to have visited in a high school in Tijuana, Mexico.[20] The recruiter had apparently turned up after following a conversation with two potential recruits. "The U.S. Army does not recruit here. We don't endorse them coming here," claimed a spokesman. But the Mexican newspaper *Milenio* called the sergeant's efforts "an intense campaign to recruit young high school students." Other local newspapers contended that the recruiter handed out promotional literature to students, claims denied by the US. In 2005, activists reported ads on Facebook that offered a Green Card in exchange for military service, highlighting the fact that the US military didn't just want foreigners, it wanted young foreigners, perhaps to make up for all the retirees it was letting in. The young were also impressionable and full of romantic ideas about the American Dream. Within the US, it was a similar story—with recruiters bribing young illegal immigrants in the nation's schools. Arlene Inouye, a high school teacher in the Los Angeles unified school district, said: "It's well-known, common knowledge that military recruiters do promise or offer to our undocumented students fake Green Cards." A student at the same school, Salvador Garcia III, added: "They offered they would bring my father back from Mexico if I served a four-year tour in the United States military."[21] In 2007, civil rights activist Ildefonso Ortiz Cabrera reported that while he was in Phoenix, Arizona, army recruiters suggested he go to a military base; he refused and instead returned to El Burrion, his town in Sinaloa, north Mexico.[22] Not everyone was so strong-willed but we never heard about them—they ended up in the Middle East.

The promise of citizenship was a serious incentive. For many young Latinos this was the only shot for them and their family. In April 2008, Green Card holder Arturo Huerta-Cruz, twenty-three, of the Tenth Mountain Division, was on patrol near Tuz in northern Iraq, when he was killed by an IED. Huerta-Cruz was originally from a small rural town called Hidalgo, Mexico, but moved to Florida when he was ten. His motives for fighting were accurately outlined by the *Tampa Bay Times*, which said his death "will further opportunities for his younger cousins, including [his] baby Arturo, who is a U.S. citizen," adding, "The infant child will have opportunities never available to Huerta-Cruz. He can vote for president; he might become president. He can work for the government—as Huerta-Cruz once hoped—or he might pass along his name to the family's growing list of natural-born U.S. citizens."[23] The headline of the article was typical of the "patriotic foreigner" narrative the military and media pushed: "Mexican Citizen Died in Iraq Serving U.S., His Beloved New Land," it read. But the American Dream had started to look very different during the War on Terror: it was no longer affluent suburban life in Middle America, but indigent war life in the Middle East. Sergeant Ernesto Hernandez, twenty-six, a Mexican from Temple, Texas, saw the military as the only way out of working in dead-end job with the threat of deportation. His fear, he said, was forever "working at Wal-Mart, changing oil or working at McDonalds." Hernandez became a vehicle mechanic for the 101st Airborne, and was deployed to Kuwait soon after. "It's not a bad deal," Hernandez said. "Especially with everybody speaking English, you pick it up like that."[24] Despite all this testimony of desperation, the military claimed that the granting of citizenship was not among the main reasons for immigrant enlistment. "Money for education, wanting to serve the country, and to learn a skill are the top three motivations," said Douglas Smith, Public Affairs Officer at the US

Army Recruiting Command, contradicting everything the recruits were actually saying.[25]

On top of this the military claimed immigrants were actually better soldiers because they had a *better understanding* of American democracy and freedoms than those born in the country. It was a desperate attempt to put a positive spin on the "barbarization" of the military. "In many cases, they have a personal experience from living in an area where they didn't have that freedom and liberty," said Lieutenant Colonel Keith Pickens, chief of staff for the division rear command of the 101st Airborne. "They're a lot closer to the American founding fathers than the average American might be," he added.[26] It was the same rhetoric that accompanied the wars in Iraq and Afghanistan: foreigners can only grasp freedom when they see American bombs. Some of the soldiers might have realized that in their native countries—including Guatemala, among many others—democracy had been repressed by the US government. But the patronizing tone continued. Military leaders lauded the "cultural sensitivity" of foreigners—compared to the high levels of chauvinism among the regular troops anyway. "The American Army finds itself in a lot of different countries where cultural awareness is critical," said Lieutenant General Benjamin C. Freakley, the top recruitment officer for the army. The CNA added, "Legal permanent residents, or green card holders, are more racially, ethnically, linguistically, and culturally diverse than citizen recruits. This is valuable on many levels, particularly at a time when the military is addressing the challenges of fighting terrorism."[27] But this new love for multiculturalism and diversity had its drawbacks. In the case of José Gutierrez, it can be argued that his lack of English contributed to his death. "He was holding security on one building, as they picked up he was on other side of building," said his platoon sergeant. "He didn't hear the verbal command ... to get up and move."[28] Or he didn't understand it.

Life Is Cheap

The move to get foreigners to fight America's wars was controversial among immigrant groups, as it was essentially an extension of the already lopsided ethnic demographics of the US military during the War on Terror, in which minorities were disproportionately enlisted. It had unnerving echoes of the Vietnam War, where black soldiers were asked to fight to "defend" a democracy in which they had few rights: the new battalions of Green Card soldiers were fighting the same fight. Foreigners' lives are cheap—that is traditional imperial ideology, so it was clear quite early on that these recruits would not be stuck biting their fingernails at US bases for long. Many were sent straight into combat with no other option. The situation was made worse by a strange 2009 report from the Rand Corporation which found that Latinos were actually *underrepresented* in the US military. This increased efforts to find a way to get more of them in.[29] "For us, that's a huge problem. Mainly because in the invasion in 2003 in Iraq, 20 percent of the casualties in the invasion were Latino," said Marco Amador, a filmmaker.[30] But only 15.1 percent of the US population are Latino: if they are underrepresented in the military, how can 20 percent of those killed be Latino? The obvious answer is they are assigned more dangerous missions while on active duty. The charge that Green Card soldiers were merely cannon fodder looked uncomfortably true. For many in the immigrant communities it was the final straw as their communities had been gradually degraded by criminalization and deportations. "We have grown up with the trauma of having our family members and friends detained, jailed, and deported. But we are strong and determined, so we keep onwards," said one Latino rights group.[31] The reaction was similar to that of the parents who were fighting the militarization of childhood and education—the militarization of immigration was being equally resisted. A strange ideological alliance was spawned in opposition as immigrants' rights groups concerned with the blackmail received support from the anti-immigrant right-wing wary of a "flood" of immigration. It's "another example of the exploitation of cheap labor," said Jorge Mariscal, Vietnam veteran and professor of Latino studies at the University of California, San Diego.[32] It was another way to replicate the injustices of wider American society in its fighting force. "This is what the US military has always done. This is nothing new. They use the Latino community or the poor working class community in this country as their cannon fodder," added Amador.[33] Then there were the right-wing arguments. "We should go to any length to avoid developing a kind of mercenary army, made up of foreigners loyal to their units and commanders but not to the republic," Mark Krikorian, executive director of the Center for Immigration Studies, which aims to bring down immigration, wrote in the conservative *National Review*. "It didn't work out well for the Romans."[34] He felt the profession would be sullied by the involvement of too many foreigners, putting American citizens off serving, similar way to the way Americans don't want to work fruit-picking. "If enlisting were a way to get legalized or a way to get into the United States," he continued later, "soldiering would become a job Americans would not do very rapidly."[35] There were frequent charges that Green Card soldiers were merely mercenaries, whose loyalty to the US military and the country more generally made them a risk. Recruiting a large number of non-citizens could change the main purpose of the military from that of defending the country to being "a way to get a foot in the door of the United States," the argument went. Those same critics didn't seem to mind the multiple private security firms who were populating the occupations of Afghanistan and Iraq (and other parts of the world); firms whose soldiers were *literally* mercenaries being paid private salaries without any government oversight, free from the legal constraints on normal US soldiers.

In fairness to the critics, it *was* true that the entrance of foreigners from far-flung countries—from Pakistan to Malaysia—into the US military posed serious concerns about the security of the troops—a priority extremely low down on the Pentagon's list when compared with bolstering the number of soldiers. With the evident US military insouciance towards extremism—including Islamic fundamentalism—it was the perfect opportunity for terrorist elements or foreign intelligence agents to penetrate the force. Egyptian double agent Ali A. Mohamed, who had served in the army as a supply sergeant at Fort Bragg in North Carolina in the late 1980s, did exactly that, providing Osama Bin Laden and his Al-Qaeda network with high-level information for terrorist attacks against US targets. The military had been extremely slow to come alive to his threat and it would end tragically. "Mr. Mohamed's story . . . is one of appalling oversights by American national security, including the C.I.A., the F.B.I. and the Army," said the *New York Times*.[36] His role in the September 11 attacks is unclear, but he has been charged with helping to plan the 1998 car bombing of the US Embassy in Kenya, which killed 224 people and injured 4,500. It appeared the army hadn't learned its lesson. During the War on Terror, a new program was designed that specifically targeted immigrants skilled in medicine and languages: the first time since Vietnam that those on temporary visas would be allowed to serve. Recruits would receive US citizenship within just six months of service. The fact that the military was desperate for Arabic speakers added to the perceived risks. Of course, the Bush administration didn't care. In fact, they were getting so desperate that it wasn't just their natural right-wing aversion to immigrants that was being compromised. Even homosexuals, who had for decades been the target of discrimination by the Republicans, were enjoying a quiet renaissance. There was, however, one American patriot, fluent in Arabic himself, who would be among the last hauled from the military for the "crime" of being gay.

ASK, TELL

People will look at Afghanistan and Iraq as the moment when lesbian and gay service members proved themselves to be part of the US military.

Victor Maldonado, Servicemembers Legal Defense Network, 2008

Bleu Copas had always been a patriotic American but on September 11, 2001, that changed. As the carnage unfolded on his television screen that morning he moved from being simply a patriot—he now wanted to be a warrior. "I decided right then that as I had the ability and desire I would go ahead and serve my country, that I would act on my patriotic flair," says Copas, a twenty-four-year-old from Johnson City, Tennessee. At the time, he was studying for his masters in counseling at East Tennessee State

University, but he decided to put his studies on hold. "I felt like my country needed me then, and it couldn't wait," he tells me. Copas was young, educated, well built, and passionate about serving his country. He was the perfect candidate. There was only one problem: he was gay. "I was prepared to lie and keep it secret," he says. At the time the military operated a "Don't Ask, Don't Tell" (DADT) policy which dated back to 1993. It stipulated that homosexuals in the military must keep their orientation secret and if they bucked this rule or were "outed" by colleagues they would be discharged. It all went according to plan for Copas. He was put on active-duty service and, via the Defense Language Institute in California, he arrived at Fort Bragg, North Carolina, in 2004 and became part of the Eighty-Second Airborne division. He didn't even have to be overly private. "Throughout this whole time in the military, my colleagues realized my orientation but it was never a problem," he says. Until 2005, that is. Then an anonymous email campaign targeting Copas started up, circulating correspondence in which Copas had divulged his sexuality. Even then he was shown sympathy by his superiors. "My command tried to sweep it under the rug, they tried to get rid of it because they wanted to keep me, I had been promoted very quickly when they realized my skills," he says. But the emails continued unabated and spread to his colleagues. Eventually the command gave Copas an honorable discharge with health benefits. "They had no choice, they had to discharge me then," he said. But Copas realizes he was just very unlucky after his easy start. "I think, ironically, everything now is falling into place regarding discrimination against homosexuals," he said in 2008. "I was just the victim of a very aggressive campaign, I would have been fine otherwise," he added. He was also lucky to get an honorable discharge, which meant holding on to the benefits he was entitled to—a luxury not everyone enjoyed.

Figures obtained through the Freedom of Information Act support Copas's claims about the military turning a blind eye. The DADT policy had resulted in hundreds of discharges every year since it was enacted, but in the period of the wars in Afghanistan and Iraq, the numbers of discharges fell precipitously. In 2001 there were 640 discharges for homosexuality; in 2006 it was 282—a 56 percent reduction.[37] Homosexuals were serving almost without hindrance. "I think that people will look at Afghanistan and Iraq as the moment when lesbian and gay service members proved themselves to be part of the US military," said Victor Maldonado of the Servicemembers Legal Defense Network (SLDN), an organization which campaigns against military discrimination against homosexuals. "The conflict will be the Rubicon for gays and lesbians in service and there will be no going back. More and more service members are serving openly and having no repercussions, they simply are gay, and it evidently does not affect their relationship with their colleagues or command." The situation was so open that, Copas added, "At one point in the barracks in Monterrey [California] I was staying on a floor with eight rooms, and gay people were in half of them. In fact they were everywhere, especially at the language institute. And there are several that I know serving openly in the desert right now."

Before the DADT legislation, the extent of regulation on homosexuals was a 1982 DOD directive which stated that "homosexuality was incompatible with military service,"[38]— around the same time it was decided that being a Nazi was not compatible with military service. When he first came to power in 1992, President Clinton announced an executive order designed to completely overturn the discriminatory policy. In response, the Republican-controlled Congress put forward legislation that would have enshrined the existing directive in federal law, making it impossible for any president to overturn. The 1993 DADT policy was the resulting fudge. Clinton can't be blamed for the intransigence of his Republican opposition, and the compromise was a huge improvement on what went before; but it was still one more twist in the long history of formalized discrimination against homosexuals in the armed forces. In the Korean and Vietnam wars homosexuality had been labeled a "mental defect," and the military barred recruits based on medical examinations, much like modern-day Turkey does. But troop needs ebbed and flowed: during wartime the military quietly ignored its strict regulations on gays, only to revive them again in peacetime. This is why the gay civil rights movement was so intent on achieving its goal (repeal of DADT) during a period when the War on Terror—with its *de facto* repeal of the law—had shown gays could serve openly at no detriment to the military.

Arguments Against

The case against homosexuals serving openly is primarily a moral one derived from religious dogma, a dominant feature of the Bush administration. The strength of deep-seated moral opposition even within the military brass was strong throughout the war years. In 2007 one of its top commanders came out in favor of DADT and likened homosexuality to adultery. "I believe homosexual acts between two individuals are immoral and that we should not condone immoral acts," said Marine General Peter Pace, Chairman of the Joint Chiefs of Staff. "I do not believe the United States is well served by a policy that says it is OK to be immoral in any way."[39] Although that was the real reason for opposition to the repeal, the critics invented logistical problems in an attempt to give their opinions legitimacy. Some said, for example, that enlisting openly gay service members would be detrimental to morale and cause problems with shared bedding in the barracks and bases. It was implied that gay soldiers would be unable to handle the living conditions, with military guidelines noting that the armed forces are a "specialized society" where the same laws for civilian society don't apply—military service, of course, is "characterized by forced intimacy with little or no privacy."[40] Critics of the repeal also pointed to attrition rates. In a 2009 article for the *Washington Post* a group of retired military officers wrote that the "repeal of this law would prompt many dedicated people to leave the military," citing a *Military Times* poll that indicated 58 percent were opposed to the repeal and that 10 percent wouldn't reenlist if it went through.[41] They didn't mention that the new Irregular Army meant many homosexual soldiers were serving openly anyway—estimates put it at 65,000. But with a tenuous bit of extrapolation they arrived at a figure of 228,600 for the potential loss of military personnel. "We don't need a study commission to know that tensions are inevitable in conditions offering little or no privacy, increasing the stress of daily military life," they concluded.

But what they should have been more worried about was the attrition rate of *gay* service members themselves, who comprised a significant portion of the fighting force. Many of them could not understand why they had to hide their identity and personal life while risking their lives for their country. Jennifer Hogg, a New York National Guard Member, said, "Being a lesbian on 9/11 is what initially led me to begin to question my involvement in the military and the military's involvement in the world," before adding, "If on 9/11, I did not have the freedom to hug my girlfriend goodbye before we left as a unit for NYC, then what freedom was I protecting? What freedom could we offer to the world if we treat it so restrictively based on who a person falls in love with?"[42] During the War on Terror this struggle for freedom took the same form as the civil rights struggle in the 1960s, when young black men were being sent to fight for a democracy they couldn't vote in. Patriotic homosexuals had served in all of America's wars anyway, bypassing the persistent efforts to disenfranchise them. Some of America's most revered fighters, like Baron von Steudben, were reportedly gay. He had been a Prussian military officer who served as inspector general during the American Revolutionary War, passing on his expertise to guide the Americans to victory. Navy doctor Tom Dooley was another: his humanitarian mission in Southeast Asia made him a legend in his lifetime.

The available evidence also contradicted the arguments of the critics of the repeal of DADT. A 2010 poll of veterans of Iraq and Afghanistan by the Vet Voice Foundation found that 41 percent of service members under the age of 35 favored gay and lesbian soldiers being able to serve openly, to 35 percent against.[43] Over-thirty-fives came in 36 percent against, to 31 percent in favor. A Zogby poll in 2007 found 73 percent of troops who had served in Iraq or Afghanistan were comfortable in the presence of gays. They had also proved themselves particularly loyal and fastidious in duty. Lesbians serve proportionally more than the rest of the female population. Between 1990 to 2000 lesbians aged eighteen to twenty-seven had three times higher rates of service than their straight peers. And they served longer, too:

82 percent report serving for two or more years, compared to 74 percent for the wider population.⁴⁴ Attitudes were changing in the general population as well, as the *de facto* repeal of DADT proved it could work. In early 2010 a poll by CNN and the Opinion Research Council found that 69 percent of the public were in favor of allowing homosexuals to serve openly, with just 27 percent against.⁴⁵ That was a big step forward. In 1994, the year after DADT was instituted, the figure had stood at 53 percent in favor. Around the world, the experience of the US's closest allies was adding further pressure. In 2000, the UK lifted its ban on gay soldiers after a ruling from the European Court of Human Rights called it a "grave interference" into people's private life.⁴⁶ Israel was even further ahead of the curve, ending its restriction in 1993, the same year as DADT was instituted. Research has shown that serving openly had no detrimental effect on the morale or effectiveness of the Israel Defense Forces. "It's a non-issue," said David Saranga, a former IDF officer. "There is not a problem with your sexual tendency. You can be a very good officer, a creative one, a brave one, and be gay at the same time." There had been many attempts to overturn the policy within Congress, most effectively from Representative Patrick Murphy, who was the first Iraq war veteran elected to Congress. His experience there with British forces convinced him that open serving would only improve the service. He sponsored a bill for the repeal. "I take it as a personal affront to our warriors," he said. "To say that other countries' soldiers are professional enough to handle this and American soldiers aren't is really a slap in the face."⁴⁷

Faced with this mass of evidence, attitudes in the military establishment were slowly thawing, with probably its biggest name, former Joint Chiefs of Staff chairman Colin Powell, who had originally supported DADT, coming out in support of its repeal in 2009. "The policy and the law that came about in 1993, I think, was correct for the time," he said. But, he added, "Sixteen years have now gone by, and I think a lot has changed with respect to attitudes within our country, and therefore I think this is a policy and a law that should be reviewed."⁴⁸ John M. Shalikashvili, chairman of the Joint Chiefs of Staff from 1993 to 1997, and formerly a staunch supporter of DADT, wrote an op-ed in the *New York Times* in which he described a similar Damascene conversion. "I now believe that if gay men and lesbians served openly in the United States, they would not undermine the military efficacy of the armed forces," he concluded. But unlike Powell he subtly revealed the real reason for his change of heart. "Our military has been stretched thin by our deployments in the Middle East," he wrote, adding "we must welcome the service of any American who is willing and able to do the job."[49] It was, in other words, a numbers game. Gays would get their rights: but only because it was too costly to keep them out. Although happy with the sea change, the gay community was not fooled as to the reasons for their newfound acceptance. "Now that the Army needs recruits for a violent, unpopular war, we are more welcome," wrote Andrew Hiller in a bitter letter to the *New York Times* in response to Shalikashvili's article.[50] "It is more apparent than ever before that, as we conduct a global war on terror and face tremendous personnel shortages, that the 'don't ask, don't tell' law is undermining our military readiness," chimed Democrat Representative Martin Meehan (D-MA), who introduced a bill to repeal DADT.[51] In the Bush administration's order of priorities, a commitment to bigotry seems to have ranked pretty high, but meeting army recruitment targets was even more important. Money was also a factor. It was calculated in a 2005 GAO report that the DADT policy had cost the military 9,488 service members since 1993 with 322 of them highly skilled linguists the military could ill afford to lose (like Bleu Copas).[52] In fact, 757 of them were deemed "critical." The cost of training a soldier is between $90,000 and $150,000. For this reason, the SLDN didn't take any particular joy in the figures from the War on Terror. "We don't necessarily recognize it as a success," said Maldonado. "During a time of war, when the military needs men and women to fight in Afghanistan and Iraq, lesbians and gays deserve basic rights because they are among the frontline defending our country. But during times of peace when threats are not proximate dismissals under DADT increase."

But what should have been more concerning for Powell and Shalikashvili than all this was that the DADT policy had created a climate of rampant homophobia in the US military during the War on Terror. The Pentagon's own inspector general released a report in

2009 which showed the horrendous treatment being meted out to gay service members and the climate of fear in which many lived. It found that "offensive comments about homosexuals were commonplace and the majority believed these offensive comments were tolerated to some extent within the military."[53] The secrecy necessitated by the DADT policy meant many were targeted by McCarthyite-style witch-hunts. A full 40 percent of soldiers "felt they had witnessed, or been a target of, harassment for perceived homosexuality." Eighty percent said they had heard offensive speech, derogatory names, jokes, or remarks about homosexuals in the last twelve months. Even more—85 percent—thought this abuse was tolerated by the military brass. "This behavior is not acceptable and will not be tolerated in the military," said a Pentagon spokesman. "We need to do more work on this policy," he added, but didn't blame DADT explicitly. SLDN did. A report it authored documented 968 cases of anti-gay harassment—including murder and assault—in the period from February 1999 to February 2000, an increase of 142 percent on the previous year. As the military was opened up to extremists and gangs, this hit an all-time-high level. The alleged Wikileaks source, Bradley Manning, was one gay soldier who reported being a victim of the rampant abuse during the War on Terror—bullying that may have been a factor in his alleged whistle-blowing. "It took them a while, but they started figuring me out, making fun of me, mocking me, harassing me, heating up with one or two physical attacks," Manning wrote to his friend on a chat website. He continued, "The army took me, a web dev, threw me into a rigid schedule, removed me from my digital self. The army . . . threw me in the forests of Missouri for 10 weeks with an old M-16, Reagan-era load-bearing equipment and 50 twanging people hailing from places like Texas, Alabama, Georgia, and Mississippi . . . joy. What the hell did I put myself through?" It was a good question. Independent journalist Dahr Jamail, who did much important work on the subject, believed that homophobia had in fact become the worst kind of discrimination in the military during the War on Terror. "Homophobia arguably manifests itself in the worst form of discrimination in the military, surpassing even racism," he wrote.

Instead of enabling recruits to vanquish their prejudices and strengthening the individual and the collective spirit, all military training
seems to be geared towards invoking the darkest elements in human
nature—fear, hatred, pettiness, insecurity and similar aberrations.
Under normal conditions, such an orientation legitimizes unacceptable behavior; under harsh and hostile conditions, it makes beasts of
men. It is immaterial whether one is at the perpetrating end or the
receiving end of unjust behavior. Of greater significance is the general
air of violence and inequality that gets normalized in the process.[54]

It wasn't just homosexuals, either. The kind of Christian fundamentalism expressed by General Pace's comments about homosexuality's "immorality" was prevalent across the military brass, and meant
other groups were marginalized as well. Religiosity was increasingly
prevalent in the military as it provided a glue to keep together all the
disparate groups the loosening of regulations had allowed in, and
was abused for this purpose. In 2008, Specialist Jeremy Hall sued the
DOD for its "discrimination" against atheists because of the unconstitutional definition of the US military as a "Christian Army." He
revealed a culture of proselytizing among the commanders and
soldiers which put atheists in an invidious position. "They don't
trust you because they think you are unreliable and might break,
since you don't have God to rely on," he said.[55] "The message is, 'It's
a Christian nation, and you need to recognize that.'" The accusa-
tions in the lawsuit were shocking. "Immediately after plaintiff made
it known he would decline to join hands and pray, he was confronted,
in the presence of other military personnel, by the senior ranking . . .
staff sergeant who asked plaintiff why he did not want to pray, where-
upon plaintiff explained because he is an atheist," it read.[56] "The
staff sergeant asked plaintiff what an atheist is and plaintiff responded
it meant that he (plaintiff) did not believe in God. This response
caused the staff sergeant to tell plaintiff that he would have to sit
elsewhere for the Thanksgiving dinner. Nonetheless, plaintiff sat at
the table in silence and finished his meal."

Civil Rights Struggle

As momentum gathered pace and an increasing number of public figures showed support, the gay rights movement found a new hero in the Democratic presidential candidate Barack Obama. He took it on as one of his flagship issues and wrote an open letter to the LGBT community promising the repeal of DADT. "I'm running for President to build an America that lives up to our founding promise of equality for all—a promise that extends to our gay brothers and sisters," he wrote. "It's wrong to have millions of Americans living as second-class citizens in this nation. And I ask for your support in this election so that together we can bring about real change for all LGBT Americans."[57] But halfway through his term he still had not come through on the promise and the movement turned against him. During one of his speeches in April 2010, the president received an angry response from disgruntled activists from GetEQUAL, an LGBT rights group. "What about 'don't ask, don't tell'?" one protester shouted, to which Obama replied: "We are going to do that."[58] Former army sergeant Darren Manzella had already written an impassioned letter to the new president as part of *Stories from the Frontlines: Letters to President Barack Obama*, a new media campaign launched to highlight the need for more presidential leadership in the fight to repeal DADT. "I served two tours of duty in the Middle East in support of Operation Iraqi Freedom as a Soldier in the United States Army. I was promoted to sergeant, was a team leader of a medical squad, and conducted over 100 twelve-hour patrols in the streets of Baghdad, treating wounds and evacuating casualties of sniper fire and roadside bombs," he wrote. "But, today, instead of protecting my fellow Americans, I sit working in a university development office because I was discharged under DADT."[59] Depending on your point of view, Manzella had been either extremely foolhardy or extremely brave. In 2008, he took time out from his duties as a medical liaison specialist with his division in Kuwait to appear on CBS's flagship *60 Minutes* program. He was on his second deployment to the region after serving in a medical field artillery unit in Baghdad in 2005 and receiving a combat medal for giving treatment under enemy fire. Despite his stellar credentials, Manzella was aware that he was still an outsider in the army, not because of his dedication, patriotism, or competence, but thanks to his sexuality. In the thirteen-minute section of the program Manzella talked openly, without permission, about being gay. He told CBS that he had taken his boyfriend out with his army pals and painted a picture of a military that had come to accept gay members for who they were. Nothing happened in the aftermath. But he was eventually the target of another malicious anonymous email campaign that instructed him to tone down his "ostentatious" behavior. He decided to consult his commanding officer who told him that for the crime of telling the truth he would have to report Manzella to his superiors. "I had to go see my battalion commander, who read me my rights," he said. "What a Catch-22. You go and tell your lieutenant the truth and now you violated the army's rule." True to his trailblazing attitude, Manzella held nothing back in the investigation, providing photos of him with AJ, his boyfriend, including pictures of them kissing. But despite all this, Manzella was told to resume work in the military. "The closest thing that I was given by my superiors was, 'I don't care if you're gay or not,'" Manzella said. Even after the CBS show aired on national television Manzella was allowed to stay in the military. Nevertheless, in 2008 he was eventually discharged as the case became too embarrassing for the military to ignore. But they had wanted to ignore it—and there were thousands more Manzellas serving openly in the US military.

Things heated up in September 2010 when the DADT policy was ruled unconstitutional by a judge in California. A lawsuit had been brought by the Log Cabin Republicans which moved to order an injunction against the policy. In conclusion US District Court Judge Virginia A. Phillips wrote forcefully:

> The Don't Ask, Don't Tell Act infringes the fundamental rights of United States servicemembers in many ways ... The Act denies homosexuals serving in the Armed Forces the right to enjoy "intimate conduct" in their personal relationships. The Act denies them the right to speak about their loved ones while serving their country

in uniform; it punishes them with discharge for writing a personal letter, in a foreign language, to a person of the same sex with whom they shared an intimate relationship before entering military service; it discharges them for including information in a personal communication from which an unauthorized reader might discern their homosexuality. In order to justify the encroachment on these rights, Defendants faced the burden at trial of showing the Don't Ask, Don't Tell Act was necessary to significantly further the Government's important interests in military readiness and unit cohesion. Defendants failed to meet that burden. Thus, Plaintiff, on behalf of its members, is entitled to judgment in its favor on the first claim in its First Amended Complaint for violation of the substantive due process rights guaranteed under the Fifth Amendment.[60]

At the same time, the movement had found another brave and eloquent spokesman in the form of Lieutenant Dan Choi, from the Army National Guard, who had served bravely in Iraq and was a graduate of West Point before being discharged under DADT. Choi was particularly critical of the survey the Obama administration had set up to gauge military attitudes to homosexuality, which he saw as another betrayal on the president's part. "That the commander in chief [was] the first [from a] racial minority to achieve that rank and that position was a signifying moment for all of us, whether we're racial minorities, whether we're sexual minorities, whether we're American citizens or not even yet American citizens, it was an absolute moment of vindication for a lot of people," he said. But, he added, "Nobody ever polls the soldiers on whether we should go to war or not. Nobody ever says, 'What do you think about your commander in chief being African-American?'"[61] Choi was adamant about taking advantage of the judge's verdict and the obvious fact that the policy was becoming untenable for the military. In October 2010, he went to reenlist in the marines at Times Square in New York City, trailed by a sizeable media contingent. He took advantage of a new Pentagon statement that "recruiters have been given guidance, and they will process applications for applicants who admit they are openly gay or lesbian."[62] There was increasingly nothing the military could do in the face of this tidal wave of activism. In a stunning victory for the gay community in the US and around the world, seventeen years of struggle to get DADT repealed finally came to a head in December 2010 when Congress passed a law repealing the policy. "No longer will our country be denied the service of patriotic Americans who are forced to leave the military, no matter their bravery or zeal, because they happen to be gay," said President Obama as he signed it into law.[63] It was a bittersweet victory: a wonderful civil rights triumph, but one that would have been impossible without the military's desperate need for troops allowing homosexuals to serve honorably and basically openly for the first time. Obama admitted as much, commenting that the repeal will be introduced "in a way that only strengthens our military readiness" (read: more troops). In the end, homosexual service members got their rights, but it took risking their lives in ever-greater numbers in wars started by an administration that believed their sexuality was a moral abomination. The Bush administration's lack of principle across the board had ironically laid the ground for the one positive thing to come out of America's Irregular Army.

The Aftermath

The story didn't end there, however. President Obama rapidly moved from hero to villain after the bill was signed, coming under intense pressure from gay civil rights groups about the languid pace at which the repeal of DADT was proceeding. Months on from the repeal, gay service members were still being discharged under the policy as all branches of the military remained in the "training" phase aimed at preparing existing service members for the change in policy. For many gay soldiers the "integration process" was bogus because they were already in there serving openly. The SLDN started a clock on their website to count every second that has passed since the repeal was signed until it is finally enforced. "I find it offensive that it takes nearly a year to make the transition," Aubrey Sarvis, executive director of the SLDN, told me. Many straight troops knew already who was gay or lesbian within their platoon or company so this was not news, which made the delays even harder to understand.

The chorus of criticism from gay groups of Obama and his administration reached fever pitch when the President and his wife refused to invite Servicemembers United, the largest gay military group by members, to an event at the White House in early 2011. "It was the first military event at the White House since repeal and we asked for a representative to be included," said Alexander Nicholson, executive director of Servicemembers United. "First they didn't think of it themselves, but when we pointed out and asked to have a representative they specifically refused, which was disappointing and puzzling," he told me. Many put this down to political calculus on Obama's part as he tried to leverage his positions on the economy and health care. But snubs like this, alongside the fact it had taken him two years to come through on the campaign pledge, turned the tide of popularity against the president. Criticisms of the fact that the repeal did not go far enough started in earnest. The final repeal, for example, did not include the non-discrimination mandate clause, which would have made gay service members a protected class and had profound legal ramifications. If a gay soldier is discriminated against based on their sexuality in terms of a promotion or another injustice, they still do not have the venue to complain using equal opportunity legislation as someone with a religious or racial complaint would. Without that in place, a new president who wanted to reinstate DADT would have authority to do it. Feasibly there could be an administrative directive from a future White House that curtails open service policy after certification or outright reverses it. In essence, the repeal bill took away the law enacted in 1993, but before that the gay ban was completely regulatory. With the 1993 law gone, the issue was back in regulatory space, which, while most expected the Pentagon to continue an open service policy, left open the possibility that in a decade or so, with troop needs back to being manageable, they could adopt a discriminatory policy again. "Given the doublespeak of the White House, its supportive but never too supportive, people are skeptical, nobody is 100 percent trusting of the fact we are done yet. Everybody is waiting," added Nicholson.

The Defense of Marriage Act, or DOMA—which the Obama administration had pledged to stop defending in court—also continued to draw ire because it still meant that while gay people can die for their country their spouses or significant others would not be honored in the same way as spouses of their straight colleagues, or receive the same benefits. There are even *Republican* groups pushing for the Obama administration to go further. "The biggest criticism for us is that President Obama has refused to suspend the discharge proceedings as the certification is taking place," said Clarke Cooper, executive director of the Log Cabin Republicans, who served openly in Iraq and was later appointed by George W. Bush as a diplomat. In many ways, the military appeared more effusive than the Obama administration about the changes, perhaps because they had seen it operating during the War on Terror with no real drawbacks. General James Amos, a Marine Corps commandant, had been against the repeal initially, but told Congress in the midst of the training process that the repeal was going forward with few problems. "I've been looking for issues, but honestly we haven't seen it," he said.[64] "There hasn't been the recalcitrant pushback. We haven't seen the anxiety over it from the forces in the field." The surprise for progressives was that the only anxiety about it was coming from the White House.

Epilogue: Indiscriminate Trust

On the careful choice of soldiers depends the welfare of the Republic, and the very essence of the Roman Empire and its power is so inseparably connected with this charge, that it is of the highest importance not to be entrusted indiscriminately.

Flavius Vegetius Renatus, fifth century[1]

You go to war with the Army you have. They're not the Army you might want or wish to have at a later time.

Secretary of Defense, Donald Rumsfeld, 2004[2]

Sometime in the early fifth century an aristocratic Roman thinker with no first-hand experience of war sat down to write what would become the most important military rulebook in history. The short tract, *Concerning Military Matters*,[3] ripped up conventional ideas about military affairs and the art of war, casting a long shadow over the following millennium of fighting. Its lessons were varied, ranging from instructions on how to manage raw and undisciplined troops to notes on legionary musical etiquette. But many were also timeless—centuries later in the war-ravaged Middle Ages the rulebook was still treated like gospel by a rogues' gallery of despots and their generals. Its author was Flavius Vegetius Renatus, a self-effacing young man who regarded his work as a clarion call to an empire of awesome power but with problems coming into sharp focus on the horizon—particularly, Vegetius believed, concerning the military. He addressed his preface for the first book directly to Emperor Valentinian with typical coyness: "I do not presume to offer this work to Your Majesty from a supposition that you are not acquainted with every part of its contents," he assured his master.[4] While his humble tone and faith in his leader's intelligence can perhaps be admired, it would prove to be a wrongheaded assumption. Over the next century, Vegetius's revolutionary lessons on how to run a successful military machine would be spurned by the leaders of the world's most powerful empire, an oversight that would prove fatal as the Roman colossus fell from a position of unrivalled global dominance to a barely recognizable shell power. It was the biggest fall from grace history has seen to date.

In his classic work *The Rise and Fall of the Roman Empire*, the eighteenth-century historian Edward Gibbon describes the empire's pinnacle in glowing prose: "In the second century of the Christian era, the Empire of Rome comprehended the fairest part of the earth, and the most civilised portion of mankind," he writes. "The frontiers of that extensive monarchy were guarded by ancient renown and disciplined valour."[5] Yet from this redoubtable position, just three centuries later in 410, Rome, the imperial capital, the symbol of all that was great and good in the empire, was sacked by the "barbarians" who had been its slaves just decades earlier. Historians have spent the last millennium trying to work out why and how this happened with such speed, but despite the amount of painstaking research undertaken there remains significant debate about why the fall came when it did. "Although the topic has been popular, and myriad reasons have been offered to explain Rome's fall, no consensus has emerged, and historians of the twentieth century have multiplied the variety of explanations many times over," writes one historian.[6] Explanations range from the insidious influence of Christianity from the first century on, to a generalized rupture in the moral fabric of Roman society. But one strain of thought stands out about all others—the military explanation. Vegetius was a pioneer in this regard. In his book, he observed that "so many defeats" as the Romans suffered at the time can "only be imputed" to the "careless choice of our levies."[7] He feared that the careless attention paid to stocking the fighting force with upright and well-trained warriors could prove the death of the empire he loved. He was further alarmed at the "inclination so prevalent among the better sort in preferring the civil posts of government to the profession of arms."[8] At the Battle of Châlons, at around the time Vegetius was writing, Rome's military had been shown up as a shadow of its former self. The enemy commander Attila had the gall to inform his troops that Rome's warriors were nothing but a ragtag army of nonentities. It was an unthinkable charge. "The dust of battle overwhelms them while they fight in close formation under a screen of protective shields," he taunted as his soldiers laughed.[9] The descent culminated when the imperial city was sacked for the first time in 800 years, as one of the barbarian Germanic tribes that had been tormenting the empire, the Visigoths, stormed into Rome and looted for three days.

As he looked back centuries later, Gibbon saw the same trajectory as Vegetius. "In the purer ages of the Commonwealth," he wrote, "the use of arms was reserved for those ranks who had a country to love, a property to defend, and some share in enacting those laws which it was their interest, as well as duty, to maintain."[10] Gradually, though, things changed. "The common soldiers, like the mercenary troops of modern Europe," writes Gibbon, soon became "drawn from the meanest, and very frequently from the most profligate, of mankind."[11] The Roman military had also opened its doors to the conquered enemies—a process referred to in the field as "barbarization," which allowed mercenaries to receive Roman largesse in exchange for fighting the elite's increasingly avaricious wars. The new additions created endless problems for a military that had been the envy of the world. As historian Arthur Ferrill, author of *The Fall of the Roman Empire: The Military Explanation*, writes, "Despite the impact of barbarization, Roman forces continued to fight according to traditional Roman tactics, yet those tactics, previously so superior, seemed absurd to the barbarians of the fifth century."[12] It had a significant and detrimental impact on the ability of the army to do its job. "To fight effectively in close order, troops require intensive drill and rigorous discipline," says Ferrill. "Romans of the fifth century apparently maintained the old formations but abandoned the necessary training. As a result they combined the worst features of the Roman and barbarian styles of fighting."[13] The importance of the "careful choice of levies" has continued to occupy all the most renowned military thinkers. Sun Tzu wrote in *The Art of War* that one of the ways "in which a ruler can bring misfortune upon his army" is by "employing the officers of his army without discrimination."[14] While Nicolo Machiavelli warned in his classic *The Prince*, "If a prince bases the defense of his state on mercenaries he will never achieve stability or security. For mercenaries are disunited, thirsty for power, undisciplined, and disloyal; they are brave among their friends and cowards before the enemy."[15] Both books were apparently favorites of American military planners before and during the War on Terror.

False Prophet

History doesn't repeat itself exactly, but it often resonates and in the psyche of the country at large 9/11 assumed similar proportions to the sacking of Rome centuries earlier. Unlike the destruction of Rome, however, it wasn't a verdict on the military weakness of the country—the US still had thousands of bases around the world and its defense budget was nearly as much as that of the rest of the world combined. But it did precipitate the War on Terror which, this book has shown, saw the decline and "barbarization" of the US military with the inclusion of domestic "undesirables" on a scale comparable to the later years of Rome. In fact, the American military's deterioration has been considerably quicker and more dangerous, and the failures in Afghanistan and Iraq could foreshadow the diminution of American power along Roman lines. There has been a pervasive feeling since the War on Terror and financial crisis that power is slipping away. "American Decline" is now a vogue topic across the media and academia. But it may not be terminal. In Vegetius's second address to the emperor he made a plea: "The expense of keeping up good or bad troops is the same," he wrote, "but it depends wholly on You, most August Emperor, to recover the excellent discipline of the ancients to correct the abuses of later times. This is a reformation the advantages of which will be equally felt by ourselves and our posterity."[16] He could easily have been addressing US President Barack Obama in January 2009 on his ascension to power. Like the Roman Emperor, Obama was inheriting a military broken by the "abuses of later times"—or, more specifically, by the Bush administration. Its troops were scarred, many mentally unstable and untreated, ravaged by two wars and the subsequent occupations which the Pentagon was ill-prepared for. Countless families across the nation were (and are) dealing with loved ones who have changed forever, while the military had reached the lowest point in its history. "We're on the brink," said Thomas White, former Secretary of the Army, earlier in the War on Terror. "We are in a situation where we are grossly over-deployed, and it is unlike any other period in the 229-year history of the Army. We have never conducted a sustained combat operation with a volunteer force, with a force that we have to compete in the job market to hire every year."[17] It was a task without historical precedent and it fell to Obama to fix for posterity what had been so disastrously broken. "I thought by the end of Vietnam . . . we had broadly destroyed the US Army," White added.[18] "The non-commissioned officer leadership had vanished. Indiscipline rates were way, way up. We needed a complete rebuilding of the force from bottom to top. And that's precisely what we engaged ourselves in for the next 20 years or so." The US military establishment now has to engage itself for the next decade (and probably longer) doing the same thing.

The auguries for the Obama presidency were good. Despite all the public-relations hype surrounding his election campaign, in the military there were real reasons to hold out hope for change. As we have seen, Obama was forceful in denouncing the use of veterans as guinea pigs to test new drugs on. He had come out equally strongly against the discriminatory Don't Ask, Don't Tell policy on homosexuals. He had backed the post-9/11 GI Bill, proposed by Jim Webb, which would pay out $78 billion in education benefits to veterans who had served in the military after September 11. John McCain, his presidential opponent, was against it. Obama's soaring rhetoric was even sweeter. "What this new generation of veterans must know is this," he opined. "Our nation's commitment to all who wear its uniform is a sacred trust that is as old as our republic itself. It is one that, as President, I consider a moral obligation to uphold."[19] Obama announced a new twenty-first-century Veterans Health Administration which would make it easier for veterans with PTSD to receive the medical benefits they deserved, while the GI Bill would also open up educational opportunities and job training to those coming back from Iraq and Afghanistan. It seemed he was aware that if the government continued to get the reintegration of its soldiers back into civilian society wrong, it would have disastrous effects for America for decades to come.

But it didn't take long for cracks to appear in the shiny veneer. Obama had originally opposed the war in Iraq and his campaign had been built partly on his ironclad commitment to end the war. "As a candidate for this office, I pledged I would end this war. As President, that is what I am doing," he said in August 2010. "We have brought home more than 90,000 troops since I took office. We have closed or turned over to Iraq hundreds of bases. In many parts of the country, Iraqis have already taken the lead for security."[20] But, in fact, many of the Bush administration's most destructive policies were simply kept in place. The final 40,000 non-combat US troops were brought home in 2011, but many called it the privatization of the occupation, as security contractor numbers continued to rise. At the same time, Obama ratcheted up operations in the other front in the War on Terror: within a year of his inauguration he announced a "surge" in Afghanistan which would increase troop levels by 30,000, keeping up the pressure on the broken military. In 2011, just 34 percent of veterans of Iraq and Afghanistan believed the wars had been worth fighting. At the same time, both veterans and active-duty personnel were less likely to approve of Obama than the rest of the population.

The Corporate Model Wins Out

The wars in Afghanistan and Iraq have been the longest combat operations in American history. Millions of lives have been destroyed in the process and whole societies traumatized. The project ended up as a humanitarian catastrophe for the occupied populations but, contrary to popular belief, it wasn't a failure for the ideologues who started the conflagrations. Rumsfeld's vision of an eviscerated civilian military was, in the end, and at great human cost, realized. Trying to keep the army small when the wars demanded large numbers of troops meant the military acted more and more like a corporation; unfortunately it was a corporation without enough employees. Morten G. Ender at the Military Academy in West Point, New York, put it this way: "What's new is the all volunteer force. The military now has to rely on the corporate model. If people don't come to your business you have to compromise your standards or lower your expectations."[21] In power, Obama ended up using more private security contractors than even the Bush administration had, despite early concerns about what journalist Jeremy Scahill calls their "unconstitutional" use. In truth it was impossible to do without them: the broken US military could not long stand on its own two feet. The fact that its armed forces have become US military Inc. should be extremely worrying for the American public, for the military planners whose concern is projecting power around the world, and for those who may be next on the receiving end of their bombs.

It is clear from the stories in this book that the military's drop in standards unleashed a significant tranche of mentally unstable, extremist, and violent individuals upon the Iraqi and Afghan populations. Many of the most sickening of the atrocities committed by US service members—from the Abu Ghraib torture scandal to the Mahmudiyah massacre—were directly related to the loosening of standards. It might be a felon who had received a "moral waiver" but couldn't shake off his criminal impulses, or a neo-Nazi granted a newfound freedom in the military. It could be a drunk soldier who picked up his weapon in the middle of a binge and went out to take pot-shots at the locals. This in itself has profound implications for the pretext of the whole War on Terror, billed as a moral crusade to bring democracy to the benighted Middle East. Indeed, it shifts the entire frame through which we should look at the whole venture. For modern military occupations, destruction of the occupied society is usually *de rigueur*. But the evidence strongly suggests that a military

rife with alcoholics and gang-bangers is even more likely to griev-
ously harm the society it occupies. The Irregular Army also ended up
as the largest anthropological experiment in history, with US service
members as the guinea pigs. In 1992, as Secretary of Defense Dick
Cheney had said, "The military is not a social welfare agency . . . We
aren't there to run social experiments. We are there to fight and win
wars," but under his administration's watch a "social experiment" is
what it became.[22] It bought together groups that would never come
across each other in their everyday lives. Neo-Nazis from Iowa broke
bread with gang-bangers from Chicago in Baghdad, and alcoholics
supped "hajji juice" with the mentally ill in Fallujah. It engendered
weird alliances. In November 2010, for example, it was reported that
Mexican drug cartels were enlisting white supremacists to smuggle
illegal drugs across the border.[23] Members of both of groups had
been enlisted in the military in considerable numbers during the
War on Terror. Did the relationship begin there? The military's
recruitment policy will contribute to social degeneration back home
for decades to come. From the mentally scarred soldiers who are
refused treatment (many of whom end up in the criminal justice
system) to heavily trained gang-bangers stalking the streets of US
cities, the "barbarization" of the US armed forces will be a theme
that returns again and again as it touches on so many of the ills
plaguing US society.

The FBI reported that it had carried out over 14 million background checks on Americans wanting to purchase weapons and
explosives in 2009, up 10 percent from 12.7 million the year before.
That represents more guns than the number held by the biggest mili-
taries in the world—combined.[24] As I write this, Jared Loughner, a
delusional young loner, has just murdered six people in Arizona and
nearly killed Congresswoman Gabrielle Giffords with a semiautomatic weapon. It has since transpired that Loughner had tried
to join the military in late 2008—and his experience is instructive.
He was refused entry, which would seem to contradict the thesis of
the Irregular Army. In truth, it was a demonstration of all the military shortcomings outlined above. Loughner passed the ASVAB easily
and was soon in one of the Military Entrance Processing Stations

(MEPS)—which gauges recruits' applicability—where he was asked the standard question of whether he had "used illegal drugs or abused prescription drugs."[25] He answered honestly that he used marijuana, and according to the military they barred him on this basis. But he could have lied about it—as thousands of others had done in the War on Terror and before. He could also have been the recipient of a "medical waiver" or "moral waiver" even if he had a conviction. In other words, had he been smart he could have gotten in with no problem and been sent off to war. "It's bizarre," a military official said. "I certainly wouldn't go through the whole process only to say, 'Hey, I've been smoking marijuana for the past couple of years.'"[26] There are undoubtedly many other Loughners who were smarter and went on to serve—maybe some of them appear in this book. Over the coming decade, with military training and access to weapons, they will be stalking the streets of both the US and the Middle East. America will pay for this in the blood of its own citizens as will the subject populations of the countries its military occupies. A warning shot was fired in March 2011 when the FBI arrested Kevin William Harpham, a thirty-six-year-old member of the neo-Nazi National Alliance, in Spokane, Washington, on suspicion of planting a bomb at a Martin Luther King Day celebration which if detonated would have killed hundreds of people. Harpham had served in the US army for two years in the mid-1990s.

Lies Into Iraq

But pointing the finger is too easy. We have to take some blame ourselves, as we were as indiscriminate in our trust in our leaders as they were with their choice of soldiers. As the wars went on, we believed their crocodile tears when American troops died. We bought their soaring rhetoric about their commitment to service members, when in fact they were often cutting veterans' access to benefits and health care. It was just a continuation of the lies we were told to take us into war in the first place. For people like Charlie P. Gaffney Jr., who picked up a gun again at the age of forty in an effort to help bring democracy to the people of Afghanistan and Iraq, these lies ended their lives. While the Bush administration cast the invasion as a "liberation" to "free the Iraqi people from the tyranny of Saddam Hussein," the uncomfortable fact that during the 1980s the US had supported Hussein was scrubbed from history. Declassified files show that the Reagan administration and its special Middle East envoy, Donald Rumsfeld, had done "little to stop Iraq developing weapons of mass destruction in the 1980s, even though they were fully aware that Saddam was using chemical weapons 'almost daily' against Iran," reports the *Guardian*. The declassified documents detail how Reagan and Rumsfeld had allowed the export of biological weapons, including anthrax, ingredients for chemical weapons, and cluster bombs. In 1983, the then Secretary of State George Shultz received intelligence of "almost daily use" of chemical weapons by Iraq. A mere twenty-five days after this information was received, Reagan gave a secret order allowing the administration to do "whatever was necessary and legal" to help Iraq win the war over Iran. In December of that year, Rumsfeld met Saddam in Baghdad and stated the United States' desire to restore diplomatic relations. This support and flow of arms continued long after the end of the Iran–Iraq war, right up until the first Gulf War in 1990—even after Saddam had shelled the Kurdish town of Halabja in March 1988 with gas bombs, killing an estimated 5,000 civilians and maiming thousands more.

The lie was no different in the UK. In December 2009 I was sent by my newspaper at the time, the *Financial Times*, down to the National Archives in Kew Gardens, London, to write a series of articles based on secret British state documents, which were then being released under the thirty-year disclosure rule. I would be viewing documents from 1979, the same year Saddam Hussein became president of Iraq in a bloody coup. I was particularly interested in how the British had viewed the event, and reading the reactions of the British ambassador to the coup was an eye-opening experience. Saddam became president in July 1979 in what the ambassador described as "the first smooth transfer of power in Iraq since 1958," when a group of army officers had overthrown the monarchy.[27] The ambassador noted, however, what this "smooth transfer" had involved: Within the first twenty-four hours of Saddam's rule, "21 prominent Iraqis, including five members of the ruling Revolutionary Command Council, [were] executed." Britain was confident of Saddam's ability to crush dissent. "Strong-arm methods may be needed to steady the ship," wrote a Foreign Office official. "Saddam will not flinch." A Foreign Office briefing said Saddam was "personable in appearance" and wore "well-cut clothes, reputedly London-made." He was said to elicit "fear mixed with grudging admiration" and gave "an impression in conversation of quiet but determined concentration, unusual in the Ba'ath leadership."

The archives included a document sent by the embassy to London that detailed a day in the new president's life. "It is not often we are permitted a glimpse into the personal lives of Iraq's leaders," said the letter to the Foreign Office, "so by way of introduction, I enclose a touching account of a day in the life of President Saddam Hussein." Badly translated from Arabic, it read: "The early morning workers often exchange tales of how President Hussein surprised them at work site, how he chatted with them, smiled to them or asked them and listened to them . . . Tales full with love and admiration growing day after day in their hearts." On January 1, 2010, the day the thirty-year embargo was up and the newspapers printed our articles, I went to my local newsagent and checked all the other papers nervously to see if I had missed any big stories buried in the documents. Luckily, there were none. Everyone looked to have found the same sort of things—except, funnily enough, the one about Saddam Hussein. My article in the *Financial Times* (headline: "Saddam Was Well-regarded by British") was the only one that even referenced the documents related to Iraq. It was an example of our deeply biased reporters ignoring the ugly truth of what our government stood and stands for in the world. The British had, in fact, been honing their methods of domination for decades—methods copied by the US. They were spelled out quite clearly by Lord Curzon who, when installing King Faisal in Iraq in 1921, wrote that the British need an "Arab facade ruled and administered under British guidance and controlled by a native Mohammedan and, as far as possible, by an Arab staff . . . There should be no actual incorporation of the conquered territory in the dominions of the conqueror, but the absorption may be veiled by such constitutional fictions as a protectorate, a sphere of influence, a buffer state and so on."[28] Nothing has changed in the twenty-first century.

The wars in Iraq and Afghanistan also had profound effects on the UK military, the only other country in the coalition fighting the War on Terror whose armed forces were stretched even close to those of the US, and the most generous partner in terms of providing troops. A high of 9,500 British service members were deployed to Afghanistan in 2009, while the Iraq war saw an initial force of 46,000. So far, 179 UK soldiers have been killed in Iraq and 407 in Afghanistan.[29] For a country with a population a fifth of that of the US, it was a substantial commitment and the biggest military operation since the end of World War Two. The UK military experienced some but not all of the problems that Rumsfeld and the Pentagon presided over in the US, and the differences are instructive. For example, there have been very few reports of a proliferation of neo-Nazis and white supremacists in the British military, although members of the fascist British National Party have joined up. Little substantial investigative work has been conducted on the matter and it remains an open but worrying question. The leader of the BNP, Nick Griffin, has said that his party is popular among British soldiers. "I'm the one who talks to the families of young squaddies and large numbers of ex-servicemen and they all say that almost everyone at the coalface, fighting in Afghanistan, vote for the British National Party," he said in 2009.[30] But gangs are considerably less prevalent in the UK and their members have not been enlisted to any worrying degree in its military. Likewise the rules on recruiting criminals were not tweaked to swell the ranks.

Where the UK military did suffer was in the susceptibility of its troops to alcohol and drugs and the concomitant problems of PTSD. There was a fivefold increase in UK soldiers failing drug tests in the period 2002–8, although their drug of choice was different from that of their American colleagues.[31] On the whole it was cocaine and ecstasy, with a move in later years to mephedrone, which is cheaper and more easily accessible. In 2006 the *Daily Telegraph* revealed that the armed forces had in fact scrapped, in secret, its policy of automatic dismissal for those caught using Class A drugs. The Ministry of Defence claims, like the DOD, that it doesn't tolerate any drug use, but by 2008 it had allowed 1,300 drug users to stay in the military.[32] Alcohol is not strictly banned by the UK military and it developed into a big problem during the War on Terror—one in seven soldiers reported being driven to alcohol by their experience in war.[33] PTSD also became a big problem for UK soldiers, though dwarfed by comparison with the US. One study found that American soldiers were seven times more likely to get PTSD than their British counterparts. UK rates for PTSD stayed at around 3–4 percent during the War on Terror, compared to 30 percent in the US military. "PTSD seems not to be a 'universal stress reaction', arising in all societies across all time," wrote Neil Greenberg, author of the study. "Evidence from both world wars suggests that the ways in which service personnel communicate distress is culturally determined and that the development of PTSD may be one more phase in the evolving picture of human reaction to adversity."[34] Perhaps the more important difference was the lack of health and rehabilitation services available to US troops as the military unraveled—something the UK didn't experience on the same level. Likewise, German soldiers in Afghanistan had PTSD levels at 2 percent for returning soldiers.[35]

In terms of the general physical condition of UK troops, the picture was not pretty: the only soldier whose death was officially linked to obesity was British. In 2009 a leaked army memo complained that thousands of British troops could not be deployed to Afghanistan because they were too fat.[36] Operational readiness, the memo noted, was being undermined by the lack of fitness of British troops, who are required to do a minimum of just two hours of exercise per week. Unlike in the US, there's no proof they stopped kicking out overweight troops. Homosexuals were already allowed to serve in the UK military before the War on Terror began, so that engendered no change, and tellingly no problems either. Foreigners—notably in the form of Nepalese Gurkhas—had fought in the British military since the time of the empire. The issue attracted a high-profile campaign when the British government refused to allow Gurkha veterans to live in the UK after service—a controversy similar to that which arose when the government had refused to let Iraqi translators and other workers in danger settle in the UK. The Gurkhas were joined by others during the War on Terror, although the regulations were not changed to allow more of them into the UK. Figures released in 2009 show that one in ten new recruits to the army were born abroad, three times the number in 2000. In 2008–9, 1,320 service members born outside Britain joined the military, compared with 540 in 1999–2000.[37]

Heroes and Villains

The majority of this book (excepting the heroic civil rights victory for gay service members) will have been a depressing and a sobering read for patriotic Americans and those around the world concerned with human rights and decency. But it has also revealed a heroes gallery of lawmakers, activists, active-duty soldiers, and veterans who refused to accept the degrading treatment that has been meted out by the military brass and their colleagues in Washington. Henry Waxman was one member of Congress who stood up to highlight the outrageous proliferation of felons in the military, while Marty Meehan tried his damnedest to pass civil rights legislation that would allow gays to serve openly. They were widely traduced and attacked at the time. Active-duty troops included Justin Watt, who alerted his superiors to the Mahmudiyah massacre and risked his life in order to see justice done for the family involved. He was mocked and ignored by the military initially but kept his steel. Then there are the kids of Bushwick, Brooklyn, who have fought valiantly against the *de facto* conscription the Bush administration imposed on the poor children of America by allowing recruiters to take over their schools. Private First Class Bradley Manning, the alleged source of the Wikileaks cables and war logs, is another. So angered was he at being ignored by his senior officers when he told them about the illegal activity he saw, he thought he had to do something about it—and changed the course of history at the same time.

Unfortunately brave individuals like Manning have been the exception. There has been a concerted effort by the military brass and their political allies to ignore the problem or simply deny it even exists. In every case where the military acknowledged there had been a loosening of standards it was presented officially as a victory for democracy or civil rights—permitting older recruits, for example, confirms a commitment to non-discriminatory practices based on age. It was the same tactic as is used generally for US foreign policy: every action, by definition, has to be spun as altruistic. While finishing this book, the Wikileaks release of the Afghanistan and Iraq war logs gave the public an unprecedented look at the anatomy of those wars and the toll they had taken on civilians. I decided to check out the SIGACT ("significant activity") reports related to some of the events I was writing about. It became clear quite quickly that although a vital tool in revealing the true brutality the war inflicted on Iraqis, the reports did not come close to conveying the true horror of what had taken place. One of the distinctive features of US war-waging, as in Vietnam, is that specific massacres and murders are held up by the Pentagon as unfortunate exceptions, the transgressions of a few "crazy" lowlife troops. The perpetrators are then made an example of. In Iraq, those massacres were Haditha and Mahmudiyah (and in 2012 Panjwai district in Afghanistan). In Vietnam, after the investigative work by Seymour Hersh, it was My Lai (an "American tragedy" according to *Time* magazine). The great lie, then as now, is that these are the exceptions when in fact they are commonplace. Cold-blooded murder, taking pot-shots at the locals: it's all par for the course if you talk to veterans who have been at the sharp end of the conflict. In interviews published in the *Nation* magazine in 2007, veterans of Iraq described the true horror the invading army had inflicted on the civilian population. Chris Hedges and Laila Al-Arian, the interviewers, concluded that indiscriminate killings were "common," "often go unreported—and almost always go unpunished."[38] They were right. Even the atrocities that were reported had been initially hushed up by the US military.

Take the case of Lance Corporal Delano Holmes—who stabbed his Iraq colleague Private Hassin to death while on sentry duty. He received a joke sentence handed out by a farcical court-martial system, but typical of the justice afforded to what was viewed as just "collateral damage." How was the murder of Hassin reported in the log? One host nation soldier killed, it says. "Prior to an Iraqi guard post change . . . the Marine and the IA were arguing over the off-going soldier smoking in the post. Smoking is prohibited inside the post due to the enemy sniper threat," it begins, as if excusing what is to come. "The arguing changed to shoving each other at which time the oncoming Iraqi soldier arrived and joined in the shoving. The [redacted] of the off going IA was fired [redacted] times inside the post, at which time the Marine believing his life was threatened stabbed the off-going Iraqi soldier with a knife resulting in [redacted]."[39] But at the court-martial, the prosecutors said Holmes had fired Hassan's AK-47 afterwards to make what was a cold-blooded murder look like self-defense—the same lie reported by the SIGACT. In other words, the SIGACT is entirely misleading. The Wikileaks logs gave a glimpse of the horror, but only a glimpse. Behind every report, there was another world of truth obfuscated by the pared-down and tendentious military reportage. Often the truth looked more like that of the "kill team" in Afghanistan, whose reign of terror in Kandahar was made public in 2011. Twelve men were charged with the indiscriminate murder of civilians after they had posed for photos with the dead bodies. When one of the soldiers was asked by the judge what he had intended to do with the shootings, he replied: "The plan was to kill people." Some of them were also charged with staging killings to make it appear as if they had been defending themselves against Taliban assaults. It is safe to assume that many others got away with this tactic.

The reaction from the American public when such truths are revealed is always one of disgust, which is why the truth has to be kept from them. In 2004 about three-quarters of the US population believed it was not right to invade Iraq if it had no weapons of mass destruction or links to Al-Qaeda. But nearly 60 percent still believed Iraq had WMDs, or programs for them in development, *and* links to 9/11, thanks to the Bush administration propaganda (and a pliant media).[40] The national press parroted the lie that these wars needed to be undertaken for our own protection. The opposite was the case. A classified US intelligence report *Trends in Global Terrorism: Implications for the United States* revealed the huge effect the war in

Iraq had on increasing Islamic radicalism and spreading it to a new generation of young Muslims who would now be more likely to attack Western targets. In Britain, a report by the Joint Terrorist Analysis Centre—composed of officials from MI5, MI6, Government Communications Headquarters, and the police—stated that "events in Iraq are continuing to act as motivation and a focus of a range of terrorist-related activity in the UK."[41] The amount of money spent in the twin occupations has also helped to bankrupt America. The esteemed economist Joseph Stiglitz has estimated that all-told the war in Iraq alone will end up costing in total $3 trillion.

I hope reading this book will rouse that anger, because the veterans and the occupied populations deserve the truth to come out at the very least. The FBI and other investigative bodies outside the US military—like the GAO—have been alive to the problems of the Irregular Army and done important work to address them. For the military itself, however, it has been too painful to look into the mirror; no one will ever know the number of personal tragedies on both sides this dereliction of duty has caused. It is a national and international scandal. The benefits of empire are always unequally distributed at home—benefits that come to the imperial country as a result of war and occupation are generally concentrated among the economic elite. In the US there remain very sharp differentials in income, and the polarization of wealth and poverty as a result of imperialism got worse during the War on Terror. When foreigners look at the US, they see the riches, but they tend not to see the other side. The recruitment for the Irregular Army preyed on this other side—the most vulnerable and poor Americans—while the financial benefits of their sacrifice filtered back to the rich and powerful.

Using the Military

The US is at a crossroads. After the trauma of September 11, the biggest ever attack on its homeland, it was taken on a dangerous, violent, and reckless journey by a group of nationalist extremists. It is getting sicker as the wars continue to consume the nation, but it's not terminal. With the will and fortitude of the American people, there can be a reckoning with the forces that have destroyed so many lives in both the US and the Middle East. According to some estimates, over a million Iraqis died as a result of the invasion, while Afghanistan is poorer than ever and sees little hope of redemption (we don't keep count of the number of people we kill). But as I write this at the turn of 2011, 4,408 American soldiers have been killed in Iraq since the invasion, and 1,339 have perished in Afghanistan, while all the issues raised in this book are alive as ever and continue to blight the US military. As we move on to new "theaters of conflict" like Iran we need to look unflinchingly at what we've done and who we've destroyed in process. The lives lost will be in vain unless the truth of what was done to both military service members and the occupied populations enters the historical record unvarnished. The people who did this to us, to them, must face their crimes and their victims: the veteran who has just committed suicide after being denied treatment for PTSD; the Afghan children murdered in their beds by drugged-up airmen; the next generation ravaged by military-trained gangs and neo-Nazis in American cities. And they must look into the mirror and accept it was all a huge mistake: for history has shown that imperial hubris and the degradation of the fighting force only ends one way.

Amid the possibility of a ground force intervention in Libya in early 2011 and continued troop increases in Afghanistan, a split emerged between the Obama administration and the Pentagon over how large the US army should be and what it should be capable of in the future. In a debate which mirrored closely what happened in the build up to the war in Iraq, Secretary of Defense Robert Gates publicly said that "any future defense secretary who advises the president to again send a big American land army into Asia or into the Middle East or Africa should have his head examined."[42] He added that large-scale conflicts with other big countries will likely be fought mainly with air and naval forces. But as he made those comments during a lecture to future army officers at West Point, the soon-to-depart army chief of staff, General George Casey, pointedly cautioned against the "hollowing out" of the armed forces after deployments to Iraq and Afghanistan come to an end.[43] Whichever school of thought wins out will define American expansionism over the next century. In January 2012, Obama seemed to side with Gates. Recognizing the dreadful toll the Irregular Army had taken on the US, in terms of both its soldiers and its ability to project power, Obama outlined a historic change in direction for the military, specifically moving towards a "leaner" military force and away from the troop-heavy ground warfare which defined the War on Terror. He said he wanted "smaller conventional ground forces," which reflected his abandoning what he called "outdated cold war-era systems." "Yes our military will be leaner," he added, "but the world must know the United States is going to maintain our military superiority with armed forces that are agile, flexible, and ready for the full range of contingencies and threats."[44] It sounded exactly like Donald Rumsfeld in 2001.

The US is now profoundly aware of its waning power and how this could impact its future. "Owing to the relative decline of its economic and, to a lesser extent, military power, the US will no longer have the same flexibility in choosing among as many policy options," concluded the National Intelligence Council (which gathers information from all US intelligence agencies) in early 2009.[45] And this weakness will be exploited. Sun Tzu wrote: "When the weapons are dulled, your ardour damped, your strength exhausted and your treasure spent, other chieftains will spring up to take advantage of your extremity. Then no man, however wise, will be able to avert the consequences that must ensue."[46] There's a healthy dose of irony in the fact that Tzu was himself Chinese, the country which is slowly challenging America's role as the world's sole superpower. "When the army is restless and distrustful, trouble is sure to come from other feudal princes," he continues. "This is simply bringing anarchy into the army, and flinging victory away."[47] An anarchist's distrust of bureaucracy and state power is an apt description of Rumsfeld's attitude towards the military.

The decline of the ability of the military to handle combat or even recruit enough troops has seriously compromised the ability of the US to project its power and secure victories. Memories of the returning soldiers' treatment will be hard to shake, and this will likely lead to a version of Vietnam Syndrome, in which many Americans will spurn the military. Even the war-booty expected from the occupations has largely evaded the American imperialist class this time around. Analysis of the two rounds of oil and gas contracts in Iraq shows that US companies won only two of the eighteen contracts, both in joint ventures with other companies. The original plan by the Bush administration was for the Iraqi government to pass a new oil law which would have indirectly privatized Iraq's hydrocarbons through an unconventional type of contracting called "production sharing agreements," which would have given foreign oil companies shares of production and exclusive control over Iraq's oil fields for up to thirty-two years. But the Iraqi constitution requires the parliament to ratify laws, and because of the internal dynamics in the country at the time the parliament ended up being controlled by nationalist parties with anti-occupation politics. Despite the fact that the ruling parties in the Iraqi executive branch were very happy with the Bush oil law, the other parties controlling the legislative branch were opposed to it and ended up blocking it. The Iraqi government then had to revert to an older law that only allows for "technical service agreements," which kept the oil under Iraqi ownership while giving foreign oil companies a flat rate in exchange for services.

As I write this, the US and the world are still in the grips of the crisis that has rocked the global economy since the collapse of Lehman Brothers in September 2008. Unemployment in the US has stayed stubbornly high, which, according to some, has put the issues raised in this book on a temporary back burner as people who can no longer find work turn to the military for salvation. But it would be a mistake to assume this will solve the deep problems in the military. What the War on Terror has shown is that the Pentagon is prepared to dispense with both its regulations and its moral compass when faced with the need to stock any future wars with soldiers. Whatever regulations have been brought back as the wars have wound down—not many, in truth—are therefore still at threat of being ignored again should the situation demand. And this war isn't near to being at its close, either. The wars in Iraq and Afghanistan have radicalized thousands of Muslims to take up the fight against the West, it has emboldened Iran through the deposition of the Sunni minority in Iraq, and it has been prosecuted so badly that the invincibility of American power is no longer an illusion that pervades the world. Unfortunately, however, a wounded tiger is much more dangerous than a healthy one.

The US needs to re-evaluate its role in the world and move away from the use of military force which has, in recent history, become self-perpetuating thanks to its competitive advantage. In his auto-biography, the former Secretary of State Colin Powell notes how Clinton's Secretary of State Madeleine Albright asked him, "What's the point of having this superb military you're always talking about if we can't use it?"[48] With China rapidly closing in on the US economically, this massive military machine will prove even more dangerous: if you have the means of violence in place, there's a very strong temptation to use it. This is new. America has fought dozens of wars since 1945, but during the Cold War nearly all were fought through "proxy forces," meaning that the US government provided financial and military support to an element in a foreign country that was fighting the "Red Menace." The tactic was used by both the US and the Soviet Union essentially because they both wanted to avoid direct military conflict, and this was met with moderate success.

But at the end of the Cold War, with the Soviet deterrent gone, US planners failed to realize that the military was not designed for the direct interventions and occupations of foreign countries that would now be much easier to execute. Their theory went that with the threat of the Soviet Union gone, the US would be able to use its "full-spectrum military dominance" to entrench its "economic rights." Since the economic supremacy of the US was being chal-lenged, planners were intent on fighting back by exploiting their biggest advantage: the military. In many ways the US turned to attacking Iraq because it could no longer control the global econ-omy and was seeking to regain ground by military means, trying to stem a decades-long structural decline by sending its guns around the world. This was the express philosophy of the lobby group called Project for the New American Century, many members of which became part of the George W. Bush administration. The most informative document produced by this think tank, *Rebuilding America's Defenses: Strategies, Forces and Resources for a New Century*, noted: "The United States has for decades sought to play a more permanent role in Gulf regional security" and "the unresolved conflict with Iraq provides the immediate justification ... for a substantial American force presence in the Gulf."[49] But it wasn't what America was good at. "The US in terms of its offensive fire power and global deployment remains absolutely unrivalled, but its weakness is that its forces are not well suited for policing activities," historian Michael Mann tells me. In other words, it has the ability to defeat foreign armies and conquer their cities, but it doesn't have the ability to bring them under control afterwards.

There are a number of reasons for this: first, the US military has no policing record—unlike, for example, the British army in Northern Ireland—while pacification is mostly a political not a military problem. Throughout the Cold War, the US only intervened in foreign countries where there were local allies who with American help could run their countries for them—"even in Vietnam it wasn't implausible that the South Vietnamese government, which had an army of over 200,000 men, could be propped up and successfully pacify the country," adds Mann. The Muslim world is different: the US never had such allies in Iraq or Afghanistan, but launched pre-emptive strikes anyway. But there is another profound problem that renders old-style imperial American power anachronistic: the country has a domestic culture which is not conducive to long-drawn out wars of aggression, as demonstrated by the turmoil during the Vietnam War in the 1960s and 1970s. "American kids are not brought up to be as racist, as stoic in combat, as self-denying in crisis, or as obedient to authority as British kids once were," writes Mann.[50] That lack of an imperial American culture is a proud tradition: its citizens don't want to be part of the Empire however much they are pressured to take up arms for it. I want to give the final word to them.

Never Did, Never Will

One afternoon while I was living in Harlem, New York City, I decided to visit Brownsville, one of the poorest neighborhoods in the city, to talk to local people and find out how the War on Terror had affected them. I walked down Pitkin Avenue, which divides the neighborhood into two neat but equally deprived enclaves, an experience miles away from postcard New York with its narrative of gentrification and urban renewal. Homeless addicts pleaded for some change, children pushed each other off rusty bikes, an old woman pulled her luggage behind her, trying to dodge splinters of urban decay. Brownsville was the silent New York City. "We never get journalists here, apart from shootings," the old woman told me. Overwhelmingly populated by people of Afro-Caribbean lineage (78.2 percent), with one of the worst crime rates in the United States, one of the highest infant mortality indicators, and stellar points in every department of deprivation, it was a military recruiter's dream.

In the national conversation on Iraq that has cluttered newspapers and magazines to the point of saturation over the past decade, the academics and journalists conducting it have been men and women mostly from a similar class and with narrow ideological differences, used to getting finicky over minor points of disagreement. Most of them didn't have children in Iraq and haven't served in the armed forces themselves. Most of them don't use the public welfare systems and none of them, we can be sure, live in places where the child mortality rate is 11.8 percent. In short, for them, the war and its consequences remains an abstract idea. In Brownsville, New York City, this abstract idea condenses into something very real. People talk effortlessly about how the war has impacted their lives in a tangible and often tragic way. Decquan Copeland, seventeen, is a student on the Acorn program for social justice. He grew up in Brownsville and lives in one of the housing projects off East New York Avenue. "The war has been a disaster for this country and it is still causing so many problems," he told me. He is a devout Christian and practices at the Mount Sinai Cathedral, the main place of worship in the area. "I know about fifteen people at the Cathedral who have lost uncles, fathers and cousins in the war. And what for?" He pauses and clears his throat. "We often pray for them at Mount Sinai, but it just gets me so angry, that these people have died for nothing."

Copeland is the prime age for recruitment to the army, and mentions that he has been approached by recruiters on numerous occasions with all of the usual incentives on offer. Brownsville Recruitment Center is located on Pitkin Avenue, an oasis of calm among the chicken shops and street-sellers. In the window are pictures of hardened men and women in combat regalia, affecting faces taut with strength. "There's strong," goes the strap, "Then there's army strong." US Army Recruiter Sergeant Christopher M. Penrod is reluctant to talk and clams up when I mention I'm a journalist. Before speaking to the press, recruiting officers have to receive approval from higher authorities, which is not forthcoming. Inside, the offices are decrepit and decorated with more yellowing pictures of combat action shots. "I am a Warrior," reads another poster.

"I can't deal with death, that's why I'd never join the army," says Copeland. What about his friends? "They have all seen what has happened and I think they are probably scared and angry; the thing is, the recruiters are everywhere around here, in our schools, in our streets, in our stores. They tell us we can get some money, make something of ourselves. All that. Some kids fall for it." In a community district with 50.9 percent of the population on some form of income support, the military is still an appealing career path. Saskia Wilson, sixteen, is a student at Flushing High School. I find her watching television in a laundromat on Legion Street. She wants to go into the military when she finishes school. "It doesn't scare me; you know, my uncle was in the military, I remember he used to talk about it all the time and I remember getting excited about it. I've always been interested in the military—I watch movies and all that shit. When 9/11 happened I thought they were gonna come here, to Brownsville. So you got to defend your country, they came and bombed us so we bomb them back." Was she talking about Iraq? "Oh sure, it was Iraq that bombed us, so I want to protect my country." I wondered if her uncle was in Iraq now. "Oh no, my uncle died, he died in the military." And that doesn't scare her? "I'm not gonna feel safe, but everybody gotta die someday, it's not like it's heaven here in Brownsville." Her mother is a post office worker, and her father does "nothing," according to Saskia. Her other uncle is in the military in South Carolina. "I used to want to be a teacher," she says. "But that was when I was very young, ever since I was twelve, I've wanted to be in the military, they take care of you."

I find Stevery Carrington, forty-seven, outside Microhousing off Rockaway Avenue. He has been a heroin addict for thirteen years and is living in sheltered accommodation. His eyes burn with real intensity when the subject of Iraq is brought up. "I don't know if I should care," he says. I wondered if the war had affected him personally. "Well, hell yeah, look at all the homelessness around, look at this program," he says, and points to the shelter behind him. "There's subsidized programs, day programs, all these things helping people get their life back on track and they wasting all this money on the war—they could be putting it in here. I've relapsed four times for drug abuse, I need the help, I can tell you." I suggest that the people of Brownsville seem like they have strong feelings about the conflict. "They don't care!" he shouts back. "You live here, you shit here, you fuck here, if anybody know anything they don't say shit, nobody gives a fuck, but the war comes to them through deaths of people they know. That's my relationship with the war—seeing my brothers come back in coffins."

Brownsville has a large Muslim community, mainly African American converts, but there are a sizeable number of believers and an active mosque. I spoke to Abdullah Aziz, fifty-two, who was sitting on Pitkin Avenue outside his friend's shop. He had converted to Islam thirty years ago and worked as a plumber and drug counselor. "I have a son in Iraq," he begins. "He just went, he's in Kuwait until weather conditions allow him to go into Iraq for a year. I think the invasion was politically incorrect, it was unjust, it was for oil, but it's the power that be, and that's it, it is, it be's, so we can't do nothing about it. They talk about due processes, but they are the process!" It was strange that a devout Muslim, against the war morally, would allow his son, twenty years old, to go to the Middle East to fight for the US. "He wanted a career, there's not much else he could do," he says. "The decision was his—he understands he's Muslim and the Koran says Muslims shouldn't kill other Muslims, but then look at Iraq that's what's happening. It's a job to him, they get you young and dumb, but he's also a grown man so we're supporting him. Of course, every parent is worried about it, but you can't do anything, he's got to find his own way, a lot of kids round here do the same shit."

Many people in Brownsville are employed off the record, using anything they have or can get hold of to make money. Melvin Ford, twenty-six, is selling grubby second-hand teddy bears on the main thoroughfare, along with coverless Sudoku and coloring books. He has some strong opinions on the war and gives a historical context on the whole operation: "Well, Bush senior did some stupid shit," he says. "He let Saddam make all that money and get away with it. People forget," he adds, "that's not our oil . . . They should leave Iraq alone," he expands, "bring the troops home and let the Iraqi President deal with it." It transpires that Ford has two cousins who have been in Iraq. One, Lans Franklin, was sent home for going AWOL while the other, Richard Franklin, remains there. "Richard don't know anything," says Ford. "He's been there since 2004, or whenever it started and now I think he's switched to Kuwait or something. He sends letters, tells us he's doing good, how wonderful it all is. But it's the school he went to: they trained him for guns and war, told him how good all that shit is." Richard Franklin has five children, three boys and two girls. They haven't seen him for four years. His brother, Lans, went AWOL and was discharged by the military after going out to Iraq. "He fucked up and it turned him a little crazy, and they said, 'You are gonna drop a fucking bomb on us one day so we're sending you home, we don't need you.'" Lans, from the Bronx originally, had been back for about six months; he has problems hearing, after a bomb went off nearby when he was asleep. "I don't know if he's changed at all," says Ford, getting agitated. "He was definitely drinking more than usual when I last saw him: 'Let's get a six-pack, blah blah,' that kind of shit. He was drinking two six-packs and liquor every day when I saw him last. He's kind of crazy now, but the military don't help him." He pauses and looks down. "Never did, never will."

The War Comes Home

Just weeks before the hardcover edition of *Irregular Army* came out in September 2012, a neo-Nazi US Army veteran walked into a Sikh temple in Oak Creek, Wisconsin, and shot dead six worshippers. A topic that had never managed to hold the interest of the American media during the War on Terror—the extremists being trained by the country's military—suddenly moved front and center.

Many Americans wondered how this white supremacist could have survived in the military for so long; surely something must have gone wrong. But the Wisconsin shooter, Wade Michael Page, was merely one of many far-right radicals who have used the US military over the past two decades to gain access to the highest-grade weaponry in the world, alongside attendant training. The Springfield semiautomatic 9mm handgun used by Page in Oak Creek was, for instance, very similar to the Beretta M9, the civilian version of the pistol issued by the US military. And neo-Nazi veterans, like Page, were explicit about wanting to use their new military skills in the coming race war they hoped would ignite in the US. Page's heavy-metal white-power band, called End Apathy, was itself a call to arms. According to a 2010 interview he gave to a white supremacist website, he wanted to "figure out how to end people's apathetic ways"; the band was meant to "be the start towards moving forward."[1]

As details emerged, they seemed to confirm what I had written in this book. The most shocking part of Page's story was that he was completely open about his neo-Nazi views while serving in the army during the 1990s, a decade before the War on Terror. Page was no army private either—he was assigned to the esteemed psychological operations ("psyops") branch. But despite this senior status, the independent American military newspaper *Stars and Stripes* wrote in the aftermath of the shooting that Page was "steeped in white supremacy during his army days and spouted his racist views on the job as a soldier."[2] Page served from 1992 to 1998. The latter part of this period putatively witnessed the US military taking a strong stand against white supremacism within the ranks after neo-Nazi active-duty paratrooper James Burmeister murdered an African American couple near Fort Bragg, North Carolina, in 1995.

Page's story actually bore an uncanny resemblance to that of one of the main characters in *Irregular Army*: Forrest Fogarty, the War on Terror veteran I spent time with in Tampa, Florida. Like Page, Fogarty was a neo-Nazi; like Page, he was a member of the Hammerskins, the most violent skinhead group in the US; like Page, he served in the US military (in Fogarty's case in Iraq from 2004 to 2005); and like Page, Fogarty was the lead singer in a neo-Nazi rock band. Fogarty had in fact signed up to the US army, complete with racist tattoos, in 1997, around the same time Page was denied reenlistment for alcoholism (not neo-Nazism). In fact, as I looked into the history of Page I even came across images of him playing his racist rock with Fogarty himself: they performed in the same band at neo-Nazi concerts. The US military, it would seem, has a penchant for Nazi rockers.

The media ate up the Pentagon's reflexive lies during the fallout from the massacre. When Al Jazeera interviewed me, they asked the Pentagon for clarification of their policy on extremists. A spokesman told them that "participation in extremist activities has never been tolerated."[3] The media interest endured for a couple of weeks, then the silence returned. But over the subsequent two years, the threats I warned about in the book played out with frightening regularity. Many of the predictions of "blowback" from a decade (and more) of unchecked extremist and criminal infiltration were coming true. Not long after the Sikh Temple massacre, an anti-government militia of active-duty soldiers at Fort Stewart—where Fogarty had been based—was discovered. This heavily armed group had already murdered an active-duty soldier and his wife and was planning to assassinate President Barack Obama. According to prosecutors, the soldiers had spent nearly $90,000 on guns and bomb components.

Not long after this cell was discovered, a Missouri National Guardsman admitted to helping train a white supremacist group, American Front, whose members were preparing for a domestic race war. These extremists, court documents detailed, were alleged to have committed hate crimes alongside paramilitary training in "furtherance of a civil disorder."[4]

The steady beat of tragedies kept coming. In April 2014, an Army veteran and "grand dragon" of the Carolina Knights of the Ku Klux Klan, Frazier Glenn Miller, killed three people at two Jewish centers in a suburb of Kansas City. Miller had retired from the Army in the 1990s as a master sergeant after twenty years of active duty, including two tours in Vietnam and thirteen years as a member of the elite Green Berets. These cases were particularly scary because they showed the long lineage of this problem. In the book I had focused on the War on Terror years because in that period even the light regulations that were in place were lit up in flames, but Page and Miller demonstrated the long incubation period allowed for these errant extremist veterans to turn into cold-blooded murderers. Over the next two decades, US society will doubtless endure other versions of these massacres— involving veterans from Iraq and Afghanistan this time round. The scars from these wars are long, deep and may be impossible to salve. The US military has refused to take seriously the dangers posed by the radicals in its service—and its own soldiers, alongside the population they are meant to defend, are paying a heavy price. Many more ticking time bombs—unlike Miller and Page, not yet detonated—are now settling back home after a decade of hard combat training.

A toxic mix

But it was not just white supremacist soldiers and veterans who were proving dangerous. Many of the other problems outlined in the book—from the US military's failure to deal with post-traumatic stress disorder (PTSD) or the economic hardship of the veteran community—were coming back to bite the US populace. In Wade

Page's case, for example, it was a confluence of factors that turned him into a murderer. Like many veterans, his house had been foreclosed on in the aftermath of the financial crisis. This toxic mix involving PTSD, extremism, the financial crisis and its tragic aftermath was a recurrent theme. In May 2014, Marine Corps Sgt. Andrew Tahmooressi, who had served in Afghanistan and was being treated for PTSD in a VA hospital, was arrested in Mexico with a huge cache of heavy weaponry. If Mexican police hadn't picked him up, who knows what carnage he could have caused south of the border with his training, weapons skills and troubled psyche—all courtesy of the US military.

Disaster at the hands of a mentally troubled US service member struck again in September 2013, when an aviation electrician in the navy, Aaron Alexis, walked into a secure navy yard in Washington, DC, and shot dead twelve people. Alexis was in a lot of ways emblematic of many of the problems afflicting the US military as it dealt with the fallout from over a decade of war and occupation. He had been decorated with two of the most respected medals bestowed by the US military, and he served it honorably for four years. But he had been arrested twice on firearm offences: first, in 2004, before he signed up to the navy, and then in 2010, which precipitated his discharge from service. He was also receiving treatment from the Veterans Association for mental health problems. Alexis's father told detectives his son had "anger management problems" associated with PTSD.

As explored in this book, the scourge of PTSD is estimated to afflict upwards of 30 percent of veterans, and while resources have been added, treatment for psychological ailments is sorely lacking. The will to sort this mess out is not there in Washington. One Iraq war veteran, Omar Gonzalez, was so angry he invaded the White House and got through five rings of security in September 2014 before being caught by security. He had, like so many others, been diagnosed with PTSD after three arduous tours of Iraq during which he lost part of his foot. When he came back to the US it did not get any easier: his marriage broke down and he started living on the street. While traumatized veterans are mainly a threat to themselves—it is estimated that twenty-two veterans in the US commit suicide every day[5]—it's increasingly common for them to take their anger out on others. Still, the military paid no heed.

In the aftermath of the Navy Yard massacre, a Pentagon inspector general found that fifty-two convicted felons had "routine" unauthorized access to military facilities, "placing military personnel, dependents, civilians, and installations at an increased security risk."[6] No media reports mentioned the huge numbers of felons, and other criminals, who had been knowingly recruited by the US military when its troop needs were most serious, as detailed in the book.

The Navy Yard massacre was the second largest murder spree on a US base in history. The record in that regard was the Islamic radical Nidal Malik Hasan, who killed thirteen of his fellow soldiers at Fort Hood in November 2009. The unchecked threat to domestic military installations from US soldiers was reinforced in April 2013, when Ivan Lopez, another US soldier taking military-prescribed medication for depression and anxiety, went on a shooting rampage, again at Fort Hood in Texas, which killed three people as well as him. Investigators concluded that, like Alexis in his DC rampage, Lopez's "fragile" state of mind had been the cause of the shooting spree, remarking, "We believe that is the fundamental, underlying causal factor."[7] It was found that he hadn't been given any serious psychological treatment. Instead he was prescribed pills, the military's preferred method of care for its service members. Lopez, who served in Iraq, hadn't even been considered for early discharge based on his problems. It was a familiar story for a desperate military, and showed that their claim to have "cleaned up their act" in the wake of withdrawal from Iraq was a lie. Lopez had actually bought the .45-caliber pistol at the same store in Killeen, Texas, where Hasan had bought his own five years before.

Enduring problems

Most of the murders described above became infamous because Americans were killed en masse. But the slow-burn violence involving gangs and US military personnel continued as well, with terrible human consequences. The New York *Daily News* reported in 2013 that "Mexican drug cartels are recruiting American soldiers to act as clandestine hit men in the United States, paying them thousands of dollars to assassinate federal informants and organized crime rivals."[8] The story was picked up across the US. "We have seen examples over the past few years where American servicemen are becoming involved in this type of activity," Fred Burton, vice president for Stratfor Global Intelligence, told Fox News. "It is quite worrisome to have individuals with specialized military training and combat experience being associated with the cartels."[9] It had taken nearly a decade for this story to make it to the mainstream, and only because it was now Americans that were under threat from their military's recklessness. The unsayable truth is that criminal gangs are increasingly attractive to veterans, who often find the job market impossible to break into.

Los Zetas is a Mexican cartel that actually grew up out of disaffected former elite Mexican Special Forces, some of whom had received training at Fort Bragg. American soldiers on the same base are now joining them. The drug cartels often seek to hire *sicarios*—hit men—from the ranks of former US, Mexican, and Guatemalan military forces. The horrific "drug war" in Mexico is slowly moving over the border into the southern US states. In May 2013, four Mexican nationals were caught and charged for their part in a large methamphetamine trafficking organization. It was a vision of the future. This unfolding story with gangs in the US military remains largely unreported because they are killing only each other. That could, of course, change at any time.

In this book, I outlined cases like that of former Pfc. Michael Jackson Apodaca, who carried out a contract killing for the Juárez Cartel in 2009 while an active-duty soldier at Fort Bliss. Apodaca, who served in Afghanistan, was sentenced in an El Paso District Court to life in prison, with a chance of parole after thirty years. With the pressure of two occupations now lifted, the US military now admitted openly that it had allowed all sorts of criminals and gangs to join when they were short on numbers. "A person like Apodaca would not even be allowed to enlist today," said Army Maj.

Joe Buccino, spokesman for Fort Bliss. "We're more selective than during the height of Iraq."[10] Unfortunately even that wasn't true, but it was the updated excuse from the war years.

But the silence was proving harder to uphold. In May 2014, Juan Jesús Guerrero-Chapa, a former lawyer for the Gulf Cartel, was mowed down in a well-to-do suburb of Fort Worth, Texas. "Obviously, the nature of this homicide, the way it was carried out indicates—and I said indicates—an organization that is trained to do this type of activity," Southlake Police Chief Stephen Mylett said following the attack. "When you're dealing with individuals that operate on such a professional level, certainly caution forces me to have to lean toward that [sic] this is an organized criminal activity act."[11] Mylett conceded that the murder was a "targeted affair conducted by professional killers," but refused to be drawn on if the killers had military training. "The case is still being investigated," he added. It was even reported that two members of Los Angeles street gangs had gone to fight alongside militias linked to Syrian dictator Bashar al-Assad in the country's civil war, maybe for the same reason they had infiltrated the US military: training and weapons.[12]

The reason these events hit the news is that they happened in the US. But you do not need too much of an imagination to picture similar crimes that were inflicted on the people of Iraq and Afghanistan during a decade of occupation. How many Sikh temple massacres, Navy Yard shootings, Fort Hood rampages were there in Iraq and Afghanistan? We will never know. All the known massacres committed by US troops were initially denied, until the truth finally came out. The US military's ethos is: deny, deny, deny—until that becomes untenable because of the weight of contradictory information. The vast majority of times, we found out about US soldiers' criminal activities only when they erred back home, where the rule of law could not be so easily discarded. That fallout will keep coming.

Maybe as a result of the new military sophistication of the criminal underworld, the militarization of domestic US policing has also ramped up. This has dangerous implications not just for the hyperviolent drug gangs, but also for any American who wants to exercise his or her First Amendment rights. They are now up against militarized and heavily armed law enforcement bringing the behavior and conduct suitable to the warzone back to Main Street. The Judge Dredd–lookalike police force that was trying to "pacify" the black community in Ferguson, Missouri in 2014—after the shooting of an unarmed black teen by the police—was a portent of the future.

The absent media

The media continued to ignore the deep-rooted problems within the US military because this story so glaringly contradicted the fairytale narrative of the War on Terror. This narrative was one the US mainstream media itself had done so much to support and construct. Individual massacres and atrocities were covered to the point of saturation, but the context was missing. It was also inconceivable that the people who had been at the top of government and turned a blind eye, people like former defense secretary Donald Rumsfeld, might share some blame. Perhaps this is why there is such surprise every time there is a violent attack: Americans are inevitably told it is an outlier, not the product of a US military that allows extremism and ignores its marginalized veterans. The longer that debate is pushed off the table the worse the problem will become, and the worse the resulting violence.

In the spring of 2014, after the anti-Semitic attack near Kansas City, the *New York Times* broke the mold and bravely printed a stinging op-ed that highlighted the problem of radicalized soldiers and veterans. Its author, Kathleen Belew, a doctoral student working on a book on Vietnam and the far right, asked: "Would [Miller] have received greater scrutiny had he been a Muslim, a foreigner, not white, not a veteran? The answer is clear, and alarming."[13] She was subjected to a torrent of abuse for impugning the whole veteran community—something she went to great pains to avoid. It was the standard tactic used to shut down debate on the topic and entirely predictable. American Legion National Commander Daniel Dellinger called it a "poorly researched and agenda-driven piece," adding that "the *New York Times* should be above the slanderous stereotyping of the men and women that have defended us against the racist ideology that Ms. Belew and the *NY Times* no doubt oppose."[14] But further vindicating Belew's piece just a month later was news that recruitment fliers imploring soldiers to fight for a "white nation" in the coming race war had been discovered on Fort Carson in Colorado. "Ever wonder if you are fighting for the right side?" the flier asks, urging the soldiers to help "secure the existence of our people and a future for White children." One further report said that a surge of KKK members with military experience had allowed the Loyal White Knights to conduct combat training for the first time in its history. In this case, Allen West, a former Republican congressman and retired military officer, gave the usual line intended to shut down debate: "Why do I question this? Because I know the tactics of the liberal progressive Left, and besmirching the military to prove their long-held thesis is very important," he wrote.[15] I don't think it is too strong to say that when this "blowback" hits the next innocent Americans, the people who tried to impugn the Cassandras will bear part of the responsibility.

There is, in fact, barely anyone who spoke critically of the situation in the US military from the inside who has come out with his or her career or reputation intact. After publication of *Irregular Army*, I got to know a number of whistleblowers who had bravely exposed this issue during the War on Terror. When a Department of Homeland Security report warned in 2009 of the threat posed by far-right extremism, Secretary Janet Napolitano apologized to veterans for the report's imputation that those with military experience were especially susceptible to solicitations from far-right groups. Daryl Johnson, the senior analyst who wrote the report, was put out to pasture after a ferocious backlash from department officials, the military and some politicians on Capitol Hill. Despite the fact that Johnson's clarion call now looks increasingly prescient, he had to leave the DHS and is now a consultant. It was the same story with other whistleblowers, from Army Reserve Sgt. Jeffrey Stoleson, who alerted his superiors to the gangs in this unit, and had his life destroyed, to former DoD gang investigator Scott Barfield, who was attacked mercilessly for raising the alarm on white supremacist infiltration of the US military.

When I was interviewed by the US mainstream media, the focus was nearly always on what the findings of the book meant for Americans. No one thought it was of interest what the effect was on the populations of Iraq and Afghanistan. Ten seconds before I was to appear on MSNBC opposite a retired colonel, the producer spoke through my earpiece. "Try to keep it light on rape and massacres, please, Matt," he said. I half-laughed, but he was deadly serious. When I got over the temptation to start my first sentence with "We all know there were a lot of rapes and massacres in Iraq," I pulled no punches, despite the host saying I had written the book to make money.

These wars themselves are far from over, as the bombing of Islamic State (IS) positions in Iraq and Syria make clear. Similarly, after touting for years a complete withdrawal from Afghanistan at the end of 2014, President Obama announced, as the deadline hovered on the horizon, that 9,800 troops would be kept in the country until 2016, the year he will leave office. Many predict that as soon as withdrawal happens, the Taliban will follow IS's course and reestablish control of the country. As in Vietnam, years of war, millions of lives destroyed, gargantuan sums of money spent will have achieved nothing but a more dangerous world. The US withdrew from South Vietnam in 1973, and the embassy in Saigon was overrun in 1975. The US withdrew from Iraq in 2012, and IS militants took northern Iraq in 2014. It would not be foolish to believe that when the US finally leaves Afghanistan in 2016, a still-strong Taliban will take over in 2018. Such are the problems of an occupying power trying to impose its will on the natives. The past thirteen years of war have been a long black nightmare for the people of Iraq and Afghanistan, alongside the US soldiers occupying their countries. The future does not look much brighter—for them or for Americans now facing a new threat from their own soldiers and veterans.

London, August 2014

Notes

INTRODUCTION

1 Christopher Griffin, "The War at Home," *Armed Forces Journal*, March 2006.

2 http://www.defense.gov/speeches/speech.aspx?speechid=430.

3 Pierre Tristam, "Private Contractors in Iraq Still Double Overall Troop Presence," *About.com*, August 29, 2010; http://middleeast.about.com.

4 See Jeremy Scahill, *Blackwater* (Nation Books, 2007) and Naomi Klein, *The Shock Doctrine* (Picador, 2008).

5 Michael O'Hanlon, "Come Partly Home, America: How to Downsize U.S. Deployments Abroad," *Foreign Affairs*, March/April 2001.

6 President Bush Speaks at Naval Academy Commencement, May 25, 2001; http://www.washingtonpost.com/wp-srv/onpolitics/transcripts/bush-ext052501.htm.

7 Press Release, "One In Five Iraq and Afghanistan Veterans Suffer from PTSD or Major Depression," Rand Corp., April 17, 2008.

8 "TOP SECRET POLO STEP," The National Security Archive; http://www.gwu.edu/~nsarchiv/NSAEBB/NSAEBB214/index.htm.

9 "The Invasion and Occupation of Iraq: Conversation with Harry Kreisler"; http://globetrotter.berkeley.edu/people6/Gordon/gordon-con3.html.

10 "Army Chief says 200,000 Troops Needed to Keep the Peace," *Los Angeles Times*, February 27, 2003.

11 "TOP SECRET POLO STEP," The National Security Archive.

12 Ibid.

13 Ann Scott Tyson, "Two Years Later, Iraq War Drains Military," *Washington Post*, March 19, 2005.

14 Andrew F. Krepinevich, "The Thin Green Line," Center for Strategic and Budgetary Assessments, August 14, 2004, p. 1; http://www.observulsion.com/docs/B.20040812.GrnLne.pdf.

15 Ibid., p. 7.

16 Ibid.

17 Ibid., p. 15.

18 Ibid., p. 18.

19 Bryan Bender, "Military Considers Recruiting Foreigners," *Boston Globe*, December 26, 2006.

20 "Stray Voltage," *Armed Forces Journal*, June 1, 2005.

21 Press Release from Rangel Office, "Rangel Reintroduces Draft Bill," February 14, 2006; http://www.house.gov/list/press/ny15_rangel/CBRStatementonDraft02142006.html.

22 "Statement on House of Representatives Action on Legislation To Reinstate the Draft," *Weekly Compilation of Presidential Documents*, October 11, 2004; http://connection.ebscohost.com/c/articles/14975065/statement-house-representatives-action-legislation-reinstate-draft.

23 "Americans Reject Reinstating the Military Draft," March 18, 2006; http://www.angus-reid.com/polls/11567/americans_reject_reinstating_the_military_draft/.

24 Christian G. Appy, *Working Class War* (University of North Carolina, 1993), p. 6.

25 Ibid., p. 15.

26 Ibid., p. 32.

27 Ibid., p. 15.

28 "More Troops to be Deployed to Iraq: About 37,000 Will Come From Guard, Reserve Units," *Associated Press*, May 4, 2004.

29 http://www.unitedforpeace.org/article.php?id=2887.

30 http://www.randproject.org/news/press/2010/06/14.html.

31 "Need Help With a Down Payment? Ask the Army," *Associated Press*, August 9, 2007.

32 Jamie Wilson, "US Lowers Standards in Army Numbers Crisis," *Guardian*, June 4, 2005.

33 "Rep. Susan A. Davis Holds a Hearing on Army Recruiting and Retention—Committee Hearing," *CQ Transcriptions*, August 1, 2007.

34 "Army, Marines Allow More Convicts to Enlist," *Reuters*, April 21, 2008.

35 "Rep. Susan A. Davis Holds a Hearing on Army Recruiting and Retention—Committee Hearing," *CQ Transcriptions*, August 1, 2007.

36 All unattributed quotations in the book are drawn from interviews conducted by the author.

CHAPTER 1: THE OTHER "DON'T ASK, DON'T TELL"

1 "Screening for Potential Terrorists in the Enlisted Military Accessions Process," Defense Personnel Security Research Center, April 2005, p. 12; http://www.fas.org/irp/eprint/screening.pdf.

2 Andrew Macdonald (pseudonym), *The Turner Diaries: A Novel* (Barricade Books, 1996).

3 "Guidelines for Handling Dissident and Protest Activities Among Members of the Armed Forces," *DOD Directive 1325.6*, 1969; http://www.dtic.mil/whs/directives/corres/pdf/132506p.pdf.

4 (SPLC President) Richard Cohen, "Letter to Secretary Gates: Extremists Continue to Infiltrate Military," November 26, 2008; http://www.splcenter.org/get-informed/news/letter-to-secretary-gates-extremists-continue-to-infiltrate-military.

5 "Extremist Activities," *Department of the Army Pamphlet 600–15*, June 1, 2000; http://www.apd.army.mil/pdffiles/p600_15.pdf.

6 "Screening for Potential Terrorists in the Enlisted Military Accessions Process," Defense Personnel Security Research Center, April 2005, p. xiv.

7 The phone calls were made in March 2008, from New York City.

8 Dan Ephron, "The Guard Who Found Islam," *Newsweek*, March 21, 2009.

9 "Army Command Policy," *Army Regulation 600-20*, 18 March 18, 2008; http://www.apd.army.mil/jw2/xmldemo/r600_20/main.asp.

10 "Colonel is Top-ranking Officer Killed in Iraq," CNN, October 31, 2005.

11 Curtis Krueger, "Policing the Peace is Just Part of War," *St. Petersburg Times*, April 12, 2003.

12 "The Hammerskin Nation," Extremism in America, Anti-Defamation League; http://www.adl.org/learn/ext_us/Hammerskin.asp?LEARN_Cat=Extremism&LEARN_SubCat=Extremism_in_America&xpicked=3&item=hn.

13 David Holthouse, "A Few Bad Men: Racist Extremists Infiltrating US Military," *SPLC's Intelligence Report*, Issue 122, Summer 2006.

14 J.D. Leipold, "Army Changes Tattoo Policy," *Army News Service*, March 18, 2006.

15 Jon Ronson, "Conspirators," *Guardian*, May 5, 2001.

16 Stephen Lemons, "AZ Neo-Nazi Icon Elton Hall Hit by Vehicle While Protesting Salvador Reza's Day-labor Center," *Phoenix New Times*, February 10, 2008.

17 Mark Potok, "Rage on the Right: The Year in Hate and Extremism," *SPLC Intelligence Report*, Issue 137, Spring 2010.

18 www.newsaxon.org.

19 *www.bloodandhonour.com.*

20 Sonia Scherr, "Leaked Neo-Nazi E-mails Show Contacts With Military Personnel," *SPLC blog*, September 3, 2009.

21 Wikileaks release: NSM private emails; http://file.wikileaks.info/leak/ nsmfargo-hotmail-emails-2009/msg00273.html.

22 http://www.npr.org/news/images/2008/feb/08/eastpage1.html.

23 "US Soldier Says he Randomly Shot at Iraqis," *Associated Press*, January 9, 2008.

24 Dan Edge, "Fort Carson Soldiers' Killing Spree After Iraq Combat," *BBC News*, August 25, 2010.

25 Matt Kennard, "Neo-Nazis are in the Army Now," *Salon*, June 2009.

26 "US Marine Sniper Unit Photographed With 'Nazi SS' Flag," *BBC News*, February 10, 2012.

27 "Rightwing Extremism: Current Economic and Political Climate Fueling Resurgence in Radicalization and Recruitment," Department of Homeland Security, April 7, 2009; http://www.fas.org/irp/eprint/rightwing.pdf.

28 "White Supremacist Recruitment of Military Personnel Since 9/11," FBI report; http://cryptome.org/spy-whites.pdf.

29 "Gang-Related Activity in the US Armed Forces Increasing," National Gang Intelligence Center, January 12, 2007; http://militarytimes.com/ static/projects/pages/ngic_gangs.pdf.

30 Holthouse, "A Few Bad Men," *SPLC*, Summer 2006.

31 (SPLC President) Richard Cohen, Letter, June 7, 2011; http://beforeit-snews.com/story/696/459/SPLC_Exclusive:_DHS_Has_Stopped_ Investigating_Right-wing_Extremists.html.

32 Michael Miller, "Armed Neo-Nazis Now Patrolling Sanford, Say They Are 'Prepared' For Post-Trayvon Martin Violence," *Miami New Times Blog*, April 6, 2012.

33 Holthouse, "A Few Bad Men," *SPLC*, Summer 2006.

34 http://www.splcenter.org/get-informed/intelligence-report/browse-all-issues/2006/summer/a-few-bad-men/pentagon-in-denial.

35 Holthouse, "A Few Bad Men," *SPLC*, Summer 2006.

36 Figures obtained by the author from the DOD in 2008 through the Freedom of Information Act.

37 Summary of Investigative Activity: Reports obtained by the author from CID through the Freedom of Information Act in 2008 (from which the following quotations are taken).

38 Ibid.

39 "Screening for Potential Terrorists in the Enlisted Military Accessions Process," Defense Personnel Security Research Center, April 2005.

40 Thelma Gutierez, "Gangs in the Military—Part 1," CNN, May 9, 2007; http://transcripts.cnn.com/TRANSCRIPTS/0705/09/pzn.01.html.

41 "Former Airman Charged in Soldier's Death," *Associated Press*, February 11, 2009.

42 Steve Mraz, "Slain Soldier's Family Still Waiting for Justice," *Stars and Stripes*, May 30, 2006.

43 Tech. Sgt. Kati Garcia, "Little Rock Airman Convicted, Sentenced in Court-martial," Air Force website, January 27, 2009; http://www.af.mil/news/story.asp?id=123132916.

44 "Armed Services Defendant Arrested and Charged With Second Degree Murder of Army Sergeant Juwan Johnson in Hohenecken, Germany," Department of Justice, February 6, 2009; http://www.justice.gov/usao/dc/Press_Releases/2009%20Archives/February/09-034.html.

45 "Former U.S. Air Force Airman Convicted of Second Degree Murder of Army Sergeant in Germany," *US Fed News*, November 16, 2010.

46 "Soldier Convicted in Gang Beating Death of Sgt.," *Associated Press*, February 26, 2009.

47 "Verdict in Gang-initiation Death Trial Angers Victim's Mother," *Stars and Stripes*, February 27, 2009.

48 Garcia, "Little Rock Airman Convicted, Sentenced in Court-martial," Air Force website, January 27, 2009.

49 Steve Mraz, "Soldier Says Life Threatened for Speaking Up," *Stars and Stripes*, February 10, 2007 (from which the following quotations are taken).

50 "Gang-Related Activity in the US Armed Forces Increasing," National Gang Intelligence Center, January 12, 2007 (from which the following quotations are taken).

51 Rod Powers, "Army Criminal History Waivers," *About.com*; http://usmilitary.about.com/od/armyjoin/a/criminal.-u59.htm.

52 "Gang-Related Activity in the US Armed Forces Increasing," National Gang Intelligence Center, January 12, 2007.

53 Gustav Eyler, "Gangs in the Military," *The Yale Law Journal*, Vol. 118, 2009.

54 Seth Robson, "FBI Says U.S. Criminal Gangs are Using Military to Spread Their Reach," *Stars and Stripes*, December 7, 2006.

55 Eyler, "Gangs in the Military" (from which the following quotations are taken).

56 "Gang-Related Activity in the US Armed Forces Increasing," National Gang Intelligence Center, January 12, 2007.

57 Ibid.

58 "Exclusive: Gangs Spreading in the Military," CBS News, July 28, 2007.

59 Robson, "FBI Says U.S. Criminal Gangs are Using Military to Spread Their Reach."

60 "Local Police Say Fort Sill Has a Gang Problem," *Associated Press*, November 10, 2008.

61 Ron Jackson, "Fort Sill Gang Dispute Intensifies," *Newsok.com*, November 11, 2008; http://newsok.com/fort-sill-gang-dispute-intensifies/article/3320983.

62 Josh Gerstein, "Army Transfers Could Trigger A Gang War," *New York Sun*, March 16, 2006 (from which the following quotations are taken).

63 H.R. 4986: National Defense Authorization Act for Fiscal Year 2008; http://www.govtrack.us/congress/bill.xpd?tab=summary&bill=h110-4986.

64 Leo Shane III, "Bill Would Ban Gang Membership in Ranks," *Stars and Stripes*, December 15, 2007.

65 Ibid.

66 Eyler, "Gangs in the Military."

67 "National Gang Threat Assessment 2009," National Gang Intelligence Center, January 2009.

68 Ibid.

69 Ibid.

70 James M. Klatell, "Are Gang Members Using Military Training?," *CBS News*, July 28, 2007.

71 "Inside the FBI," podcast, February 6, 2009; http://www.fbi.gov/news/podcasts/inside/gangs/view.

72 "Gang Activity in the Military," KFOX TV, March 13, 2006; http://www.kfoxtv.com/news/7978035/detail.html

73 "Gang Members in the Army, Part I," California Department of Justice, November, 2005; http://img2.tapuz.co.il/forums/1_90024783.pdf.

74 Garth Stapley, "Family of Slain Ceres Officer Speaks to Help Others Weather Own Tragedies," *The Modesto Bee*, January 11, 2010.

75 "Gang Members in the Army, Part I," California Department of Justice, November, 2005.

76 http://icasualties.org.

77 "National Gang Threat Assessment 2009," National Gang Intelligence Center, January, 2009.

78 Ben Conery, "U.S., Mexican Drug Gangs Form Alliances," *Washington Times*, March 26, 2010.

79 "Clinton Pledges Broader US Effort on Mexico Drugs Gangs," BBC News, March 24, 2010; http://news.bbc.co.uk/1/hi/8582497.stm.

80 "3 Teens Charged in Cartel Slaying," *Associated Press*, August 13, 2009.

81 http://articles.latimes.com/2009/aug/13/nation/na-drug-killing13.

82 "US Army Soldier Michael Jackson Apodaca Arrested for Contract Kill in Mexican Drug Cartel Murder," *New York Daily News*, August 11, 2009.

83 Geoffrey Ramsey, "Arrest of Would-Be 'Zetas' Shows Risk of US Military Infiltration," *InSight Crime*, March 29, 2012; http://insightcrime.org/insight-latest-news/item/2415-arrest-of-would-be-zetas-shows-risk-of-us-military-infiltration.

84 "Gang-Related Activity in the US Armed Forces Increasing," National Gang Intelligence Center, January 12, 2007.

85 "Soldier Accused in Gang Shootings," *Baltimore Sun*, October 17, 2007.

86 "Soldier Held in City Shooting Could be Freed," *Baltimore Sun*, October 18, 2007.

87 "Gang-Related Activity in the US Armed Forces Increasing," National Gang Intelligence Center, January 12, 2007.

88 "Gang Members in the Army, Part I," California Department of Justice, November 2005.

89 "Ex-Guard Soldier Faces Gun Smuggling Charges," *Associated Press*, September 22, 2006.

90 Linda Rosencrance, "GAO: Stolen U.S. Military Gear Sold on eBay, Craigslist," *Computerworld*, April 14, 2008.

91 Timothy Roberts, "City to Vote on Assault Rifle Buy, Cops Want an M-4 in Every Patrol Car," *El Paso Times*, January 12, 2010.

92 Eric M. Weiss, "Probe: Robbers Used Weapons Smuggled From Iraq by Soldier," *Washington Post*, July 16, 2006 (from which the following quotations are taken).

93 "Tancredo Concerned Military Officials Unaware of Gang Infiltration in U.S. Army," Rep. Tancredo's Congressional Website, April 9, 2008; http://tancredo.house.gov.

94 Art Winslow, "Review: *Black Hearts: One Platoon's Descent into Madness in Iraq's Triangle of Death*, by Jim Frederick," *Chicago Tribune*; http://www.chicagotribune.com/entertainment/books/chi-books-reviews-black-hearts-frederick,0,5714703.story.

95 Jim Frederick, "The Blackest Hearts: War Crimes in Iraq," *Guardian*, July 24, 2010.

96 Wikileaks Iraq War Logs; www.wikileaks.ch.

97 "Disabilities of Convicted Felons: A State-by-State Survey, 1996," US Department of Justice; https://www.ncjrs.gov/pdffiles1/pr/195110.pdf.

98 Michael Boucai, "Balancing Your Strengths Against Your Felonies: Considerations for Military Recruitment of Ex-Offenders," *Palm Center*, September 2007.

99 "Military Grants More Waivers to Recruits," *Associated Press*, February 14, 2007.

100 "Military Enlistment of Felons Has Doubled," *Palm Center Report*, February 13, 2007.

101 Ibid.

102 Al Baker, "Soldier Says Pardon Buoys His Hopes for Police Career," *New York Times*, January 2, 2010.

103 "A Well-earned Second Chance," *New York Daily News*, January 2, 2010.

104 Sig Christenson, "When Inmates Become US Army Soldiers," *San Antonio Express-News*, March 22, 2010.

105 Ibid.

106 Ann Scott Tyson, "Military Waivers for Ex-Convicts Increase," *Washington Post*, April 22, 2008.

107 Ibid.

108 "Military Recruiting: New Initiatives Could Improve Criminal History Screening," GAO Report, February 23, 1999; http://www.gao.gov/archive/1999/ns99053.pdf.

109 Boucai, "Balancing Your Strengths Against Your Felonies."

110 Lizette Alvarez, "Army Giving More Waivers in Recruiting," *New York Times*, February 14, 2007.

111   Lizette Alvarez, "Army And Marine Corps Grant More Felony Waivers," *New York Times*, April 22, 2008.

112   "Marine Who Killed Iraqi Set Free," *Associated Press*, December 15, 2007.

113   Russell Carollo, "Troops Linked to Crimes in Iraq War were Recruited Despite Troubled Pasts," *Macon Telegraph*, July 20, 2008 (from which the following quotations are taken).

114   Perry Jefferies, Letters, *New York Times*, February 25, 2007.

115   Alvarez, "Army And Marine Corps Grant More Felony Waivers."

116   "Waxman Requests Pentagon Docs on Recruitment," *Politico.com*, April 21, 2008; http://www.politico.com/blogs/thecrypt/0408/Waxman_requests_Pentagon_docs_on_recruitment.html.

117   "More Convicted Felons Allowed to Enlist in Army, Marines," *Associated Press*, April 21, 2008.

118   "Military Takes More Recruits with Criminal Pasts," *Associated Press*, October 10, 2007.

119   "House Panel Probes Army's Waivers for Recruits With Criminal Histories," *CQ Today*, April 21, 2008.

120   Scott Tyson, "Military Waivers for Ex-Convicts Increase."

121   Adam Liptak, "1 in 100 U.S. Adults Behind Bars, New Study Says," *New York Times*, February 28, 2008.

122   "Military Enlistment of Felons has Doubled," *Palm Center Report*, February 13, 2007.

123   "Jailhouse Recruiting," Local CBS News Channel; http://www.youtube.com/watch?v=WvXkQHuuZN0.

124   "Rep. Susan A. Davis Holds a Hearing on Army Recruiting and Retention—Committee Hearing," *CQ Transcriptions*, 1 August 2007.

125   Mark Benjamin, "Out of Jail, Into the Army," *Salon*, February 2, 2006.

126   Sig Christenson, "From Prison Stripes to Sergeant's Stripes," *San Antonio Express-News*, March 21, 2010.

127   Ann Scott Tyson, "Army More Selective as Economy Lags," *Washington Post*, April 17, 2009.

128   Ned Parker, "Sniper Unit Chief Tells of Ordering Slaying," *Los Angeles Times*, February 9, 2008.

129   Ibid.

130   Carollo, "Troops Linked to Crimes in Iraq War Were Recruited Despite Troubled Pasts."

131   Ibid.

132 "Complaint," United District Court in the Eastern District of Virginia, February 15, 2011.

133 Matt Kennard, "Pentagon Harassment Suit May Spark Further Action," *Financial Times*, April 15, 2011.

134 Elisabeth Bumiller, "Sex Assault Reports Rise in Military," *New York Times*, March 16, 2010.

135 Kennard, "Pentagon Harassment Suit May Spark Further Action."

136 "Sexual Assault in Military 'Jaw-dropping,' Lawmaker Says," CNN, July 31, 2008.

CHAPTER 2: SICK, ADDICTED, AND FORSAKEN

1 Lizette Alvarez, "After the Battle, Fighting the Bottle at Home," *New York Times*, July 8, 2008.

2 Greg Miller, "Alcohol Cited as Problem at Prison," *Los Angeles Times*, July 13, 2004.

3 Ibid.

4 Statistics obtained from the DOD by the author via the Freedom of Information Act.

5 Paul von Zielbauer, "For U.S. Troops at War, Liquor Is Spur to Crime," *New York Times*, March 13, 2007,

6 Ibid.

7 Gregg Zoroya, "More Soldiers Seek Drug Abuse Help," *USA Today*, November 21, 2008.

8 Ibid.

9 Alvarez, "After the Battle, Fighting the Bottle at Home."

10 Paul von Zielbauer, "In Iraq, American Military Finds it Has an Alcohol Problem," *New York Times*, March 12, 2007.

11 Ibid.

12 "Study: Binge Drinking Common in Military," CBS News, February 13, 2009; http://www.cbsnews.com/stories/2009/02/13/health/main4800944.shtml.

13 Corey Pein, "US Military's Party Budget Includes Thousands For Alcohol in Afghanistan," War Is Business website, December 31, 2010; http://www.warisbusiness.com/features/ledger/military-alcohol-in-afghanistan/.

14 Charles Laurence, "How the Iraq War is Destroying America's Fighting Men," *Daily Mail*, March 20, 2007.

15 Ibid.

16 Ibid.

17 "Afghan Alcohol Ban After Nato Staff Were 'Too Hungover' to Give Explanation for Airstrike that Killed 70 Civilians," *Daily Mail*, September 9, 2009.

18 "Alcohol Banned on Afghanistan Base After Troops Party Too Hard," *Daily Telegraph*, September 8, 2009.

19 "Alcohol Abuse on Rise Among US Soldiers: Reports," *AFP*, June 19, 2009.

20 Ewen MacAskill and David Batty, "US Embassy Bans Alcohol at Guards' Quarters After Claims of 'Lewd' Parties," *Guardian*, September 3, 2009.

21 Ibid.

22 "Report: U.S. Sailor Arrested in Killing in Japan," *Associated Press*, April 3, 2008.

23 "Drunk American Kills Prized Bengal Tiger," Sky News, September 20, 2003.

24 "Afghan Drug Trafficking Brings US $50 Billion a Year," *Russia Today*, August 20, 2009.

25 Shaun McCanna, "It's Easy for Soldiers to Score Heroin in Afghanistan," *Salon*, August 7, 2007.

26 http://www.heroin-detox.org/drug_czar.htm.

27 McCanna, "It's Easy for Soldiers to Score Heroin in Afghanistan."

28 Robert Lewis and Kate McCarthy, "War Vets Fighting Addiction," ABC News, November 26, 2007.

29 Lisa Daniel, "October is Drug Abuse Prevention Month," American Forces Press Service, October 16, 2010.

30 Hugh C. McBride, "Alcohol Abuse on the Rise Among Combat Veterans"; http://www.drug-rehabs.com/addiction_alcohol-abuse-among-combat-vets.htm.

31 Gregg Zoroya, "More Soldiers Seek Drug Abuse Help," *USA Today*, November 21, 2008.

32 Ibid.

33 Brad Knickerbocker, "Military Looks to Drugs for Battle Readiness," *The Christian Science Monitor*, August 9, 2002.

34 Elliot Borin, "The U.S. Military Needs Its Speed," *Wired*, February 10, 2003.

35 Ibid.

36 Melody Petersen, "U.S. Military: Heavily Armed and Medicated,"

MSNBC, May 19, 2009; http://www.msnbc.msn.com/id/30748260/ns/health-health_care/.

37 Ibid.

38 Ibid.

39 "U.S. Soldiers Involved in Drug Smuggling Ring," ABC News, October 26, 2005.

40 Ibid.

41 David Adam, "Ecstasy Trials for Combat Stress," *Guardian*, February 17, 2005.

42 "PTSD Symptom Reduction by Propranolol Given After Trauma Memory Activation"; http://clinicaltrials.gov/ct2/show/NCT00645450.

43 Ibid.

44 Clayton Dach, "America's Chemically Modified 21st Century Soldiers," *Alternet*, May 3, 2008.

45 Brandon Keim, "Uncle Sam Wants Your Brain," *Wired*, August 13, 2008.

46 Brian Ross and Vic Walter, "'Disposable Heroes': Veterans Used To Test Suicide-Linked Drugs," ABC News, June 17, 2008.

47 Jake Tapper and Maddy Sauer, "Obama on Vet Drug Tests: 'Outrageous'; Meanwhile WH Slams ABC News Report," ABC News, June 17, 2008.

48 Tony Newman, "Support the Troops: Especially When They Come Back with Substance Abuse Problems," *Commondreams.org*, August 2, 2005; http://www.commondreams.org/views05/0802-21.htm.

49 Alvarez, "After the Battle, Fighting the Bottle at Home."

50 Lewis and McCarthy, "War Vets Fighting Addiction."

51 McCanna, "It's Easy for Soldiers to Score Heroin in Afghanistan."

52 Lizette Alvarez, "Concerns Grow About Treatment for Veterans," *New York Times*, July 9, 2008.

53 Alvarez, "After the Battle, Fighting the Bottle at Home."

54 www.thatguy.com.

55 Penny Coleman, "Pentagon, Big Pharma: Drug Troops to Numb Them to Horrors of War," *Alternet*, January 10, 2008.

56 Petersen, "U.S. Military: Heavily Armed and Medicated."

57 Paul Harasim, "Grieving Family Hopes Army Finds What Prompted Suicide," *Las Vegas Review-Journal*, September 11, 2007.

58 David Olinger and Erin Emery, "Waging Internal War," *Denver Post*, August 27, 2008.

59 Ibid.

60 Ibid.

61 "Rep. Berkley Issues Statement on Truth about Veterans' Suicides," *US Fed News*, May 6, 2008.

62 Olinger and Emery, "Waging Internal War."

63 Lizzette Alvarez, "Suicides of Soldiers Reach High of Nearly 3 Decades," *New York Times*, January 29, 2009.

64 Mike Mount, "June Was Worst Month for Army Suicides, Statistics Show," CNN, July 15, 2010; http://www.rawa.org/temp/runews/2010/07/15/june-was-worst-month-for-army-suicides-statistics-show.html#ixzz18Bwhrq67.

65 Aaron Glantz, "After Service, Veteran Deaths Surge," *New York Times*, October 16, 2010.

66 Michael Riley and Tom Roeder, "Intense Combat Tied to Homicides by Ft. Carson GIs," *Denver Post*, July 16, 2009.

67 Tom Roeder, "Fort Carson Report: Combat Stress Contributed to Soldiers' Crimes Back Home," *The Gazette*, July 16, 2009.

68 Ibid.

69 Bill Berkowitz, "The Military's Mounting Mental Health Problems," *Alternet*, April 30, 2004.

70 Mark Benjamin, "Army Sent Mentally Ill Troops to Iraq," *UPI*, March 12, 2004; http://www.upi.com/Business_News/Security-Industry/2004/03/12/Army-sent-mentally-ill-troops-to-Iraq/UPI-97331079131967/.

71 "Army Tours in Iraq to be Extended, Gates Says," MSNBC, April 11, 2007; http://www.msnbc.msn.com/id/18059112/ns/world_news-mideast_n_africa/t/army-tours-iraq-be-extended-gates-says/#.T3nSBL9rPNo.

72 William Yardley, "Killings Add to Worries at Soldier's Home Base," *New York Times*, March 11, 2012.

73 "Report: Suicidal Troops Sent into Combat," *Associated Press*, May 13, 2006.

74 Rick Rogers, "Some Troops Headed Back to Iraq are Mentally Ill," *Union-Tribune*, March 19, 2006.

75 "Report: Suicidal Troops Sent into Combat," *Associated Press*, May 13, 2006.

76 Army Maj. Gen. Raymond Palumbo, "Resiliency is the Key to Success," Joint Base Elmendorf-Richardson Website, November 10, 2011; http://www.jber.af.mil/news/story.asp?id=123279673.

77 Petersen, "U.S. Military: Heavily Armed and Medicated" (from which the following quotations are taken).

78 "WikiLeaks Accused Bradley Manning 'should never have been sent to Iraq'," *Guardian*, May 27, 2011.

79 Evan Hansen, "Manning-Lamo Chat Logs Revealed," *Wired*, July 13, 2011.

80 Elizabeth Curlee, "Mental Illness in the Military on the Rise," CBS News, June 15, 2007.

81 Ibid.

82 "Democrats Slam Budget Cuts for Veterans' Services," CNN, March 19, 2005.

83 Thomas B. Edsall, "Funds for Health Care of Veterans $1 Billion Short," *Washington Post*, June 24, 2005.

84 "Bush FY 2006 Budget Proposal Might Mean 'Deep Cuts' in Veterans' Health Care," *Kaiserhealthnews.org*, February 13, 2005; http://www. kaiserhealthnews.org/Daily-Reports/2005/February/11/dr00028116.aspx.

85 Editorial, "Veterans Without Health Care," *New York Times*, November 9, 2007.

86 Ibid.

87 Ann Scott Tyson, "Pentagon Report Criticizes Troops' Mental-Health Care," *Washington Post*, June 16, 2007.

88 Bob Egelko, "Veterans Not Entitled to Mental Health Care, U.S. Lawyers Argue," *San Francisco Chronicle*, February 5, 2008.

89 Linda D. Kozaryn, "President Honors Veterans, Families at USS Intrepid Ceremony," *American Forces Press Service*, November 11, 2008.

90 Matt Kennard, "Obama Under Pressure Over Veterans Benefits," *Financial Times*, March 3, 2011.

91 Matthew Kauffman and Lisa Chedekel, "Slipping Through the System Special Report: Mentally Unfit, Forced to Fight," *The Hartford Courant*, May 15, 2006 (from which the following quotations are taken).

92 Michael de Yoanna and Mark Benjamin, "I am Under a Lot of Pressure to Not Diagnose PTSD," *Salon*, April 8, 2009.

93 Roeder, "Fort Carson Report: Combat Stress Contributed to Soldiers' Crimes Back Home."

94 "Study Finds Toops Shy Away From Mental Health Care," CNN, April 30, 2008.

95 Sgt. Joshua Risner, "Tour Raises Awareness of Mental Illness," *Army News Service*, September 9, 2009.

96 "One in Five Iraq and Afghanistan Veterans Suffer from PTSD or Major Depression," Rand Corp., April 17, 2008.

97 Ann Zieger, "U.S. Mental Health Spending Rising Rapidly," *Health News*, August 6, 2009.

98 Wendell Marsh, "Jobless Rate Among Veterans Highest in Five Years," *Reuters*, February 5, 2011.

99 Kennard, "Obama Under Pressure over Veteran Benefits" (from which the following quotations are taken).

100 Robert Longley, "VA-HUD Issue First-Ever Homeless Veterans Report," *About.com*, February 14, 2011; http://usgovinfo.about.com/od/resourcesforveterans/a/Homeless-Veterans-Report.htm.

101 "Boxer Joins Colleagues, Veterans Advocates to Oppose Extreme GOP Proposal to Deny Housing to 10,000 Homeless Veterans," Press Release of U.S. Senator Barbara Boxer, March 10, 2011.

102 Craig Roberts, "HUD-VASH Vouchers Survive Budget Cut," *The American Legion*, April 13, 2011.

103 Rick Maze, "18 Veterans Commit Suicide Each Day," *Army Times*, April 22, 2010.

104 Matt Kennard, "US Companies in Iraq: Touting for Business," *Financial Times' Beyond Brics blog*, August 30, 2011.

CHAPTER 3: PLUMP, YOUNG, DUMB— AND READY TO SERVE

1 "Too Fat to Fight? Obesity Becomes National Security Issue, Weight Would Disqualify Many Potential Military Recruits," *University of Buffalo News Release*, November 27, 2002; http://www.buffalo.edu/news/fast-execute.cgi/article-page.html?article=59700009.

2 "An Overweight Army," *The Douglass Report*, September 26, 2005; http://douglassreport.com/2005/09/26/an-overweight-army/.

3 "Too Fat to Fight? . . .," *University at Buffalo News Release*, November 27, 2002.

4 Medical Surveillance Monthly Report, Volume 16, Number 01, Armed Forces Health Surveillance Center, January 2009.

5 "Top Army Recruiter Weighs Fat Camp for Recruits," *Associated Press*, January 12, 2009.

6 Julia Sommerfeld, "Battling the Bulge," *Knight Ridder News Service*, May 12, 2003.

7 Ibid.

8 Chris Ayres, "US Troops are Losing Battle of the Bulge," *Times*, November 18, 2002.

9 Ibid.

10 Alvarez, "Army And Marine Corps Grant More Felony Waivers."

11 Douglas Belkin, "Struggling for Recruits, Army Relaxes its Rules," *Boston Globe*, February 20, 2006.

12 Matt Kennard, "Army Discharge Stats Suggest that Wartime Breeds a New Attitude Towards Soldiers Who are 'Different,'" *Columbia News Service*, April 15, 2008.

13 "Top Army Recruiter Weighs Fat Camp for Recruits," *Associated Press*, 12 January, 2009 (from which the following two quotations are taken).

14 Bo Joyner, "Fit to Fight: Program Pushes Reservists to Pursue Healthier Lifestyle," *Citizen Airman*, August 2004.

15 Andrew Tilghman, "New Rules Allow More Body Fat With Age," *Marine Corps Times*, March 31, 2008.

16 "Obesity in the Military on the Rise," *RedOrbit.com*, February 11, 2009; http://www.redorbit.com/news/health/1637795/obesity_in_the_military_on_the_rise/.

17 Documents obtained by the author from the Pentagon through the Freedom of Information Act.

18 Ibid.

19 Letters, *Army Times*, January 28, 2010.

20 Sandra Jontz, "More Servicemembers Fighting Battle of Bulge," *Stars and Stripes*, February 11, 2009.

21 Oliver August, "'Battle of the Bulge' Begins as US Troops Stand Easy," *Times*, November 13, 2009.

22 Ibid.

23 Mark Townsend, "British Army Changes Rules to Allow Obese Recruits to Enlist," *Observer*, August 2, 2009.

24 Ibid.

25 Neva Grant, "Helping Dropouts Break the Cycle of Poverty," National Public Radio, March 27, 2006; http://www.npr.org/templates/story/story.php?storyId=5300726.

26 First Lt. Kyle Key and Spc. Austin Hurt, "Guard's Patriot Academy Gives Dropouts Second Chance," *Army.mil*, August 27, 2009; www.army.mil/article/26681/ (from which the following quotations are taken).

27 Sgt. Brad Staggs, Indiana National Guard, "First Student Arrives for First Patriot Academy Class," *NationalGuard.mil*, June 3, 2009; http://www.nationalguard.mil/news/archives/2009/06/060309-First.aspx.

28 "Readiness Subcommittee Hearing on Budget Request for Army Reserve, Army National Guard and Air National Guard Training and Operations," *Gpo.gov*, April 27, 2010; http://www.gpo.gov/fdsys/pkg/CHRG-111hhrg58105/html/CHRG-111hhrg58105.htm.

29 Diana Penner, "Centerpiece; Taking on a Challenge," *Indianapolis Star*, August 27, 2009.

30 Sgt. Mike R. Smith, "Guard's Education and Youth Programs Take Center Stage in Atlanta," *National Guard Bureau*, July 28, 2009.

31 Sgt. Robert G. Cooper III, "Patriot Academy Offers Soldiers Second Chance at High School Diploma," *Arng.army.mil*, August 26, 2009; http://www.arng.army.mil/News/Pages/PatriotAcademy.aspx.

32 Sgt. David Bruce, "Patriot Academy Diversifies Student Body," *Army.mil*, July 13, 2010; http://www.army.mil/article/42178/.

33 "Ready, Willing, and Unable to Serve," A Report by Mission: Readiness; http://d15h7vkr8e4okv.cloudfront.net/NATEE1109.pdf.

34 Ibid.

35 James J. Heckman and Paul A. LaFontaine, "The Declining American High School Graduation Rate: Evidence, Sources, and Consequences," The National Bureau of Economic Research, February 13, 2008.

36 Neva Grant, "Helping Dropouts Break the Cycle of Poverty," *NPR*, March 27, 2006; http://www.npr.org/templates/story/story.php?storyId=5300726.

37 Mark Thompson, "Army Recruiting More Dropouts," *Time*, January 23, 2008.

38 Henry Giroux, "Obama's Betrayal of Public Education? Arne Duncan and the Corporate Model of Schooling," *Truthout*, December 17, 2008; http://www.truth-out.org/121708R.

39 Program's website: http://www.ngycp.org/.

40 Eric Eckholm, "Discipline of Military Redirects Dropouts," *New York Times*, March 7, 2009.

41 Ibid.

42 "Ready, Willing, and Unable to Serve," A Report by Mission: Readiness.

43 "Army Opens Prep School for Recruited Dropouts," *Associated Press*, August 27, 2008 (from which the following quotations are taken).

44 http://www.arng.army.mil/News/publications/fs/2008/graphics/afr_fy08_text.doc.

45 Army National Guard Annual Financial Report, FY2009; http://www.arng.army.mil/News/publications/fs/2009/index.htm.

46 Appy, *Working Class War*, p. 32.

47 Ibid.

48 Thompson, "Army Recruiting More Dropouts."

49 "US Military Heads for Crisis in Recruitment," *New York Times News Service*, June 12, 2005; http://www.taipeitimes.com/News/world/archives/2005/06/12/2003258996.

50 Mark C. Young and Leonard A. White, "Preliminary Operational Findings From the Army's Tier Two Attrition Screen (TTAS) Measure," U.S. Army Research Institute for the Behavioral and Social Sciences; http://www.dtic.mil/cgi-bin/GetTRDoc?AD=ADA481765.

51 Tom Philpott, "Army Signs More Dropouts," *Military.com*, November 22, 2006; http://www.military.com/features/0,15240,119382,00.html.

52 Eric Schmitt, "Army Recruiting More High School Dropouts to Meet Goals," *New York Times*, June 11, 2005.

53 Fred Kaplan, "GI Schmo," *Slate*, January 9, 2006.

54 Schmitt, "Army Recruiting More High School Dropouts to Meet Goals."

55 Richard Herrnstein and Charles Murray, *The Bell Curve: Intelligence and Class Structure in American Life* (Free Press, 1994).

56 Thompson, "Army Recruiting More Dropouts."

57 "DOD Instruction," March 14, 2006, http://www.dtic.mil/whs/directives/corres/pdf/130430p.pdf.

58 Thompson, "Army Recruiting More Dropouts."

59 Young and White, "Preliminary Operational Findings From the Army's Tier Two Attrition Screen (TTAS) Measure."

60 DOD Instruction, March 14, 2006, http://www.dtic.mil/whs/directives/corres/pdf/130430p.pdf.

61 Jennifer Kavanagh, "Determinants of Productivity for Military Personnel," Rand Corp., 2005; http://www.rand.org/pubs/technical_reports/TR193.html.

62 "Army Recruiter Threatens High School Student with Jail Time," *Democracy Now, August 7, 2008 (from which the following quotations are taken);* http://www.alternet.org/story/94192/army_recruiter_threatens_high_school_student_with_jail_time/.

63 Damien Cave, "Army Recruiters Say They Feel Pressure to Bend Rules," *New York Times*, May 3, 2005.

64 "School Recruiting Program Handbook, *USAREC Pamphlet 350-13*, September 1, 2004 (from which the following quotations are taken).

65 Karen Houppert, "Military Recruiters Are Now Targeting Sixth Graders. Who's Next?," *The Nation*, September 5, 2005.

66 "Detailed Information on the Junior Reserve Officer Training Corps Assessment"; http://www.whitehouse.gov/omb/expectmore/detail/10003233. 2006.html.

67 Andy Kroll, "Fast Times at Recruitment High," *Mother Jones*, August 31, 2009.

68 "Military Training Program for Teens Expands in US," *Agence France-Presse*, November 25, 2007.

69 Houppert, "Military Recruiters Are Now Targeting Sixth Graders. Who's Next?"

70 Mike McAndrew, "Teenagers, the U.S. Army Wants You," *Syracuse Post-Standard*, June 22, 2008 (from which the following quotations are taken).

71 ASVAB website; http://www.military.com/Recruiting/ASVAB/0,13387,, 00.html.

72 Ibid.

73 "Reauthorization of the Elementary and Secondary Education Act of 2001 (No Child Left Behind Act of 2001)"; http://www.notyoursoldier. org/section.php?id=13.

74 David Goodman, "A Few Good Kids?," *Mother Jones*, September/October 2009.

75 Robert Hodierne, "Concern Over US Army Recruitment," BBC News, August 23, 2006 (from which the following quotations are taken).

76 Jim Lobe, "School Military Recruiting Could Violate International Law," *Inter Press Service*, May 14, 2008.

77 Carrie McLeroy, "Army Experience Center opens in Philadelphia," *Army News Service*, September 2, 2008.

78 "Recruiting Center to Have Flight Sims, Video Games," *Stars and Stripes*, June 16, 2008.

79 Holly M. Sanders, "An Army of Fun," *New York Post*, June 15, 2008.

80 Kathy Matheson, "Flashy Army Recruitment Center in Pa. Mall Closing," *Associated Press*, June 11, 2010.

81 http://shutdowntheaec.net.

82 "Computer Games Liven up Military Recruiting, Training," *National Defense*, November 1, 2002.

83 Clark Boyd, "US Army Cuts Teeth on Video Game," BBC News, November 25, 2005.

84 Anne Broache, "Video Games in Congress' Crosshairs," June 2, 2006; http://news.cnet.com/Video-games-in-Congress-crosshairs/2100-1028_3-6079654.html#ixzz18ZzXU6HT.

85 Tom Leonard, "Boy Scouts Train for Badge in Anti-terrorism," *Daily Telegraph*, May 15, 2009.

86 Kevin Johnson, "Police Tie Jump in Crime to Juveniles," *USA Today*, July 12, 2006.

87 Damien Cave, "Growing Problem for Military Recruiters: Parents," *New York Times*, June 3, 2005.

88 Kelley Beaucar Vlahos, "Heavy Military Recruitment at High Schools Irks Some Parents," Fox News, June 23, 2005.

89 Donna Tam, "Eureka, Arcata Lose Youth Protection Act Appeal," *The Times-Standard*, December 18, 2010.

90 Lizza Minno, "Bushwick Teens Resist Recruiting," *Indypendent*, March 14, 2008 (from which the following quotations are taken).

91 Noah Shachtman, "OMG! Navy Calls MySpace Kids 'Alien Life Force' (And They Hate the War, Too)," *Wired*, September 28, 2007.

92 Michael Felberbaum, "Army Likes its Older Recruits," *Associated Press*, December 11, 2006.

93 "Slain Soldier Rejoined Army to Help Others," *Associated Press*, January 2, 2009.

94 David L. Teibel, "More Than 200 Gather to Honor Fallen Cpl. Gaffney, an ex-Tucsonan," *Tucson Citizen*, January 5, 2009.

95 Robert Smith, "Soldier Paid Tribute at Remembrance Ceremony," *The Leaf-Chronicle*, February 12, 2009.

96 Lisa Burgess, "Army Raises Maximum Enlistment Age for New Recruits from 40 to 42," *Stars and Stripes*, June 23, 2006.

97 Tom Vanden Brook, "Older Recruits are Finding Less Success in Army," *USA Today*, February 19, 2007.

98 Patrik Jonsson, "Newest Army Recruits: The Over-35 Crowd," *The Christian Science Monitor*, September 6, 2006.

99 Felberbaum, "Army Likes its Older Recruits."

100 Leo Shane III, "Army Reopens Retiree Recall Program," *Stars and Stripes*, August 14, 2009.

101 Ibid.

102 Vanden Brook, "Older Recruits are Finding Less Success in Army."

103 Shane, "Army Reopens Retiree Recall Program."

104 Felberbaum, "Army Likes its Older Recruits."

105 James Dao, "Older Recruits Challenge Army and Vice Versa," *New York Times*, June 17, 2009.

106 Vanden Brook, "Older Recruits are Finding Less Success in Army."

107 Aamer Madhani, "Schaumburg Man Served in Vietnam," *Chicago Tribune*, May 21, 2004.

108 "Army Accepting Older Recruits," *Associated Press*, August 19, 2006.

109 Brian MacQuarrie, "Older Recruits Fill Out Military," *Boston Globe*, October 23, 2006.

110 Felberbaum, "Army Likes its Older Recruits."

111 Ibid.

112 "Americans Living Longer, Enjoying Greater Health and Prosperity, but Important Disparities Remain, Says Federal Report," National Institute of Aging, March 27, 2008.

113 "Army Accepting Older Recruits," *Associated Press*, August 19, 2006.

114 "Military Draws Older Recruits," *Detroit News*, February 21, 2009.

115 Dao, "Older Recruits Challenge Army and Vice Versa" (from which the following quotations are taken).

CHAPTER 4: OUTSIDERS

1 "Militarization of US Immigrant Rights Movement Dangerous," *Russia Today*, May 26, 2010.

2 Bill Hendrick, "Troops' Deaths Bring Conflict Home," *The Atlanta Journal-Constitution*, March 23, 2003.

3 Film: *The Short Life of José Gutierrez*, Dir: Heidi Specogna, Atopia, 2006 (from which all unattributed quotes in the following pages are taken).

4 Walter LaFeber, *The American Age: US Foreign Policy at Home adn Abroad, 1750 to the Present* (New York, 1994), p. 546.

5 Ibid.

6 Ibid.

7 "Clinton: Backing Dictators was Wrong," BBC News, March 11, 1999.

8 Simon Crittle, "In Death, a Marine Gets his Life Wish," *Time*, March 28, 2003.

9 Jeordan Legon, "Fallen Marine Wanted to Give Back to Adopted Country," CNN; http://edition.cnn.com/SPECIALS/2003/iraq/heroes/jose.gutier-rez.html.

10 Bryan Bender, "A U.S. Military 'at its breaking point' Considers Foreign Recruits," *New York Times*, December 26, 2006.

11 "Non-Citizens in Today's Military Research Brief," CNA; http://cna.org/centers/marine-corps/selected-studies/non-citizens-brief (from which the following quotations are taken).

12 James Pinkerton, "Immigrants Find Military a Faster Path to Citizenship," *Houston Chronicle*, September 14, 2006.

13 "Row Over War Veterans Facing Deportation From the Country they Risked their Lives to Defend," *Daily Mail*, October 25, 2010.

14 Bryan Bender, "Military Considers Recruiting Foreigners," *Boston Globe*, December 26, 2006.

15 "Many New American Citizens Are Foreign-Born Members of US Military," *Voice of America News*, September 11, 2009.

16 "Row Over War Veterans Facing Deportation . . .," *Daily Mail*, October 25, 2010 (from which the following quotations are taken).

17 "Latin Youth Defines Dream Act as De Facto Military Draft," *Vamos Unidos Youth*; http://teachersunite.net/node/555.

18 Max Boot and Michael O'Hanlon, "A Military Path to Citizenship," *Washington Post*, October 19, 2006 (from which the following quotations are taken).

19 "Non-Citizens in Today's Military Research Brief," CNA.

20 Mark Stevenson, "Recruiter Draws Ire for Entering Mexico," *Associated Press*, May 9, 2003 (from which the following quotations are taken).

21 Film: *Yo Soy El Army: US Military Targets Latinos with Extensive Recruitment Campaign*, Marco Amador of Producciones Cimarrón and the Center for Community Communications and Big Noise media collective; http://www.democracynow.org/2010/5/18/yo_soy_el_army_us_military.

22 Stevenson, "Recruiter Draws Ire for Entering Mexico."

23 Brian Spegele, "Mexican Citizen Died in Iraq Serving U.S., His Beloved New Land," *Tampa Bay Times*, May 26, 2009.

24 Wes Allison, "Foreign Citizens Help Shoulder Military Duty," *St. Petersburg Times*, March 11, 2003.

25 "Immigrants Become US Citizens Quickly Through Military Service," *Workpermit.com*, October 18, 2006; http://www.workpermit.com/news/2006_10_18/us/military_service_citizenship.htm.

26 Allison, "Foreign Citizens Help Shoulder Military Duty."

27 "Non-Citizens in Today's Military Research Brief," CNA.

28 Film: *The Short Life of José Gutierrez*.

29 "Reasons Why Hispanics Remain Underrepresented in Military, Despite

Interest," Rand Corp., January 14, 2009; http://www.randproject.org/news/press/2009/01/14.html.

30 "Militarization of US Immigrant Rights Movement Dangerous," *Russia Today*, May 26, 2010.

31 "Latin Youth Defines Dream Act as De Facto Military Draft," *Vamos Unidos Youth.*

32 Jose Cardenas, "Recruiting the Undocumented for the Military is Proposed," *Tampa Bay Times*, April 27, 2008.

33 "Militarization of US Immigrant Rights Movement Dangerous," *Russia Today*, May 26, 2010.

34 http://www.cis.org/node/351

35 Mark Krikorian, "Green-Card Soldiers: Should the U.S. Military be Reserved for Americans?," *National Review Online*, April 22, 2003.

36 Virginia Heffernan, "Slipping Through the Cracks: Bin Laden's Mole," *New York Times*, August 28, 2006.

37 Documents obtained from the DOD by the author in 2008 through the Freedom of Information Act.

38 Rod Powers, "Don't Ask, Don't Tell—The Military Policy on Gays," *About.com*, May 5, 2010; http://usmilitary.about.com/od/millegislation/a/dontask.htm.

39 "Gay Sex Immoral Says US General," BBC News, March 14, 2007; http://news.bbc.co.uk/1/hi/6446815.stm.

40 "10 USC Chapter 37," February 1, 2010; http://uscode.house.gov/download/pls/10C37.txt.

41 James J. Lindsay, Jerome Johnson, E.G. Shuler Jr., and Joseph J. Went, "Today's U.S. Military is Still no Place for Gays," *Washington Post*, April 16, 2009.

42 Dahr Jamail, "Resisting Homophobia in the Military," *Truthout*, August 31, 2009; http://www.globalresearch.ca/index.php?context=va&aid=14998.

43 "Bi-Partisan Poll of Iraq & Afghanistan Vets," *Vet Voice Foundation*, March 15, 2010; http://www.vetvoicefoundation.com/new?id=0002.

44 Gary Gates, "Gay Men and Lesbians in the U.S. Military, Estimates from Census 2000," Urban Institute; http://www.urban.org/publications/411069.html.

45 Paul Steinhauser, "CNN Poll: 69% OK with Gays in the Military," CNN, February 22, 2010; http://politicalticker.blogs.cnn.com/2010/02/22/cnn-poll-69-ok-with-gays-in-the-military/.

46 "Services Gay Ban Lifted," BBC News, January 12, 2000.

47 "Gays in Military not an Issue for Many Nations," *Associated Press*, July 12, 2009.

48 "Time to Review Policy on Gays in U.S. Military: Powell," *Reuters*, July 5, 2009.

49 John M. Shalikashvili, "Second Thoughts on Gays in the Military," *New York Times*, January 2, 2007.

50 "'Don't Ask, Don't Tell'? No, Sir!," Letters, *New York Times*, January 7, 2007.

51 "US Military's Gay Policy 'costly,'" BBC News, February 25, 2005; http://news.bbc.co.uk/1/hi/world/americas/4296325.stm.

52 "Financial Costs and Loss of Critical Skills Due to DOD's Homosexual Conduct Policy Cannot Be Completely Estimated," GAO, February 2005; http://www.gao.gov/new.items/d05299.pdf.

53 Robert Burns, "Abuse of Gays Rampant in Military," *Associated Press*, February 11, 2009 (from which the following quotations are taken).

54 Jamail, "Resisting Homophobia in the Military."

55 Neela Banerjee, "Soldier Sues Army, Saying His Atheism Led to Threats," *New York Times*, April 26, 2008.

56 Jason Leopold, "Charges in Religious Lawsuit Against Army Detailed," *Truthout*, September 25, 2007; http://archive.truthout.org/article/charges-religious-lawsuit-against-army-detailed.

57 "Open Letter From Barack Obama to the LGBT Community," http://www.examiner.com/sex-relationships-in-national/obama-reaction-to-california-supreme-court-ruling-on-prop-8-nada?render=print.

58 Toby Harnden, "Barack Obama Heckled by 'Don't Ask Don't Tell' Protesters," *Daily Telegraph*, April 21, 2010.

59 "Stories from the Frontlines: Former Army Sgt. Darren Manzella," SLDN Website, May 19, 2010; http://www.sldn.org/blog/archives/stories-from-the-frontlines-former-army-sgt.-darren-manzella/.

60 Andy Birkey, "Judge Rules 'Don't Ask, Don't Tell' Unconstitutional," *Iowa Independent*, 10 September, 2010.

61 Amy Goodman, "Why Did Obama Fire Dan Choi?," *Truthdig*, August 5, 2010.

62 Chris Geidner, "Pentagon to Recruiters: Accept Applicants 'Who Admit They Are Openly Gay or Lesbian,'" *Metro Weekly*, October 19, 2010.

63 "President Obama Signs 'Don't Ask, Don't Tell' Repeal into Law," *New York Post*, December 22, 2010.

64 "Military: No Problems Prepping for End to 'Don't Ask, Don't Tell,'" *CNN*, April 7, 2011.

EPILOGUE

1 Flavius Vegetius Renatus, *On Roman Military Matters* (Red and Black Publishers, 2008), p. 34.

2 William Kristol, "The Defense Secretary We Have," *Washington Post*, December 15, 2004.

3 The original Latin is *De Re Militari*.

4 Vegetius Renatus, *On Roman Military Matters*, p. 6.

5 Edward Gibbon, *The Decline and Fall of the Roman Empire* (Wordsworth, 1998), p. 3.

6 Arthur Ferrill, *The Fall of the Roman Empire: The Military Explanation* (Thames and Hudson, 2001), p. 12.

7 Vegetius Renatus, *On Roman Military Matters*, p. 11.

8 Ibid.

9 Ferrill, *The Fall of the Roman Empire: The Military Explanation*, p. 152.

10 Gibbon, *The Decline and Fall of the Roman Empire*, p. 9.

11 Ibid.

12 Ferrill, *The Fall of the Roman Empire: The Military Explanation*, p. 153.

13 Ibid.

14 Sun Tzu, *The Art of War* (Filiquarian, 2006), pp. 14–15.

15 Nicolo Machiavelli, *The Prince* (Penguin Classics, 2003).

16 Vegetius Renatus, *On Roman Military Matters*, p. 11.

17 "The Future—Is the Army Broken?," PBS, October 26, 2004; http://www.pbs.org/wgbh/pages/frontline/shows/pentagon/themes/broken.html.

18 "Rumsfeld's War," Transcript of Frontline program, PBS, http://www.pbs.org/wgbh/pages/frontline/shows/pentagon/etc/script.html.

19 "Daily Compilation of Presidential Documents, Obama, Barack H," August 28, 2010; http://www.faqs.org/periodicals/201008/2138532551.html#ixzz192xMsEst.

20 "Barack Obama Says US Troop withdrawal From Iraq Keeps Campaign Pledge," *Associated Press*, August 28, 2010.

21 Nisa Islam Muhammad, "U.S. Military Accepts More Ex-felons," *Final Call*, May 6, 2008.

22 Matt Kennard, "The US Army's Enemy Within," *Guardian*, July 13, 2009.

23 Claudia Núñez, "Mexican Drug Cartels Tied to U.S. White Supremacists," *La Opinión*, November 17, 2010.

24 "National Instant Criminal Background Check System (NICS) 2009," US

Department of Justice; http://www.fbi.gov/about-us/cjis/nics/reports/2009-operations-report.

25 Mark Thompson, "How Marijuana Use Aborted Jared Loughner's Military Career," *Time*, January 10, 2011.

26 Ibid.

27 Matthew Kennard, "Saddam Was Well-regarded by British," *Financial Times*, January 1, 2010.

28 "Behind the War on Iraq," Research Unit for Political Economy, *Monthly Review*, Vol. 55, May 2003.

29 "UK Military Deaths in Afghanistan and Iraq," BBC News, April 2, 2012.

30 "BNP Claim Wide Army Support," *Press Association*, October 20, 2009.

31 Michael Savage, "Is the Army Losing its War Against Drug Abuse?," *Independent*, March 15, 2010.

32 Ibid.

33 Alastair Jamieson, "One in Seven Soldiers Driven to Alcohol by War Horror," *Daily Telegraph*, May 13, 2010.

34 Ethan Watters, "The Invisible Division: US Soldiers are Seven Times as Likely as UK Troops to Develop Post-traumatic Stress," *Independent*, April 8, 2011.

35 "Two Percent of Afghan-based German Troops Return Home Traumatized," *IRNA*, April 6, 2011.

36 Claire Ellicott, "Thousands of British Troops are Too Fat to be Deployed to Afghanistan, Reveals Leaked Army Memo," *Daily Mail*, August 3, 2009.

37 Aled Thomas and Nico Hines, "British Military Steps up Fightback Against BNP After Griffin Tirade," *Times*, October 21, 2009.

38 Chris Hedges and Laila Al-Arian, "'The Carnage, the Blown-up Bodies I Saw . . . Why? What Was This For?,'" *Guardian*, July 13, 2007.

39 Wikileaks War Logs; www.wikileaks.ch.

40 Jim Lobe, "Majority Still Believe in Iraq's WMD, al-Qaeda Ties," *IPS*, April 22, 2004.

41 Alex Barker, "Security Chief Exposes Blair's Gamble on Iraq," *Financial Times*, July 20, 2010.

42 Brad Knickerbocker, "Gates's Warning: Avoid Land War in Asia, Middle East, and Africa," *The Christian Science Monitor*, February 26, 2011.

43 Lauren Finnegan, "Army Boss Cautions Against 'Hollowing' Out of Armed Forces," *Yahoo News*, February 25, 2011.

44 Charley Keyes, "Obama Unveils Plans for Pared-down Military," CNN,

January 5, 2012, http://www.cnn.com/2012/01/05/politics/pentagon-strategy-shift/index.html.

45 "US Embassy Cables: Verdict on the Leaks About the Middle East," *Guardian*, November 29, 2010.

46 Sun Tzu, *The Art of War*, p. 9.

47 Ibid., p. 15.

48 Michael Dobbs, "With Albright, Clinton Accepts New U.S. Role," *Washington Post*, December 8, 2006.

49 Neil Mackay, "Lets Not Forget: Bush Planned Iraq 'Regime Change' Before Becoming President," Information Clearing House, September 15, 2002.

50 Michael Mann, *Incoherent Empire* (Verso, 2003), p. 27.

AFTERWORD: THE WAR COMES HOME

1 Michael B. Kelley, "A Revealing 2010 Interview With Temple Shooting Suspect Wade Michael Page," *Business Insider*, August 6, 2012.

2 Megan McCloskey, "Sikh Temple Shooter Promoted Extremist Views During His Army Years," *Stars and Stripes*, August 7, 2012.

3 Rob Reynolds, "US Neo-Nazi Music Scene Flourishing," Al Jazeera broadcast, August 24, 2012,

4 "Ex-Missouri Guardsman Trained Skinhead Group," Associated Press, August 11, 2012.

5 Melanie Haiken, "Suicide Rate Among Vets and Active Duty Military Jumps —Now 22 a Day," *Forbes*, May 2, 2013.

6 Julian E. Barnes, "Report Faults Navy's Base-Access Vetting," *Wall Street Journal*, September 17, 2013.

7 Craig Whitlock and Carol D. Leonnig, "Fort Hood Shooter Had Psychiatric Issues but Showed No 'Sign of Likely Violence,' Officials Say," *Washington Post*, April 3, 2014.

8 Deborah Hastings, "US Soldiers Accepting Cash, Drugs for Mexican Drug Cartel Contract Hits," *Daily News* (New York), September 13, 2013.

9 Joseph J. Kolb, "Mexican Cartels Hiring US Soldiers as Hit Men," FoxNews.com, August 1, 2013.

10 Ibid.

11 Ibid.

12 "L.A. Gang Members in Syria: Why They Fight for Assad," CBS News, March 11, 2014.

13 Kathleen Belew, "Veterans and White Supremacy," *New York Times*, April 15, 2014.

14 "Dellinger Responds to NY Times Op-Ed Piece," Legion.com, April 19, 2014.

15 David Edwards, "White Supremacists Distribute Fliers at Ft. Carson Asking Soldiers to Fight in Coming Race War," RawStory.com, June 12, 2014.

Index

Printed by Printforce, United Kingdom